T0330384

The Politics of Oil

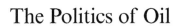

To Juana

The Politics of Oil

Controlling Resources, Governing Markets
and Creating Political Conflicts

Dag Harald Claes

Department of Political Science, University of Oslo, Norway

 Edward Elgar
PUBLISHING

Cheltenham, UK • Northampton, MA, USA

Published by
Edward Elgar Publishing Limited
The Lypiatts
15 Lansdown Road
Cheltenham
Glos GL50 2JA
UK

Edward Elgar Publishing, Inc.
William Pratt House
9 Dewey Court
Northampton
Massachusetts 01060
USA

A catalogue record for this book
is available from the British Library

Library of Congress Control Number: 2018945835

This book is available electronically in the **Elgar**online
Social and Political Science subject collection
DOI 10.4337/9781785360183

ISBN 978 1 78536 017 6 (cased)
ISBN 978 1 78536 018 3 (eBook)

Typeset by Servis Filmsetting Ltd, Stockport, Cheshire

Contents

v

Figures

Tables

Abbreviations

Aramco	Saudi Arabian Oil Company (formerly Arabian-American Oil Company)
AWACS	Airborne Warning and Control System
b/d	barrels per day (a barrel is 159 liters or 42 US gallons)
BNOC	British National Oil Corporation
CCS	Carbon Capture and Storage
CENTO	Central Treaty Organization
CEO	Chief Executive Officer
CERM	Coordinated Emergency Response Measures (IEA)
CFP	Compagnie Française des Pétroles
CIA	Central Intelligence Agency
CITGO	Citgo Petroleum Corporation
CLCS	Commission on the Limits of the Continental Shelf
CNOOC	China National Offshore Oil Corporation
CNPC	China National Petroleum Corporation
E&P	Exploration and Production
ECHR	European Convention on Human Rights
EIA	Energy Information Administration (United States)
ENI	Ente Nazionale Idrocarburi
ENOC	Emerging National Oil Company
ETI	Energy Transmission Infrastructures
EV	Electric Vehicle
FDI	Foreign Direct Investments
FEA	Federal Energy Administration (United States)
GATT	General Agreement on Tariffs and Trade
GCC	Gulf Cooperation Council
GDP	Gross Domestic Product
GTD	Global Terrorism Database
IEA	International Energy Agency
IEF	International Energy Forum
IGO	International Governmental Organization
IMF	International Monetary Fund
IOC	International Oil Company
IPE	International Political Economy

IR	International Relations
ISIL	The Islamic State of Iraq and the Levant, also IS – Islamic State, or Daesh (Arabic)
JODI	Joint Oil Data Initiative
MEND	Movement for the Emancipation of the Niger Delta
MID	Militarized Interstate Disputes
MNC	Multinational Corporation
NATO	North Atlantic Treaty Organization
NDC	National Determined Contributions (Paris Convention)
NIOC	National Iranian Oil Company
NOC	National Oil Company
OAPEC	Organization of Arab Petroleum Exporting Countries
OBM	Obsolescing Bargaining Model
OECD	Organisation for Economic Co-operation and Development
ONGC	Oil and Natural Gas Corporation (India)
OPEC	Organization of the Petroleum Exporting Countries
PDVSA	Petróleos de Venezuela
PEMEX	Petróleos Mexicanos
PLO	Palestinian Liberation Organization
PSA	Production Sharing Agreement
R/P-ratio	Reserves on production ratio
SDFI	State Direct Financial Interest (Norway)
TNC	Transnational Corporation
TRC	Texas Railroad Commission
UAE	United Arab Emirates
UNCLOS	United Nations Convention of the Law of the Sea
UNCTAD	United Nations Conference on Trade and Development
URR	Ultimately Recoverable Resources
USGS	United States Geological Survey
WTO	World Trade Organization

Preface

This book is about politics and oil. Both are complicated matters. To understand politics is as hard as it gets. When asked how it could be that the mind of man had discovered the structure of the atom but was unable to devise political means to control it, Albert Einstein replied: "It is because politics is more difficult than physics."[1] Oil, is no less of a challenge. Juan Pablo Pérez Alfonso, the Venezuelan founder of OPEC, bemoaned in 1975: "I call petroleum the devil's excrement. It brings trouble . . . Look at this *locura* – waste, corruption, consumption, our public services falling apart. And debt, debt we shall have for years."[2] On the international level, Barack Obama, before he became president of the United States, made the following observation. "Our enemies are fully aware that they can use oil as a weapon against America. And if we don't take this threat as seriously as the bombs they build or the guns they buy, we will be fighting the War on Terror with one hand tied behind our back."[3]

There are many books about the politics of oil. The most comprehensive history of the oil industry and politics is Daniel Yergin's book *The Prize* (Yergin, 1991). It has sold several hundred thousand copies, and stands out as a must read for anyone interested in the history of oil. I have numerous references to Yergin's book. Also Michael Ross's book *The Oil Curse*, has been an important inspiration (Ross, 2012). Ross is a key figure in the political science milieu focused on explaining and determining the causal links between the presence of oil resources in a country and its economic growth, type of regime and level of political violence. Following these two outstanding examples, there are many hours to be filled if one is moved to read all the literature related to 'oil' and 'politics'. Searching Google Scholar also reveals the huge academic interest in 'oil politics'. These two words generate 1.9 million hits, not far behind general political science concepts like 'government' (2.1 million) and 'international relations' (2.47 million).

I am a political scientist interested in oil. My primary interest has been the intersection between politics and markets, in particular the attempt by the oil producing states to govern the international oil market, the largest traded commodity market in the world (Claes, 2001). The ambition of this book is to show the wide variety of political aspects related to the oil industry and the international oil market. Oil and politics is connected in so many ways on so many levels, that a comprehensive analysis of oil politics would require a library. The topic of every chapter of the book deserves at least a book by itself. Nevertheless, the book is a humble attempt to cover everything you should know about oil and politics. It is divided into three sections.

The first part concerns the role of government in exercising legitimate sovereignty over oil resources, both toward other countries and their own citizens (Chapter 1). Additionally, governments perform a regulatory role over all aspects of the actual operation of transforming oil resources in the ground into a tradable commodity (Chapter 2). Finally, this part of the book discusses both the economic and political aspects of how oil states handle their income from oil (Chapter 3). This is one of the most analyzed topics in the politics of oil. Nevertheless, the conclusions regarding the so-called 'resource curse' are debated. This chapter is written together with Mads Motrøen.

The second part of the book focuses on the governance of the oil market. First, I start out with the prominent idea in the study of International Relations (IR) of the governing role of international institutions (Chapter 4). Then I turn to economic theory and oil producing companies and countries and their efforts to regulate the vagaries of the oil market. I trace the lines of producer governance back to John D. Rockefeller and the dominant role of Standard Oil in the US oil market, followed by the global role of the International Oil Companies (IOC) known as the 'Seven Sisters' (Chapter 5). A chapter is devoted to the Organization of Petroleum Exporting Countries (OPEC) currently the most prominent organization trying to govern the global oil market (Chapter 6).

The third part of the book turns the table, from examining the role of politics in the oil business and market to asking what role oil plays in political conflicts. In this section I first study the general geopolitics of oil from the perspective of the most dominant country in international politics since the Second World War – the United States (Chapter 7). Then I zoom in on the region with the highest concentration of oil resources, the Persian Gulf, and discuss the role of oil in interstate conflicts there (Chapter 8). The academic study of the resource curse has also created a very important extension studying the relations between oil and civil war. There is an extensive literature on this topic. I combine an analysis of this body of work with the not so voluminous literature on the relationship between oil and terrorism (Chapter 9). Finally, I look to the future, trying to capture what lies ahead for oil (Chapter 10). The role of oil in the future is obviously intimately tied to the prospect of climate change, or the world's ability to combat the climate effects of the burning of fossil fuels, oil included.

Another ambition with this book is to demonstrate the futility of explaining oil politics relying on a single scientific discipline. To understand oil *politics*, one needs to understand a little bit of geology, engineering, economics, philosophy, history, and more; not to mention my own home turf: political science. I am a strong believer in the value of interdisciplinary cooperation. In the field of energy studies, it is more important than ever. The attentive reader will discover several discussions based on contributions from other disciplines than economics and political science, although these two are the ones most present in the book. Not surprisingly, as I find myself comfortably placed in the field of International Political Economy (IPE). A sub-field of IR seeking to understand the intrinsic nexus between economics and politics.

This time I have tried not to burden my many good colleagues with comments and discussions of the manuscript. One reason is that this is 'a book based on books', my own from 2001, and many, many others. Another reason is that I am not trying to do something very new and innovative, but rather bring together our collective knowledge of the Politics of Oil. However, two colleagues must be mentioned. My very enthusiastic and determined research assistant, Mads Motrøen, has made a valuable contribution to the entire book, particularly Chapters 3 and 9. In the case of the Chapter 3, his contribution was so extensive that he shares the authorship. My warmest thanks to Mads. The other one is Professor Emeritus Helge Hveem. The very attentive reader will discover that Helge and I have co-authored a paper and an article that I have taken the liberty to utilize in this book. Helge has been my mentor, teacher, colleague and friend for so many years. I certainly would not have been where I am today without him. On the institutional level, I have the fortune to be part of the socially warm and academically stimulating Department of Political Science at the University of Oslo. I can hardly think of a better place to spend the working hours of my life.

I published a book titled The Politics of Oil-Producer Cooperation in 2001. Westview Press/Taylor and Francis has graciously let me use small parts of this book again. Likewise, Cogitatio Press and Helge have let me use material from our article in *Politics and Governance*, called 'From Paris to the End of Oil'. Matthew Little and Sarah Cook have significantly improved the text through their thorough copy editing. Sarah Brown has been effectively in charge of the publishing process. The editors at Edward Elgar, John Hewish and Alex Pettifer have been both patient and supportive throughout the too long writing period. Alex has to take the responsibility that follows with the fact that the whole thing was his idea. The mistakes are on me.

Dag Harald Claes
Oslo, July 23, 2018

NOTES

1. https://todayinsci.com/E/Einstein_Albert/EinsteinAlbert-PoliticsQuote500px.htm (accessed July 23, 2018).
2. "Economics focus: The devil's excrement – is oil wealth a blessing or a curse?" *The Economist*, May 22, 2003. http://www.economist.com/node/1795921 (accessed June 18, 2018).
3. "Energy Security is National Security." Remarks of Senator Barack Obama, Governor's Ethanol Coalition Washington, DC. February 26, 2006. http://obamaspeeches.com/054-Energy-Security-is-National-Security-Governors-Ethanol-Coalition-Obama-Speech.htm (accessed January 7, 2018).

PART I

Resource governance

1. Sovereignty and ownership

1.1 OIL – A FREE GIFT OF NATURE

In a free competitive market, the individual producer is unable to influence the market price, and thus only controls the quantity produced. Basic economic theory finds the producers maximize profit when they produce the exact quantity whereby price equals marginal cost – marginal cost being the cost of producing one more unit of the product. As the marginal cost is assumed to increase, the producers accrue profit from the difference between the average cost and the market price. The average costs of the individual producers might differ. Since the market price is the same for all producers, the producer with the lowest average cost will gain a higher total profit than producers with higher average costs. There are many reasons for differences in production costs, such as skills, efficiencies, labor costs, technology, productivity, and so on. The extraction of natural resources differs from this standard model of the economics of production, since nature itself provides economic value – a *resource rent*.

The extraction of natural resources provides an extra economic value in addition to the factors mentioned above. Nevertheless, David Ricardo (1821/2001, p. 51) in essence applies the same logic to the extraction of natural resources as he does for other markets, "The return for capital from the poorest mine paying no rent, would regulate the rent of all the other more productive mines . . . It will be sufficient to remark that the same general rule which regulates the value of raw produce and manufactured commodities, is applicable also to the metals." According to Ricardo, rent is "that portion of the produce of the earth, which is paid to the landlord for the use of the original and indestructible powers of the soil" (Ricardo, 1821/2001, p. 39). The excess profit from extracting or harvesting natural resources appears due to differences in production costs following differences in the quality of the goods or natural conditions, such as the fertility of different land areas. This understanding of resource rent is called Ricardian rent, or differential rent. In the case of oil, a world market price sets the price for all producers. The natural conditions are extremely varied – from easily accessible oil reserves in the Middle East, to costly reserves in deep water offshore production in Brazilian waters or in the

North Sea. Obviously, the producer of the oil fields with low production costs of a handful of dollars per barrel makes more money than producers with extraction costs of $20 or $30 per barrel.

A different understanding of resource rent was developed by Harold Hotelling (1931). He advanced a theory of the price path of non-renewable resources. The core idea is that the economic value of the extraction of exhaustible resources increases over time as the scarcity of the resource increases. Maximizing the rent of the total extraction of the given stock of the resource implies that the price should increase at an equal percentage to the discount rate. Hotelling based his understanding of the resource rent on the scarcity of the resource, not on the differences in production costs. The scarcity of the resource drives the price upwards in a continuous path. This price path is not observed in the oil market, as any scarcity of oil resources is hard to identify. I will return to the issue of scarcity in the next chapter.

The third understanding of resource rent is to some extent inherent in the two outlined above, although not explicated. Here the essence of the concept is the exclusive control the owner has over unique or non-renewable resources. Such control can generate an excess profit above normal profit – or rent – if the resource owners are able to extend their control to the entire market. In terms of natural resources, a prime example is the owner of a mine extracting rare minerals. From the beginning of modern oil production in the latter half of the 19th century, various individual oil producers or groups of producers in collusion have tried to exercise such monopoly power over the oil market, with varying degrees of success. These attempts constitute the core of the second part of this book.

It is important to note that the three variations of the resource rent can be hard to distinguish from each other. When excess profit from oil extraction is empirically identified, it is usually the outcome of a combination of all three. For example, a group of producers agreeing to cut back production with the aim of enhancing their profit from increased market prices, is an attempt to create scarcity in the market. However, the resource rent provides a strong argument for the importance of resource ownership. The next question therefore is who can rightfully claim the benefits of natural resources like oil. In other words: *who owns nature?*

1.2 SOVEREIGNTY OF NATURAL RESOURCES

"Sovereignty and ownership are the most fundamental legal concepts governing the relationship between humankind and its natural environment" (Lee, 2009, p. 1). With respect to natural resources, these two concepts are somewhat intertwined. Here, sovereignty will relate to the relationship between states and the single state's control of its own natural resources. Ownership relates to the relationship between the state and individuals regarding production or extraction of the resources, and the right to the benefits from this extraction. However, it is important to note that the two concepts are inextricably linked.

1.2.1 Property Rights and Territorial Rights

John Locke (1632–1704) developed a theory of property that has formed the backbone of most elaborated theories of territory based on individualist property rights. "They typically begin from an account of property as an individual (natural) right and then conceive of territory as arrived at by the consent of many individual property owners who agree to establish a government (legislative, executive, and judiciary) to rule over them" (Moore, 2015, p. 17).

> Whether we consider natural *Reason*, which tells us, that Men, being once born, have a right to their Preservation, and consequently to Meat and Drink, and such other things, as Nature affords for their Subsistence: Or, *Revelation*, which gives us an account of those Grants God made of the World to *Adam* . . . 'tis very clear, that God . . . *has given the earth to the Children of Men,* given it to Mankind in common. (Locke, 1689/1988, p. 286)

For the purpose of this book, it is essential that this gift also gives individuals the right to utilize the property and receive the economic rent of extracting the natural resources. However, the formation of a sovereign state presupposes the formation of a government. This is probably one of the most studied issues in political theory and philosophy, mulled over ever since Plato wrote *The Republic* in 381 bc. For Locke, *consent* is essential for the formation of governments. "Men being, as has been said, by Nature, all free, equal and independent, no one can be put out of this Estate, and subjected to the Political Power of another, without his own *Consent*" (Locke, 1689/1988, p. 330). The motive of individuals to form a community is "for their comfortable, safe, and peaceable living one amongst another, in a secure Enjoyment of the Properties, and a greater Security against any that are not of it" (Locke, 1689/1988, p. 331). Having consented to the formation of the community or government every individual "puts himself under an Obligation to every one of that Society, to submit to the determination of the *majority*, and to be concluded by it" (Locke, 1689/1988, p 332).

The essence of the individualist Lockean perspective is that while private property is a natural or moral right, the regulation of occupation of territory, transfer of rights, and regulation of harvesting or extraction of resources lies with the sovereign government, provided the individuals consent to it. The individualist Lockean theory can justify government jurisdiction over a territory, but does not justify the government's authority over those property holders who do *not* consent to the authority of the government. "In other words, this argument does not justify territorial right *as we know it*, where territorial rights and especially jurisdictional authority are consistently or evenly applied across the territory" (Moore, 2015, p. 20). Another problem that arises in moving from philosophy to empirical observations is that hardly any state is "actually legitimated through individual consent of private property holders . . . The standard for state legitimacy is set so high that no state can meet it" (Moore, 2015, p. 21).

Cara Nine (2008) has suggested a solution to this problem, by introducing a collectivist Lockean theory of territorial rights. Now the distinction between property rights and territorial rights becomes important. A property right

> gives the owner of the land the right to control access to that land and to use that land in any way that does not violate the law of nature or civil laws . . . A state territorial right, by contrast, describes a relationship between the state and a geographic region. It is a jurisdictional right – the state has the right to make, adjudicate, and enforce law within a certain area. (Nine, 2008, p. 149)

In the individualistic version of the Lockean theory "the state acquires territorial rights indirectly, only after individuals have acquired property rights to the land and then consented to the state's territorial jurisdiction over that land" (Nine, 2008, p. 155). In the collectivistic Lockean theory, however, "the state acquires territorial rights in much the same way that individuals acquire property rights" (Nine, 2008, p. 155). Based on natural law theory, Nine (2012, pp. 26–45), elaborates the argument that a "collective may claim a general right to territory, if territorial acquisition, 1. is necessary for the provision of members' basic needs, or 2. can be used by the collective (without spoilage) and does not prevent others from meeting their basic needs, or 3. all persons consent to the exclusive acquisition." The second point directs us toward the characteristics of natural resources, in particular the distributional aspects of the extraction of a natural resource like oil.

1.2.2 Property Rights and State Jurisdiction

Even with a clear-cut notion of state sovereignty, the actual relationship between state jurisdiction and private ownership – in other words, between individual property rights and the state's exercise of jurisdictional rights following its sovereignty – remains to be understood. Control of natural resources is part of the larger legal issue related to human rights, and the relationship between the state and the individual in general. "The

legal consequences of belonging to a political community with a territorial base have not changed a great deal since the seventeenth century"
(Crawford, 2012, p. 607). The relationship between property rights and
state jurisdiction reflects the fundamental tension between individual and
collective interests throughout the history of man. In the 19th century,
legal theory created the myth of absolute, exclusive, and unbounded
individual ownership, which seemingly had its roots in classical Roman
law. However, analysis of the actual application of Roman law suggests a
much more dynamic relationship. "Originally, private ownership in its full
sense (with a full bundle of property rights in the hands of individuals)
existed only on surveyed and assigned land according to Roman law. *Ager
privatus* was defined through the boundary stones, dividing it from *ager
publicus*" (Jakab, 2015, p. 120). As the use of land and exploitation of
natural resources developed, so did private enterprise. This exposed the
weaknesses in the legal framework of property rights in ancient societies.

> From the 2nd century bc on, there were more and more kinds of possible usage
> granted on *ager publicus,* which added a certain private feature to public land
> . . . Land was scarce and originally owned by the state (*populous Romanus*):
> nobody had open access to public land, and property rights to individuals could
> be granted only by the state. But a low efficiency of public exploitation and
> private interference (by force) generated several types of private usage which
> were tolerated (tacitly) by the state without a proper legal framework, therefore
> with lack of security. (Jakab, 2015, p. 121)

In medieval Europe, the relationship between private property and state
jurisdiction was largely a redundant issue, as monarchs or the papal state
owned all landed territory. The king could then grant land areas, or estates,
to lords, who then parceled out properties to tenants. None of this suggested that ownership was transferred or the tenants acquired rights of any
kind. As feudalism broke down people became formally free of a landlord,
but their freedom was constrained as they had no property themselves. The
ideas of John Locke reflect the ideas of freedom and human rights that
emerged during the Enlightenment, but both the ideas and political forces
advocating individual human rights emerged earlier.

During the English Civil War (1642–1651), 'the Levellers' argued
that the King had violated the people's natural rights during the war.
They regarded property rights as deriving from a person's work on their
property and thus as the fruit of their labor. It was therefore "sacred under
the biblical injunction, 'thou shall not steal'"(Ishay, 2008, p. 91). Bernard
Mommer (2002, p. 9) notes a remarkable debate in the National Assembly
in Revolutionary France in 1791. It was assumed that "the Nation was
entitled to fully benefit from all its natural resources. Regarding the

surface, [the Assembly] concluded that the best way to achieve this end was by granting private property rights to the occupiers. . . . Regarding the subsoil, however, doubts were raised about whether this would be enough." The subsequent Mining Act of 1791 gave the surface owner the right to "mine all minerals that could be worked in the open-air . . . with excavations down to the depth of one hundred feet" (Mommer, 2002, p. 9). Due to the costs and the knowledge required, deeper mines remained in the public domain, declared as '*utilité publique*' (Mommer, 2002, p. 10).

Almost replicating the Roman Empire, Revolutionary France performed a balancing act between individual property rights and the goals and jurisdiction of the state, with the innovation that property was now part of the concept of human rights. "Regarded as a radical human rights affirmation in the seventeenth century, the right to property would become a major source of contention in nineteenth- and twentieth-century human rights discourse" (Ishay, 2008, p. 91). As demonstrated in the previous section, the sovereignty of states over their natural resources has become a fundamental part of international law. The same is not the case regarding individual property rights over natural resources. Article 1 of the 1952 protocol to the 1950 European Convention on Human Rights (ECHR), for example, states:

Every natural or legal person is entitled to the peaceful enjoyment of his possessions. No one shall be deprived of his possessions except in the public interest and subject to the conditions provided for by law and by the general principles of international law.

The preceding provisions shall not, however, in any way impair the right of a State to enforce such laws as it deems necessary to control the use of property in accordance with the general interest or to secure the payment of taxes or other contributions or penalties.[1]

The wording, "entitled to enjoyment of his possessions" seems a carefully formulated phrase. The two paragraphs of the article taken together, demonstrate, once again, the same balancing act between individual property rights and the judicial rights of the state that occurred in ancient Rome and Revolutionary France. The individual right to property is not absolute and the state has wide degree of discretion to limit these rights by law, in order to serve the common good.

1.2.3 The Distribution of Resource Rights

As Figure 1.1 shows, oil resources are far from equally distributed among the countries or citizens of the world. Three countries hold 46 percent of the proven reserves, and the top eight reserve holders control more than 80 percent of the total proven oil reserves. Almost every country in

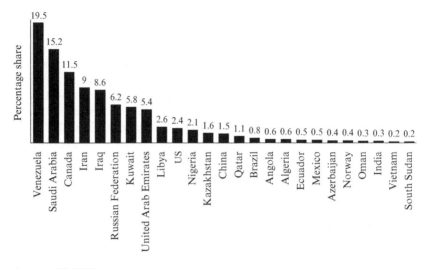

Source: BP (2017).

Figure 1.1   Percentage share of total proven oil reserves 2016

the world consumes oil, and the number of individual consumers nearly corresponds to the number of people on the planet. Oil is the dominant fuel for mechanical transportation, and thousands of consumer products are partly based on oil-derived substances. Oil is an integrated part of the modern economy and life in general in most parts of the world.

The fundamental assertion by John Locke quoted above, that God gave nature to humankind in common, prompts the question: Who has the right to oil resources, and why? This goes beyond the discussion of territorial rights and addresses the distributional aspects of natural resources. "A theory of natural resource justice will define and allocate a set of resource rights, determining who can justly derive which benefits in which circumstances, or who has the right to make decisions, say, about how resources shall be used" (Armstrong, 2017, p. 15). Armstrong then develops a set of core resource rights. These encompass both individual property rights and states' rights of property or jurisdiction. In line with the discussion above, he distinguishes between what he calls 'first-order rights', the rights describing "the ability to directly enjoy or transfer benefits from a resource" (Armstrong, 2017, p. 30), and 'second-order rights', which are "rights to distribute, condition or constrain the ways in which others can derive or transfer benefits" (Armstrong, 2017, p. 30). Some of these rights, such as the right to access, understood as the right to visit a resource and enjoy it in a non-damaging way, are outside the scope of this book. Since oil is regarded here as an economic resource, the two relevant rights are the right to derive income from natural resources and the right to regulate that income. It is also important to distinguish between the concepts of rights and rules (or regulation). Schlager and Ostrom (1992, p. 250) make the following distinction: "'Rights' refer to particular actions that are authorized . . . 'rules' refer to the prescriptions that create authorization." The authority to regulate the benefits derived from the utilization of the resource rests with the state's government, based on its jurisdictional rights or power, as outlined above. But if the oil resources of the world belong to mankind in common, the right of the oil-rich sovereign states to utilize their resources for the sole purpose of benefitting only their citizens seems unjust. A counter argument could be that if oil resources were the common heritage of mankind they would not be utilized, at least not in an effective way.

Let us assume, in line with Locke's justification of private property, that natural resources were held by mankind in common, without governmental rule. In that case nobody would have the incentive to invest time, money or effort in order to develop them or improve the productivity of land in general (Moore, 2015, p. 165). Nevertheless, "it seems unjust if one group's land is large, fertile, and resource-rich, while another group's land is meager, barren, and resource-poor" (Moore, 2015, p. 176). To correct this injustice "Thomas Pogge . . . proposes a tax on natural resources, designed to transfer substantial, but not staggering amounts of money, from well-off states to poorer ones through a small charge on certain limited natural resources" (Moore, 2015, p. 177 based on; Pogge, 2002, p. 206). In practical politics, natural resources are generally not considered the common heritage of mankind. The latter concept is in itself controversial as it challenges the sovereign right of states.

In the anarchic system of states, unfair distribution across countries seems to be the order of the day, not only with respect to oil resources, but also in terms of resources and standards of life in general. Institutions with the authority and power to execute large-scale redistribution among the states are nowhere in sight. This is different on the national level, as governments possess the authority to redistribute wealth among their citizens, although there are wide variations as to how far states pursue the role of authoritative redistributor (Esping-Andersen, 1990). Thus, the scope of distributive justice is national, not international. Most natural resources are under national sovereignty, with a few exceptions like the high seas, the deep seabed, and Antarctica.

Nine (2012, p. 123) suggests that "illegitimate or corrupt officials would not be recognized as legitimate representatives of the collective, and thus these officials could not be recognized as legitimately holding authority over resources." It follows that legitimate collective resource rights and the jurisdictional right to make, adjudicate and enforce law, presupposes democracy. Of the 25 countries with the largest oil reserves listed in Figure 1.1, only five are listed as 'free' countries by Freedom House: Brazil, Canada, India, Norway and the United States. These five hold a mere 15 percent of the world's oil reserves.

1.2.4 Natural Resources in International Law

In line with the discussion above, the generally recognized principle in international law is that natural resources "in the ground or under the seabed from the outset belongs to the state under whose territory or continental shelf the resources are found" (Alvik, 2015, p. 233). In 1962, the UN General Assembly adopted a resolution on the sovereignty over natural resources:[2]

"Permanent sovereignty over natural resources", General Assembly resolution 1803 (XVII), 14 December 1962.

1. The right of peoples and nations to permanent sovereignty over their natural wealth and resources must be exercised in the interest of their national development and of the well-being of the people of the State concerned.

2. The exploration, development and disposition of such resources, as well as the import of the foreign capital required for these purposes, should be in conformity with the rules and conditions which the peoples and nations freely consider to be necessary or desirable with regard to the authorization, restriction or prohibition of such activities.

3. In cases where authorization is granted, the capital imported and the earnings on that capital shall be governed by the terms thereof, by the national legislation in force, and by international law. The profits derived must be shared in the proportions freely agreed upon, in each case, between the investors and the recipient State, due care being taken to ensure that there is no impairment, for any reason, of that State's sovereignty over its natural wealth and resources.

4. Nationalization, expropriation or requisitioning shall be based on grounds or reasons of public utility, security or the national interest which are recognized as overriding purely individual or private interests, both domestic and foreign. In such cases the owner shall be paid appropriate compensation, in accordance with the rules in force in the State taking such measures in the exercise of its sovereignty and in accordance with international law. In any case where the question of compensation gives rise to a controversy, the national jurisdiction of the State taking such measures shall be exhausted. However, upon agreement by sovereign States and other parties concerned, settlement of the dispute should be made through arbitration or international adjudication.

5. The free and beneficial exercise of the sovereignty of peoples and nations over their natural resources must be furthered by the mutual respect of States based on their sovereign equality.

6. International co-operation for the economic development of developing countries, whether in the form of public or private capital investments, exchange of goods and services, technical assistance, or exchange of scientific information, shall be such as to further their independent national development and

shall be based upon respect for their sovereignty over their natural wealth and resources.

7. Violation of the rights of peoples and nations to sovereignty over their natural wealth and resources is contrary to the spirit and principles of the Charter of the United Nations and hinders the development of international co-operation and the maintenance of peace.

8. Foreign investment agreements freely entered into by or between sovereign States shall be observed in good faith; States and international organizations shall strictly and conscientiously respect the sovereignty of peoples and nations over their natural wealth and resources in accordance with the Charter and the principles set forth in the present resolution.

The first paragraph of the resolution can be understood as recognizing "what may be deemed the collective proprietary interest of the nation to natural resources on its territory" (Alvik, 2015, p. 234). Resolutions of the UN General Assembly are not legally binding for UN member countries. Alvik (2015, p. 234 fn. 6) notes that "no consensus was or has been reached on the exact legal consequences of the principle." However, the principle in the first paragraph, concerning the right of peoples and nations to sovereignty over their 'natural wealth', has "found an authoritative expression as common article 1 of the two main UN Human Rights Covenants" (Alvik, 2015, p. 234):

All peoples may, for their own ends, freely dispose of their natural wealth and resources without prejudice to any obligations arising out of international economic co-operation, based upon the principle of mutual benefit, and international law. In no case may a people be deprived of its own means of subsistence.[3]

Several of the paragraphs of the resolution address issues that will be discussed later in this book. The regulation of exploration (§2), the state profit (§3), and nationalization (§4), are all discussed in Chapter 2. The right of resource countries to enter into cooperation with other countries regarding the governance of their resources (§5 and §6) are both related to the topics of Chapters 4 and 6.

The final sentence in this article brings us back to the starting point above and John Locke's assertion that people have the right to preservation and subsequently to natural resources necessary for their subsistence. This philosophical and legal exposition looks upon individual access to natural resources and the state's sovereignty over territory as natural (moral) rights. The property rights of individuals and the jurisdictional rights of the state are, at least in theory, beyond the arbitrary discretion of individuals in possession of political or economic power. Power is not supposed to define rights. Furthermore, the legal regulations regarding the extraction of natural resources are based on the sovereignty of states and their self-determination over their respective territories.

1.3   GOVERNANCE OF OIL RESOURCES

The legal notion of natural resources developed above suggests that such resources are not in themselves obviously subject to private ownership. In the case of oil, one could argue that the oil deposits in the ground have economic value only after someone has invested capital and labor in order to extract the oil from them. The value of the extracted oil, for most of the reserves, most of the time, is far above the production costs, including any reasonable profit. Thus, nature provides, by itself, an economic value, the resource rent discussed in Section 1.1. "Being a resource provided by nature one might argue that it would not be just and reasonable that an individual should be able to lay claim to an exclusive and unlimited proprietary right to a petroleum reservoir merely by virtue of first discovery, appropriation, or ownership of the land in the subsoil of which the petroleum is found" (Alvik, 2015, pp. 236–237).

As discussed in Section 1.2, on territories under the jurisdiction of a sovereign state, private ownership is a result of the state exercising its sovereign right to provide the individuals with property rights following from its ownership of the territory. The property right can imply a limited or extended right to develop the resources in the ground and benefit from them. The extension of the territories under state jurisdiction has increased throughout the history of man. Today only a very few areas of the landmasses of the earth lie outside the territorial jurisdiction of sovereign states.

Some areas are contested as more than one country claims the area. In such cases, the claiming countries can agree to abstain from their claims, and thus leave the disputed area as no-man's land (*terra nullius*). In other cases, the concept of *terra nullius* has been related to the extent of the state's sovereignty in areas where indigenous people live. Antarctica is a special case of the limitation of state sovereignty over onshore territories. Antarctica has no indigenous people and very few permanent occupants (who are there almost exclusively for scientific purposes). Seven countries have made partly overlapping claims to Antarctica. The part of the continent called Marie Byrd Land is today the largest single unclaimed territory on Earth by far, with an area of 1,610,000 km^2. The 1959 Antarctic treaty strictly limits human activities on the entire continent – an area of 14,000,000 km^2. With these exceptions, and for the purpose at hand, we can regard all land territories of the world that contain prospective oil resources as being under state sovereignty. The main division in the legislation relevant for the ownership of oil resources is between oil found underground in land territory (onshore) and oil found underground in the continental shelves of coastal states (offshore). These two areas – onshore and offshore – will be discussed in sub-sections below. First, we need to provide a historical account of the development of the relationship between individual property rights and state jurisdiction concerning oil resources.

1.3.1 Private Governance of Oil Resources

The history of the US oil industry is a fascinating story which this book leaves untold, although, some of the market-related aspects are discussed in Chapter 5. Here, we will discuss some of the features, present and historical, of the almost unique US system of private governance of oil resources. There are two countries in the world, United States and to a limited degree Canada, where the property rights of private landowners include the right to explore and produce oil resources in the ground. Individuals, companies, corporations, Indian tribes, and various partnerships and organizations all hold the right to develop oil resources in the United States. In addition, the local, regional and federal governments have property rights, and thus the right to develop the oil resources. The federally owned areas are particularly important as they can easily be regulated in accordance with the policy decisions of the US government.

The recent surge in exploration of non-conventional oil resources in the US, also known as shale oil, has mainly been in land areas with private owners. This growth has brought the federal share of the oil reserves down to just above 20 percent in 2014, from over 36 percent in 2010. Almost four-fifths of the oil production in federal areas takes place offshore. In total, almost 80 percent of US oil production is in private ownership, where private actors largely control the development of their own resources, without the need to seek authorization from public bodies. This is not to say that the US industry is without any kind of regulation or taxation. However, there are striking differences between the US system and the rest of the world. Outside the US, the fundamental feature of the governance system is that the government at the outset takes full ownership of all oil resources.

In the US, the basic principle is that the owner of the land is the owner of the resources in the ground underneath that land. The landowner is usually not in a position to develop the resources on his own. He will have to enter into a contractual relationship with an oil drilling company by way of a lease. A lease is a "contract that grants the rights to explore and produce from the owner of the mineral rights (lessor) to a tenant (lessee), usually for a fee and with a specified duration" (Cleveland and Morris,

2006, p. 250). The oil company is usually the initiator, since it will have the geological knowledge indicating where oil resources are most likely located. The payment for the lease can include three elements: an up-front bonus or sign-on fee, a rental as an annual payment for the duration of the lease, and finally royalties, which are a share of the gross value of the oil produced. Historically, the standard royalty rate was 12.5 percent, but today it is often higher. If the oil company can deduct the production costs, the royalty becomes more like a split of profits.

It follows that the investments into the resources are fully in private hands. The investment decisions of the US onshore exploration and production (E&P) companies are made according to a commercial business calculation of risk and potential profit. Thus, both investments, and the subsequent level of production in the non-federal areas of US oil drilling, are much more responsive to changes in market prices than oil investments and production in countries with a publicly-owned E&P industry. The regulation of oil E&P in the non-federal areas in the US is largely left to the states. "Each state has developed common law principles and enacted statutory schemes which govern privately owned minerals and the leasing and assignment thereof" (Derman and Villarreal, 2013, pp. 277–278).

The oil under federal lands might also be developed under lease agreements. For the federal areas, the regulatory body is the Bureau of Land Management in the Department of the Interior. Privately held oil interests are regulated by the various states, through bodies like the Railroad Commission in Texas, which will be discussed further in Chapter 5 (Derman and Villareal, 2013, p. 283). Two particular legal features of the historic development of the US oil industry are the so-called *rule of capture* and the *rule of offset drilling*. "The rule of capture evolved out of common law cases where dispute arose on oil and gas fields" (Boyce, 2013, p. 156). The rule of 'capture' implies that the "owner of a tract of land acquires title to the oil and gas which he produces from wells drilled thereon, though it may be proved that part of such oil and gas migrated from adjoining lands" (Hardwicke, 1935, p. 393).

The rule of 'offset drilling' implies that the "owner of the land being drained by the operation of wells on neighboring lands cannot enjoin the further operation of the operator wells, and cannot recover damages from the operator thereof, but must protect his lines as best he can by producing from offset wells drilled on his own land" (Hardwicke, 1935, p. 393). A Pennsylvania Supreme Court decision from 1889 is generally regarded as the first leading oil and gas case, which applied the rule of capture doctrine. The court stated that water, oil and gas, in common with animals "have the power and the tendency to escape without the volition of the owner." And that they therefore "belong to the owner of the land, and are part of it, so long as they are on or in it, and are subject to his control; but when they escape . . . the title of the former owner is gone" (Kramer and Anderson, 2005, p. 906). Thus, the rule of capture dissolves the link between ownership of the soil and the fugitive natural resources in the subsoil.

In another case, the full transfer of the property of the oil through the logic of the rule of capture was explicitly stated. "If an adjoining owner drills his own land and taps a deposit of oil or gas, extending under his neighbor's field, so that it comes into his well, it becomes his property" (Kramer and Anderson, 2005, p. 907). This common law privilege of draining the oil from your neighbor's land caused unnecessary drilling because of the craving to be the first to 'capture' the oil. As everybody had the same incentive to do so, over-investment and unnecessary drilling in the oil fields was common, resulting in a loss of pressure and the production of a non-optimal amount of oil. In the early 20th century, the demand for a federal compulsory unitization statute emerged in the US oil industry. Unitization implies that the government forces the owners to operate jointly in the extraction of the oil reservoir. No such legislation emerged until 1945 when Oklahoma initiated the first comprehensive compulsory unitization statute (Kramer and Anderson, 2005, p. 902). The market implications of the rule of capture are discussed in Chapter 5.

1.3.2 Public Governance of Oil Resources

As indicated above, Canada also has private ownership of oil resources. In Alberta, about 19 percent of the oil is in private hands. The federal government owns offshore resources, while public ownership onshore resides with the states. These resources are governed in a similar way as in the rest of the world, in what we can call the system of 'public governance of oil resources'. Although the governance system of each oil-producing country has its own specific nuances, the public governance system has some basic features in common, that are generally in place in most oil-producing countries.

With state ownership, the private contractual relations that operate in the US (described above) are less relevant. The three-party relationship, with the state as regulator, the landowners as resource owners and the oil companies as operators, is replaced by a comprehensive system for regulating the two-party relationship between the state as both owner and regulator, and the oil companies set to perform the actual exploration and production (E&P) of a resource they initially do not own. In some cases, the government decides to take control of the operative aspects of the E&P by creating a state-owned national oil company, and providing this company with exclusive rights to explore and produce all oil reserves within the territory of the country. In such cases, the legislative aspects are less pronounced as the governance of the resources is, to a large extent, a matter of the relationship between the government and a subsidiary entity of the public administration of the country. In cases where state-owned oil resource is to be developed by private companies, a bargaining relationship can emerge. A model for this relationship is discussed in Chapter 2. Here the focus is on the legislative aspects.

The basis for public governance is, of course, that the state takes full ownership of the resources, in accordance with the international law recognizing the principles of UN General Assembly resolution 1803 from 1962 on permanent sovereignty over natural resources, discussed above. State sovereignty implies governmental control over resources inside the territory of the state, in relation to other states. State ownership implies governmental control over the resources in relation to domestic actors and individuals. The most effective instrument of state power and control toward its own citizens is legislation, in particular constitutional provisions. "Typically, the national constitution provides for state control and state ownership. The constitution also sets out certain rights and obligations of private actors" (Pereira and Talus, 2013, p. 9). In addition to constitutional provisions, the oil state would normally develop a body of legislation specifically for petroleum activity, including:

- Specifications of the public administration of the sector with assignment of authority and responsibilities.
- Procedures and conditions for granting licenses, including issues like work programs and the duration of licenses.
- Government take and fiscal provisions.
- Qualification requirements for operating companies.
- Codes of conduct and environmental standards for the E&P activities.
- Other provisions, such as labor standards, transparency, management requirements etc.

It is beyond the scope of this book to go into all aspects of state legislation and regulation of oil activities. However, three of the issues deserve some comments.

Public administration
The importance of the public administration of the extraction of natural resources can hardly be overestimated. As will be evident in Chapter 3, to transform natural resources like oil deposits in the ground into economic growth and the development of welfare for the entire population of resource-rich countries, is no easy task. It is considered to be one of the

most complex tasks in development, both politically, socially and economically (Kaufmann, 2017, p. 3).

The ability of the government of oil-rich states to perform 'good governance' of the oil sectors is a vital prerequisite for the resource curse to be combatted at least in political terms (Lahn et al., 2007). The Norwegian administrative system is regarded as an example of best practice in this regard (Moses and Letnes, 2017). The key feature of the so-called 'Norwegian Model' is the separation of administrative functions. The Parliament decides the framework through its legislative powers while the power of the political executive rests with the Ministry of Petroleum and Energy. The administrative functions are in the hands of the Norwegian Petroleum Directorate. The directorate is a subordinate agency of the Ministry, but exercises administrative authority over E&P activities, and has the power, under the petroleum legislation, to make decisions and adopt regulations. Finally, the state's commercial interests are handled by the partly state-owned (67 percent) national oil company, Equinor (formerly Statoil). Thurber, Hults, and Heller (2011, p. 5,366) find widespread support for "a strict separation of functions as something of a *sine qua non* of effective oil sector governance." It is another matter, though, to what extent the Norwegian administrative system can serve as a model for other oil-producing countries. Based on a comparison of 10 countries Thurber et al. (2011, pp. 5,374–5,375), draw three conclusions:

> First, serious efforts to create separation of functions rarely seem to be undertaken where political competition is low. Second, a country's ability to implement separation of functions in a meaningful way is heavily dependent of its level of institutional development. Third, countries lacking deep institutional capacity . . . early in the development of their oil sectors may benefit from *not* establishing the separation of functions model initially.

Stevens, Lahn, and Koorshy (2015, p. 12) point to the pre-existing conditions of the Norwegian case, and suggest that these cannot be expected to be present in other cases. "[T]he Norwegian example was born of very special circumstances . . . Such conditions are difficult to find elsewhere . . . the only way its [Norway's] experience can be replicated is to start with 4.5 million Norwegians."

Contract regimes

With state ownership, the operating oil company needs a contract with the state regulating the relationship akin to the leases with the landowner in the private governance system presented above. In general, there are three main models of contractual regimes, although the specific contracts or contract schemes of individual producing countries are often hybrid

Table 1.1   Key features of contract arrangements

Feature	Royalty/Tax	Production Sharing Agreement	Risk Sharing Agreement
Ownership	Transferred to IOC at the wellhead	Transferred to the IOC at delivery point	Stays with the State or NOC
IOC Control	High	Moderate to low	Low
Government Control	Low	Moderate to high	High
IOC Lifting Entitlement	Typically around 90%	Typically 50% to 60%	None
Cost Recovery Limit	None	Frequently	Rarely
Ownership of Production Facilities	IOC	Typically State/NOC	NOC/State
Limits to IOC Profitability	Few	Signinficant	Absolute

Source: Inkpen and Moffett (2011, p. 245).

versions containing elements from more than one of these models. Table 1.1 compares some of the key features of the various contract arrangements.

Concession agreements. This is the traditional type of contract, and resembles the lease contracts in the private governance system. It was used both in the United States in the 19th century and by the International Oil Companies (IOCs) in the Middle East after the Second World War. In this system, the oil company is granted an exclusive right to explore a specified area, and to develop and produce oil there. The duration of the concession is limited, but can usually be extended. Today the concession holder is under a work program obligation to perform a certain number of exploratory drillings. The production company takes ownership of the produced oil, so-called 'equity oil'. At this point, the owner – the state – receives a royalty, either in cash or in physical oil. In this system, the E&P companies assume the risks and costs of finding and developing the oil field. The costs then have to be covered by the companies' revenue after the royalty is paid to the owner (Downey, 2009, p. 86).

Production sharing agreements (PSAs). This system was first introduced by Indonesia in the 1960s (Inkpen and Moffett, 2011, p. 89). As the name suggests, this system means that the company and the owner – the state – share the produced oil. The company usually has the right to so-called 'cost oil', in order to recover its production costs. The rest of the oil, called 'profit oil' is divided according to a specified formula. The company still might have to cover all production costs and the costs of exploration, even if it is unsuccessful in finding oil. But many PSAs have a complex structure, specifying which parts of the costs are deductible and at what rate. A sliding scale can be included, detailing the change in the division of income between the state and the company over time. To some extent PSAs accommodate host countries that are reluctant to give foreign companies ownership of the oil, so-called 'equity oil'.

Service agreements. In this system the state's ownership of the oil remains at all times, including after production (Pereira and Talus, 2013, p. 12). The pure form implies that the state takes all exploration risks, notwithstanding discovery or production. The company is simply paid for its services, almost like a contractor. Thus, the state can gain or lose, dependent on the net profit from the production. In a so-called risk service contract, the company assumes the exploration risks, and is paid for its services according to the proceeds derived from the produced oil.

Fiscal regimes

The three contract regimes have some general implications for the way the state, and the companies, make money. "Royalty/tax agreements generate on average the greater takes for the E&P firms and the lowest government take . . . Service agreements generate the lowest return for E&P firms and reserve all true price or other market-based returns to the state. PSAs . . . often fall into a mid-range of balance between the IOC and the state" (Inkpen and Moffett, 2011, p. 245). Therefore, the nature of the contract regime has implications for how the revenue from oil production is distributed between the companies and the state. Even more important, of course, are the government's various mechanisms for rent extraction, and the actual percentages specified in the contracts. The taxation regimes of the different oil-producing states vary even more than the contract regimes, so also this section can only provide a brief overview. Johnston and Johnston (2010, pp. 2–5) identify four different mechanisms used by governments to gain rent from oil and gas companies:

- *Signature bonuses* are used as part of oil and gas contracts by approximately 40 percent of countries with a hydrocarbon industry.
- *Royalties* are one of the most common ways to gain governmental rent in the oil industry. They are usually based on gross revenue or gross production. Royalties are around 5 percent for PSAs and on

average 10 percent in concession systems (Johnston and Johnston, 2010, p. 4).

- *Profit-based mechanisms* take the form of corporate income tax (or other profit-based taxes) and production sharing. The former is paid in dollars, the latter in barrels of oil. Both forms often include various cost deductions for the companies. If deductions are high enough, the companies can end up not paying any tax at all.
- *Government participation* represents a smaller part of the overall government take compared to the other mechanisms above. It is usually very controversial. It works as follows: the foreign or private companies assume all costs and risks of exploration. If a profitable discovery is made, the government takes a percentage share of the production, usually via the national oil company. The government is *carried* through exploration for free.

The concept of ownership is not easily incorporated into economic models. "Modern economic science considers the ownership of natural resources irrelevant to the determination of prices" (Mommer, 2002, p. 6). The discussion above suggests that ownership does in fact have an impact on business and profits. Nevertheless, sovereignty and ownership are not only about rent and profit sharing. "The question of natural resource ownership and its relationship to prices is definitely a question of politics and not of economics" (Mommer, 2002, p. 105). It is also, and probably even more so, about state control and legitimacy in the eyes of citizens, at least in the case of democratic states. In non-democratic states, the control of natural resources is often an important issue for ordinary citizens if for no other reason than that of national pride.

1.4 LAW OF THE SEA – IMPLICATIONS FOR OFFSHORE OIL

The production of oil at sea (offshore) represents about 30 percent of world oil production, a share which has remained stable over the last decade. More than 27 million barrels per day are produced offshore in more than 50 countries. In 2015, five countries provided 43 percent of total offshore production: Saudi Arabia, Brazil, Mexico, Norway and the United States.[4] Offshore oil production is established as an ordinary part of the oil industry. Many of the aspects related to regulations and state–company relations are no different if the oil is located offshore or onshore.

The legal aspects related to offshore oil, however, are fundamentally different – in particular those related to property rights and state sovereignty. "Where petroleum is found offshore in the continental shelf, the absence of any private proprietary rights is quite logical . . . since the seabed is not subject to private ownership" (Alvik, 2015, p. 238). Since the 17th century, coastal states have claimed sovereignty over the sea adjacent to their land territory. The extension of this sovereignty was first attached to the range of canons placed next to the shore, but this was a rather imprecise measure of a territorial line. "During and after the Napoleonic wars, British and American prize courts translated the canon-shot rule into the three-mile rule" (Crawford, 2012, p. 256). Today, the UN Convention of the Law of the Sea (UNCLOS) regulates the extension of the territorial sea as 12 nautical miles from a straight coastal baseline. In addition, the content of the coastal states' sovereignty is regulated in UNCLOS. "The coastal states have all the practical rights and duties inherent in sovereignty, whereas foreign vessels have privileges, associated particularly with the right to innocent passage, which have no general counterparts in the respect of the land domain" (Crawford, 2012, p. 264).

The coastal states' sovereignty over offshore oil resources is regulated by international law, primarily UNCLOS. It is outside the scope of this book to outline the comprehensive legislative regime of UNCLOS, as oil resources are located in the seabed, the regulations of the oceans themselves are less relevant for the discussion here.

UNCLOS contains specific regulations regarding the seabed, in particular the seabed adjacent to the coastal state, known as the continental shelf. Article 76 of UNCLOS grants all coastal states a continental shelf of 200 nautical miles provided it does not meet another state's shelf.[5] This is the equal distance as the coastal states' 'exclusive economic zone' at the sea level. The coastal state enjoys exclusive rights over oil resources located in its assigned continental shelf. In cases where it is less than 400 (200+200) nautic miles between coastal states, the states will have to negotiate a delimitation line between them, including both maritime borders and division of the continental shelf. The divisons of the North Sea between Denmark, Norway and the UK, is one example of such a negotiated division. In some cases, an oil field can happen to be located so that it extends across such a territorial delimitation line. There are various models for handling this situation. One example is a so-called unitization agreement, where the parties agree to joint development of the field crossing the delimitation line.

According to the provisons of UNCLOS, a continental shelf can be extended beyond the 200 nautical miles: "The continental shelf of a coastal State comprises the seabed and subsoil of the submarine areas that extend beyond its territorial sea throughout the natural prolongation of its land territory to the outer edge of the continental margin."[6] This is known as the natural prolongation principle.

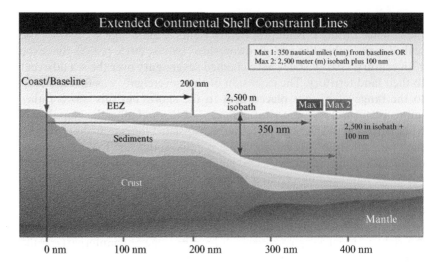

Source: NOAA (2017).

Figure 1.2   Law of the Sea regulations

Such extensions require that the geological features of the seabed accord
with the definition of such a shelf in the UNCLOS provisions, which implies
that the extension must be recommended by the Commission on the Limits
of the Continental Shelf (CLCS). The coastal state is required to present scientific data determining the geological features of the seabed, as the basis for
CLCS' evaluation and recommendation regarding the extension of the shelf.
From 2001 up until today, the CLCS has received 78 submissions pursuant
to the provision in Article 76 regarding the extension of continental shelves.[7]

It is uncertain how many of the cases of extensions of continental
shelves that involve oil resources. Coastal states can behave proactively,
and try to extend their continental shelves 'in case' oil should be discovered later. If there are no overlapping claims, the presence of oil resources
in the ground will not have implications on the process of gaining
sovereignty through the CLCS recommendation. In cases where there are
overlapping claims, oil discoveries are more likely to have an impact on
the process of gaining sovereignty. In particular since the CLCS does not
have any role in the case of overlapping claims following from extensions
of continental shelves. Where overlapping claims exist, the coastal states
must negotiate in order to determine a delimitation line, or resort to a
third party like an arbiter, a tribunal or the International Court of Justice.
These negotiations between coastal states with overlapping cliams, can be

very different with the prospect of large oil resources in the continental shelf compared to a situation without such prospects.

There are presently several overlapping claims around the globe. One prominent example is the claims in the Arctic Ocean. Russia submitted claims of extension already in 2001. The documentation was regarded as insufficient by CLCS. Thus, Russia submitted a revised documentation in 2015. By then, Denmark in 2014 had submitted documentation for an extended continental shelf overlapping the Russian claim. In addition, the expected Canadian claim will overlap parts of the same area. However, the contested area is unlikely to be very interesting for oil exploration (Claes, 2017: 91–92).

The US Geological Survey (USGS) published an appraisal of the world's oil and gas resources in 2000, in which a quarter of the remaining resources where located to the Arctic region. This created an idea in public media of an Arctic resource race. A more thorough appraisal of the Arctic in 2008 estimated the Arctic undiscovered oil resources to be about 90 billion barrels (USGS, 2008). More important is that they locate most of the resources to shallow waters, and thus within the undisputed jurisdiction of the coastal states (Gautier et al., 2009). As indicated above, conflict can arise even if the resource prospect seems weak today. The five coastal states around the Arctic Ocean have all committed themselves to abide by the UNCLOS regulation. In their joint declaration, they state that "the law of the sea provides for important rights and obligations concerning the delineation of the outer limits of the continental shelf . . . We remain committed to this legal framework and to the orderly settlement of any possible overlapping claims."[8]

Coastal states in such territorial disputes might want to engage the oil industry. Since the development of offshore energy resources requires large up-front investments, companies prefer that the jurisdictional conditions are resolved and undisputed. There have been cases where one party to a delimitation dispute has encouraged oil companies to start exploration in contested waters. Soviet authorities approached several Western oil companies for this purpose in the Barents Sea in the early 1980s (Tamnes, 1997, pp. 323–324), and in 2003 US authorities prepared to sell leases of blocks in waters where Canada had a claim.[9] In both cases, the oil companies refrained from involvement.

NOTES

1. The text is from the protocol of the Convention amended in 1952. European Convention of Human Rights, p. 31. European Court of Human Rights (ECHR). https://www.echr.coe.int/Documents/Convention_ENG.pdf (accessed July 3, 2018).
2. See https://www.ohchr.org/Documents/ProfessionalInterest/resources.pdf (accessed July 9, 2018).
3. *International Covenant on Economic, Social and Cultural Rights.* Adopted and opened for signature, ratification and accession by General Assembly resolution 2200A (XXI) on December 16, 1966. Article 1, paragraph 2.
4. EIA – Today in Energy: Offshore production nearly 30% of global crude oil output in 2015, October 25, 2016. https://www.eia.gov/todayinenergy/detail.php?id=28492 (accessed June 19, 2018).
5. United Nations Convention of the Law of the Sea (UNCLOS), December 10, 1982, 1833 UNTS 105.
6. UNCLOS, Article 76.
7. http://www.un.org/depts/los/clcs_new/commission_submissions.htm (accessed June 19, 2018).
8. http://www.arcticgovernance.org/the-ilulissat-declaration.4872424.html (accessed June 19, 2018).
9. 'US plans to tap oil in Beaufort Sea', *Alexander's Gas & Oil Connections*, April 28, 2003. http://www.gasandoil.com/news/n_america/a65f4c61aae19ce2f50b1aea23e1133e (accessed October 10, 2017).

2. Governing oil production

2.1 THE ECONOMICS OF OIL EXTRACTION

Having secured sovereignty over the territory containing potential oil resources, the next challenge for the oil state is to decide whether to explore and possibly produce the oil, or not. This might seem a redundant question, since the prospect of income from oil production represents an increase in national wealth. A prominent oil economist, Morris A. Adelman (1993b, p. 17), makes a vigorous claim that we can disregard any other motive behind oil production decisions than the economic motive:

> Some models have governments making oil production decisions for noneconomic reasons. This confuses means with ends, and getting with spending. A state seeks first to survive; then, to cultivate its garden, or spread the true faith, or bash its neighbors, or anything else. But whatever the objectives, the more wealth the better. A state that deliberately avoids wealth-maximizing is a special story, which had better be a good one. (Adelman, 1993b, p. 17)

There are other reasons for refraining from oil exploration, like a vulnerable environment for animals, proximity to densely populated areas, technical challenges related to depth or pressure conditions, and so on. Nevertheless, oil economists like Adelman generally agree about the primacy of the economic gains stemming from oil extraction. Thus, this chapter will mainly focus on the economic efficiency and the political governance of oil production. Global environmental concerns related to oil extraction, will be discussed in Chapter 10. One of the main questions in the theoretical economics of oil extraction is how to optimize the economic value of the oil resources.

Among the most influential contributions to economic theories related to oil production, is a 1931 article by Harold Hotelling (1931). It has been the starting point of theoretical economics regarding exhaustible resources ever since. The essence of Hotelling's rule is that an exhaustible resource like oil can be seen as a fixed asset that the owner can either extract immediately or leave in the ground and extract later. The challenge is to maximize the total profit of the asset. If oil is extracted immediately, and the income saved in the bank the value of it increases with the interest rate gained from the savings (Claes, 2001, p. 21). It follows that "the annual growth rate of the net price of the oil must equal the rise in the interest or discount rate to provide that profits realized by leaving oil in the ground match the profits from extracting and selling the oil" (Moors, 2011, p. 46).

The basic economic modeling following Hotelling is described by Dahl (2004, pp. 279–312). In the simplest two-period model (*now* versus *later*), the logic of the model is easy to grasp. If the oil price increases at a slower rate than the interest rate, it is better to produce more oil now, put the money in the bank, and collect the interest rate. Since there is a fixed amount of oil, more production now means less production later. Thus, the price will fall now, while later on it will increase. If the oil price increases at a higher rate than the interest rate, oil in the ground is more valuable than money in the bank. Thus, producers will reduce production now in order to produce more at a higher price in the later period. The oil price will increase as production is reduced, and fall in the later period when production is stepped up again. Remember there is a fixed amount of oil to be sold – therefore less oil sold now means more oil to sell later. Thus, it is more profitable to reallocate production until the price increases at the same rate as the interest rate. Dahl (2004, p. 285) concludes: "if producers dynamically optimize in this simple model, market forces should cause price to go up at the interest rate."

The theoretical literature following Hotelling elaborates this basic logic of why the oil price must increase at the rate of interest, to include changes in production costs, income growth, interest rates and further into dynamic models. Hotelling's work has inspired a number of economic studies, a recent example being Halvorsen and Layton (2015). As indicated above, the theoretical model has been refined, extended and discussed in many formats over the years.

Hotelling's rule relates the production decision to the increase in price, and thus it predicts the future path of the oil price. Having put money in the bank, one earns interest the following year on the interest rate earned the previous year. As the price path is assumed to follow the interest rate, the price will rise continuously. In its simple form, the rule relies on a few assumptions:

- The resources are non-renewable and exhaustible;
- The stock is completely known to the producers;
- No new discoveries are possible;
- There are no alternatives that can compete with the resource in question;
- Recycling is not possible;
- The resource is in private ownership; and
- There are constant costs of extraction.

Obviously, the empirical validity of several of these assumptions are questionable. Recent economic models have loosened some of the assumptions. However, the fundamental starting point for the economic models remain, the aim is to optimize the value of production of a fixed stock of an exhaustible resource over time (Moors, 2011, p. 335; Stiglitz, 1976).

Turning the geological fact of a fixed stock of an exhaustible resource into an economic model intended to determine the future price immediately triggers the question of scarcity – since consumption of the fixed stock implies that there is less of it left for future consumption. This was, in fact, the starting point of Hotelling's original article, as he discussed the need for regulation in the face of selfish exploitation at the cost for future generations (Hotelling, 1931, p. 137). His general observation of the challenges for economic modelling is also interesting, and he underlines the difficulty of considering exploitation of exhaustible resources over an infinite time frame without knowing future prices (Hotelling, 1931, p. 139). The problem is that a perception of scarcity leads to projections of continuous prices increases, which again are taken as evidence of scarcity. "Scarcity rent is often considered to be the most direct measure of economic scarcity of a nonrenewable resource, as it is, in principle, the price of the resource *in situ*" (Livernois and Thille, 2015, p. 60). The conclusion that follows is that "all measures of scarcity have imperfections but market price is probably the best indicator" (Livernois and Thille, 2015, p. 62). The empirical questions then arise: Is increasing scarcity observable in the oil market? Is the oil price following Hotelling's path? *Are oil resources scarce?*

2.2 ARE OIL RESOURCES SCARCE?

2.2.1 A Geological Fact of No Economic Value

Hotelling's theorem seemingly has some value, as it can explain the decision-making dilemma of an owner of an oil field or oil reserves. If the owner believes that prices will increase more than the return on investments, he or she might choose to postpone extraction. As Mabro notes, "Nobody would sell his or her shares in Shell at £5 per share today if there was a belief that the price is going to rise to £6 in a month or so" (Mabro, 1992, p. 3).

Morris A. Adelman has, on several occasions, argued against the applicability of Hotelling's rule to the international oil market: "the Hotelling Rule and Hotelling Valuation Principle are thoroughly discredited. A valid theory was joined to a wrong premise, the fixed stock. It gave results contrary to fact" (Adelman, 1993b, p. 8). The argument is partly based on an empirical observation that the physical limit of oil resources is not a restriction on the consumption of oil (cf. next sub-section). But it is also based on an understanding that the physical or geological amount of oil does not influence the workings of the oil market. "The total minerals in the earth is an irrelevant non-binding constraint. If expected finding-development costs exceed the expected net revenues, investment dries up, and the industry disappears. Whatever is left in the ground is unknown, probably unknowable, but surely unimportant: a geological fact of no economic interest" (Adelman, 1993a, p. 220).

Adelman's argument is that the market price is a poor indicator of scarcity, contrary to the conclusion of Livernois and Thille quoted above. A better signal of scarcity than the market price, is increasing costs of replacing a produced barrel of oil, so-called replacement costs: "The early-warning signal of scarcity is a persistent rise in development costs and in the in-ground value of oil reserves" (Adelman, 1993a, p. 276).

The trend in oil development costs since 1945 is not clear-cut. The over-all costs of developing oil resources have varied, and producing countries differ regarding the level of replacement costs and whether the replacement costs are rising or falling. However, it is hard to ascribe these changes to variations in scarcity. It is more likely that the market price influences the development costs. "Upstream costs follow oil prices with a time lag. In particular, a sustained 10% increase in the price of oil leads to an increase in upstream activity of about 4%, and in this way triggers a sustained 3% increase in global upstream costs after a lag of one to two years" (Naumov and Toews, 2016). Then the question is – to what extent is the market price the result of scarcity?

Figure 2.1 shows the oil price from 1861 to 2016 in 2016 dollars. In a historical perspective, the oil price has experienced three periods of dramatic price changes. The first volatile price period, from 1860 to 1880, was related to oil as a new industry in the US characterized by new discoveries of new oil provinces, which suddenly created large surpluses in the market (cf. Chapter 5). The oil price fell back and was stabilized partly due to the monopolistic role of Standard Oil. The second oil price rise in the 1970s was related to changes of market power, which shifted from the international oil companies (IOCs) to the governments of oil-producing countries, in particular those organized in the Organization of the Petroleum Exporting Countries (OPEC). The producer countries cooperated in order to achieve a higher oil price than the IOCs (cf. Chapter 6). The oil price in this period was also influenced by political turmoil in the Middle East, in particular the Iranian revolution and the Iran–Iraq

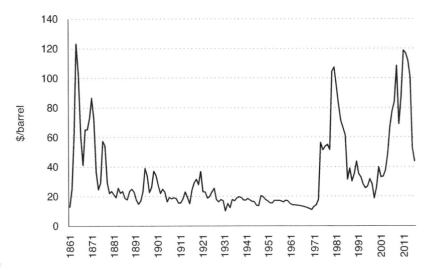

Note: 1861–1944 US Average, 1945–1983 Arabian Light posted at Ras Tanura, 1984–2016 Brent dated. $2016 (deflated using the Consumer Price Index for the US).

Source: BP (2017).

Figure 2.1 Crude oil prices 1861–2016 ($2016 $/barrel)

war. The third price increase, in the 2000s, was related to a perception in the market that existing reserves and production capacity could not keep up with rapidly increasing oil demand from emerging economies. None of these price changes can be ascribed to increased scarcity since they have all been followed by a rapid reduction in the oil price, which contradicts the Hotelling rule.

2.2.2 Are We Running Out of Oil?

Hotelling's rule also implies that there is a reduction in reserves due to the production of an exhaustible resource. Figure 2.2 shows the so-called R/P-ratio, which is calculated as global proven reserves divided by annual production. It estimates the number of years the world can continue present annual production based on the present amount of proven reserves. In the late 1970s the R/P-ratio was below 30 years compared to today's level of above 50 years. Not only have the world oil reserves been sustained, they have increased even relatively to increased production levels. The claim that the world is "running into oil, rather than out of it," still holds (Odell, 1994, p. 92).

Source: BP (2017).

Figure 2.2   Reserves-on-production (R/P-ratio), number of years

The R/P-ratio is based on estimates of proven reserves, which are those quantities that geological and engineering information indicates with reasonable certainty can be recovered in the future from known reservoirs under existing economic and operating conditions. It thus only represents those parts of the oil resources in the ground that, based on our present geological and technological knowledge, can be made available to the market with reasonable certainty and profit. This amount is very different from the geologically defined fixed stock of oil resources in the ground, also called "oil-in-place." For economic and political purposes, the interesting figure is the part of these resources that is possible to extract, the proven reserves. Oil in-place is transformed into proven reserves through technological innovation and improved geological knowledge. Oil extraction also requires profitability, so-called economically recoverable resources. This is determined by market prices and by the capital and operating costs that would be incurred during exploration and production.

Both the price increase in the 1970s and the one in the 2000s were interpreted by some as signs of a structural phenomenon indicating a fundamental shortage of oil reserves. In the consuming countries, the price rise in the early 1970s was, to some extent, seen as a symptom of a general resource scarcity. It fitted well with an influential publication from the Club of Rome called *Limits to Growth* released in 1972. Robert Pindyck

(1978, p. 36) refers to a CIA (Central Intelligence Agency) report which claimed that "a crisis is likely to occur in the early 1980s as world energy demand exceeds supply, resulting in shortages of energy, rapidly rising prices, and economic contraction in all of the industrialized countries . . . This view has had an important role in forming the rationale for the Carter administration's energy program." There was no shortage; the price increase was a result of OPEC exercising market power, not a lack of available resources. As Pindyck (1978, p. 51) concluded: "The kind of worldwide energy crisis of concern to the CIA and the Carter administration is unlikely to occur."

Nevertheless, the oil price was to increase once again. In the autumn of 1978, opposition to the Shah of Iran intensified, including strikes in the Iranian oil industry, which almost brought production to a halt in January 1979. Despite the fact that the other OPEC countries easily compensated for the disappearance of Iranian oil, demand increased as buyers clamored to secure their access to crude oil in case there was a future scarcity. From December 1978 to October 1979, the spot price increased from $13.80 per barrel to $38.35. Neither the second price shock of the 1970s can be ascribed to resource scarcity. Political factors related to the Iranian revolution, and to some extent the outbreak of the Iran–Iraq war, were obviously the triggering factors.

In 1998, the Brent oil price was $12.72 per barrel. Ten years later, in 2008, the annual average price was $97.26, with a peak in the summer of that year of $147 per barrel. Contrary to the price rise in the 1970s, this price increase had no immediate political explanation, which led some analysts to conclude that the price rise was an indication of resource depletion (Deffeyes, 2005). The idea that the price signaled fundamental resource depletion is based on an energy version of the neo-Malthusian idea that our consumption of natural resources is unsustainable given increases in population and energy consumption (Areklett, 2010; Campell, 2005). A new concept was launched – *peak oil*.

2.2.3 Peak Oil

The basic idea of Peak Oil is that oil discoveries, that is, the transformation of resources into reserves, will follow a Bell-shaped curve. Observing the point when this curve turns from an increasing to a decreasing rate of discoveries makes it possible to predict the same turning point in production. In 1956 the geologist M. King Hubbert did, in fact, predict that the peak of US oil production would occur around 1970. For many years, until the shale oil revolution caught on after 2010, this seemed to be a correct prediction. Hubbert was less accurate in predicting the global production peak in 1995 (Lallanilla, 2015). One possible explanation for the difference between predicting US production and global production is the difference in the governance system in the US and the rest of the world (cf. Chapter 1). The price increase in the 2000s triggered widespread interest in Hubbert's model and the prospect of a peak in oil production caused by reserve constraints. Several attempts to identify the peak were made, comprising both assertions that global oil production had already peaked, and predictions of future dates for the coming peak.

Noreng (2013, pp. 162–163) identifies six assumptions underlying the peak oil argument: knowledge of the world's oil reserves is complete; reserve estimates are constant; extraction inevitably takes the shape of a fairly symmetric curve; technology is constant; oil prices do not matter; all oil producers have the same revenue/profit motive and goals. As he clearly concludes: "None of these assumptions corresponds to reality" (Noreng, 2013, p. 163). The peak oil argument is based on the assumption that we have prior knowledge of how much of the world's geological resources can be turned into profitable proven reserves. The fact is that we do not know this, and Figure 2.2 suggests that we are still improving our ability to transform resources into reserves:

> Hubbert-style forecasts take URR [Ultimately Recoverable Resources] as a static variable when it is dynamic. This is a serious error. URR refers not to total resources, which is arguably a fixed amount, but to the proportion of the total which is recoverable. It is logical that this should increase over time, as technological advances raise the proportion of a field which can be recovered economically. (Lynch, 2002, p. 378)

2.3   THE DYNAMICS OF OIL RESERVES

2.3.1   Increasing the 'Fixed' Stock

A formal economic model, encompassing all relevant factors determining the optimal production level for each oil-producing country or company, is simply not attainable. "In the oil industry, important parameters are dynamic. Costs, reserves, prices, profits, competition, and regulation are constantly changing" (Noreng, 2013, p. 163). Whenever oil prices are high, doomsayers predict the end of oil because the price increase is interpreted as signaling scarcity. A prospect of a future lack of available reserves increases demand in order to secure supplies. This increased demand further raises prices, which again is interpreted as indicating scarcity. What is forgotten is that the oil market is a so-called cyclical market. When prices are low, oil consumption increases and the development of new reserves is put on hold. This combination of increased demand and reduced supply makes prices increase. When prices become high enough, demand is reduced and more reserves become profitable to develop. This combination of reduced demand and increased supply makes prices decline.

Market psychology, institutional constraints and political factors can either reduce or enhance the volatility of this cyclical movement of the oil price. Interpreting price increases as being caused by scarcity would imply a continuous increase in replacement costs, combined with reduction in proven reserves. So far this has never been seen in the history of oil. The period of high oil prices in the 2000s is adequately explained as primarily the result of such cyclical factors and short-term pressure on installed production capacity caused by an unexpected increase in demand from China, and to some extent, India. At present (2018), the potential for new discoveries of conventional oil is substantial, particularly in the Middle East. Iraq is regarded as having the second largest reserve base, having explored only a fraction of its potential oil provinces (Mills, 2008, p. 76). Furthermore, new technologies in exploration and production (E&P), have significantly improved the amount of oil extractable and reduce the cost of bringing it to the market. Breakdown of total costs shows wide variations in the cost structure of oil production. Large producers in the Middle East, like Iran, Iraq and Saudi Arabia, have low production costs and taxes, but higher transportation costs. Russia has a high tax share of the total costs. Figures presented by *The Wall Street Journal* in 2016 show a sample of countries producing a third of the world's total oil production have overall costs of less than $20 per barrel. The actual production costs, excluding taxes, capital spending and transportation are around $5 per barrel for the US, around $4 for Norway, about $3 for Saudi Arabia and Russia and around $2 per barrel in the case of Iran and Iraq.[1] Thus, it is possible to produce large quantities of oil at very low cost. In some of these countries, the geology is very favorable. In other cases, like US shale and Norwegian offshore, technological advances and efficiency gains have turned hard-to-reach resources into profitable reserves.

2.3.2 Government Production Strategies

Klare (2012, p. 24) suggests that the variation in production costs will determine distribution of extraction in time and space. "Extraction of resources, whatever the material, follows a predictable pattern . . . [P]roducers seek out and exploit the most desirable deposits of that material – those easiest to extract, purest, closest to markets, and so on. In time, however, these deposits are systematically depleted, and so producers must seek out and develop less attractive deposits." The problem is that empirical observations contradict this logic:

> [W]e should expect to see production in the lower-cost areas grow faster than the high-cost. This is precisely what we saw before 1973. Then there was an abrupt turnaround. High-cost areas expanded drilling mightily while low-cost cut back. It was water flowing uphill. The only theory which explains it is monopoly, whether of one or a small group trying to act as one, to restrain output to maintain prices. (Adelman, 1987, p. 47)

Individual oil fields do run out, but to analyze the global oil reserves in the same manner is wrong. On the contrary, the global oil reserves are expanding, as discussed above. Furthermore, producer cooperation, like OPEC, tend to enhance the price and restricts the extraction, and thus has the effect of preserving the reserves. Morris Adelman (2004, p. 18) points to the paradox that the OPEC countries "started with about 412 billion [barrels] in proved reserves, produced 307 billion, and now [2004] have about 819 billion left." Today they have 1,220 billion barrels left (BP, 2017, p. 12). Thus the last 40 years of oil extraction has not followed Klare's 'predictable pattern'.

The world will never extract the last barrel of oil from the ground. Long before we reach that point, production costs will have increased dramatically, investments in new resources will have dried up, and cheaper alternative energy sources will have taken over as the preferred choice of consumers. Furthermore, the economic models presented above are based on profit maximizing oil producers in a competitive market. The abrupt turnaround in 1973 identified by Adelman above, represented a shift in market power from the International Oil Companies (IOCs) to the oil-producing countries of OPEC. Since then the oil price has been influenced – if not set – by governments of oil-producing states trying to increase their revenues by fixing prices and/or cutting production. This has obviously affected the extraction of reserves, but also investments into development of new reserves. "Saudi Arabia alone has over 80 known fields, and exploits only nine . . . The Saudis do not invest to discover, develop, and produce more oil because more production would bring down world prices" (Adelman, 2004, p. 18). In 2005, Saudi Arabia was predicted to face an imminent decline in oil production (Simmons, 2005). The annual growth rate of Saudi Arabian oil production from 2005 to 2015 has been 0.9 percent, leading to a production level in 2015 more than one million barrels per day above the 2005 level. This has nothing to do with exhaustible resources, but is a result of market power and imperfect competition (Noreng, 2013, p. 165). We will return to the dynamics of the oil market and producer behavior in Chapters 5 and 6.

2.4 THE RELATIONSHIP BETWEEN GOVERNMENT AND COMPANIES

In the previous chapter, we established the state's sovereignty over the territory where oil resources are located, either onshore or offshore. Furthermore, we found that political authorities tend to take direct ownership over the resources, with the notable exceptions of non-federal oil provinces in the US and parts of Alberta in Canada. We also outlined the contractual and fiscal regimes of oil-producing states. In this chapter, we have established that oil is not a scarce resource in an economic and political sense. We now turn to the question of who is controlling the exploration and production of oil reserves. The immediate candidates are oil companies and oil-producing states.

In this section, we shall explore the role of the government in the development of the resources, in the industry usually referred to as Exploration and Production (E&P). The starting point for most oil-producing states is a situation of *tabula rasa*. Knowledge of anything related to exploration and production of oil is usually totally absent in the public administration, if not the country at large, when oil is discovered. This goes for all aspects – from the ability to evaluate geological and seismic information about the oil prospects, the technical requirements of the installations needed and operational aspects of E&P of oil – not to mention the financial aspects related to production costs and possible profit from the eventual sales of the extracted crude oil. On the other hand, this information is readily at hand in every oil company engaged in E&P anywhere in the world, in particular in the International Oil Companies (IOCs) who have experience and know-how of all aspects of E&P. Oil companies, especially the IOCs, also have the financial resources to handle the risk of large-scale investments in E&P in what are often remote areas in developing countries. The financial aspects are less important if oil is discovered in developed countries, but even there risking public money to develop oil resources can be hard to justify to the public at large. The government of an emerging oil state thus has to reinvent the wheel or engage the oil companies.

2.4.1 The Obsolescing Bargaining Model

In 1971 Raymond Vernon wrote a seminal book called *Sovereignty at Bay*, which focused on the relationship between host countries and the multinational companies. His empirical focus was on 187 US multinational companies and their importance, not to the US economy, but to the foreign economies where they were located. One chapter was devoted to the raw

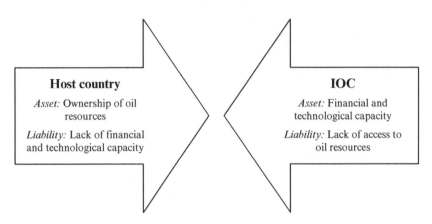

Figure 2.3   Illustration of the Obsolescing Bargaining Model

material industries. In this chapter he developed the so-called Obsolescing Bargaining Model (OBM) (Vernon, 1971, pp. 46–58), illustrated in Figure 2.3.

Vernon's model views the relationship between IOCs and host states as a dynamic bargaining game where the upper hand changes. The bases for the bargaining are the goals and resources of the parties. The host country controls access to the natural resources. In the case of oil, through a lease or license to explore and produce oil. Note that this is different in parts of the US and Canada, as discussed in Chapter 1. In most countries, the granting of licenses to explore and produce oil is dependent on some kind of up-front payment. Thus, the companies will have to be willing to spend money regardless of future discoveries. On the other hand, if none of the international oil companies choose to apply for a license to drill for oil, the host country is unable to extract the oil resources, at least in the short term. So, first the IOCs have the upper hand, because the host country is usually unable to build a petroleum industry from scratch on its own. Thus, the host country is compelled to give the IOCs lenient conditions in order to persuade them to invest in oil exploration. As discoveries are made and the companies have made their investments, the upper hand in the game changes in favor of the host country, since the investments, in the oil business in particular, are sunk costs, that is, the money spent is irretrievable. An offshore production platform is usually designed for a particular field and can hardly, if ever, be moved to another field. The company will therefore have to accept the conditions of the host country or forfeit future income. Sunk costs are irrelevant for future operative or investment decisions. The decision to continue production or abandon an oil well should only be based on expected future cash flow, not on the money spent on developing the oil field. The host country can take advantage of this and increase taxation and impose other conditions for the companies' further exploration and production of oil. "Thus, the original bargain obsolesces, giving OBM its name" (Vivoda, 2008, p. 37).

Francisco Parra (2004, p. 93) shows how governmental control over the companies was a top priority for two of the key producer countries, Venezuela and Saudi Arabia, already before the formation of OPEC. At the First Arab Petroleum Congress in Cairo in 1959, the Saudi Arabian Oil Minister, Abdullah Tariki, brought with him an American lawyer, Frank Hendryx, who delivered a paper suggesting that the host country, under certain conditions, could unilaterally alter or nullify existing concession contracts:

> Thus it seems clear that the sovereign state may by the accepted law of civilized nations, act through legislative or administrative decree, at its will, in ways which directly or in effect alter or nullify part or all of one of its existing concession agreements, so long as these actions are taken in good faith, that is, on behalf of a substantial public interest and not merely because it repents of a former bargain. (Hendryx, 1959)

To some extent, this represents a legal version of the obsolescing bargaining model. The host country could sign contracts giving the companies lenient conditions, and later exercise its sovereign right to impose stricter conditions on the companies. Hendryx's paper set the alarm bells ringing among the IOCs. There had been several specific disputes between the producing countries and the IOCs. The Hendryx paper, if acknowledged and put into practice, would have created multiple unilateral changes of contracts (Parra, 2004, p. 93). It was not put on the table, and was contested by other legal scholars, for instance Kissam and Leach, who discussed in detail Hendryx's paper and concluded as follows:

> There is no legal or moral justification for a State, after solemnly committing itself to a contract with a foreign national, seeking to avoid its responsibilities thereunder on some outworn theory that sovereignty embraces privileges only, without correlative obligations. Nothing inherent in sovereignty prevents the performance of contracts and the granting of irrevocable rights. (Kissam and Leach, 1959, p. 204)

During the 1960s, the OPEC countries made improvements to their bargaining position toward the companies, regarding price-setting, taxation, royalties and other aspects of the companies' activities in the OPEC member countries, but they did not achieve a true turn-around of the bargaining power in the sense indicated by the Obsolescing Bargaining Model.

In the early 1970s, dramatic changes in market power enfolded.[2] The changes in market power had a parallel in the domestic oil policies of the oil-producing countries. It was not only the control of the price-setting that changed hands, but also the operation of exploration and production in many oil-rich countries around the world. This coincided with a broad political focus on the relationship between Transnational Corporations (TNC) and developing countries. Neo-Marxist theories framed the operation of the TNCs as exploitation of poor countries, and in Latin-America the *dependency-school* asserted that inbound Foreign Direct Investments (FDI) made developing countries dependent on developed countries through the TNCs. During the 1970s a number of initiatives were taken to curb the influence of the TNCs over the development efforts of developing countries, culminating in the call for a *New International Economic Order*, in 1974. These general aspects of international economic diplomacy are beyond the scope of this book. However, the oil industry was an economic sector where TNCs had played a very dominant role for several decades. OPEC had so far been very modest in their demand for better terms with the companies. "The truth was that most of the member countries, especially Iran and Saudi Arabia, had no stomach for a confrontation with the companies, and by 1968, the organization seemed to have been well and truly emasculated" (Parra, 2004, p. 106). As the market power changed, so did the domestic governance of oil production.

2.4.2 National Oil Companies (NOC)

In many cases, the host country not only imposed higher taxation and other conditions on the companies, but expropriated or nationalized the entire E&P operation. An early example from just before the First World War is the UK government's purchase of a 51 percent share in the Anglo-Persian Oil Company (later British Petroleum). This was part of the geopolitical strategy of the UK. The aim was to gain access to oil resources in the Middle East in order to secure oil supplies necessary for the UK navy. For the oil industry the Mexican nationalization in 1938 and not least the Iranian in 1951, were also notable for their political implications. A large wave of nationalization of oil E&P and creations of NOCs emerged in the 1960s and even more so in the 1970s. "In the history of international raw materials markets no set of events has been as stunning as those that took place in the oil industry during the 1970s. Formal ownership was transferred from multinational firms to host-country governments . . . From 1970 to 1974 prices rose nearly 600 percent" (Krasner, 1978, p. 245). After 1971, the role of the IOCs in governing the international oil market diminished. A new group of companies emerged: the national oil companies (NOCs). "In the early 1970s several countries, including all the major producing countries in the developing world, chose to fully or partly nationalize their oil industries and replace private oil companies with national operating companies" (Nolan and Thurber, 2012, p. 145). The NOCs were initially created as instruments of government policy, whose aim was primarily to assert sovereign rights over national resources. "NOCs enable government control over the oil sector and its profits in a way that a Ministry of Energy (or equivalent) regulating IOCs does not. State control ensures easier and direct access to oil revenues" (Sarbu, 2014, p. 2). In a context of resource nationalism, they were to give the state control over the pace of exploitation and the pricing of its finite resources. NOCs also ensured that the state received an equitable share of profits (Marcel, 2006, p. 8). By the mid-1970s, therefore, most OPEC members had de facto nationalized their oil industry. In the 1970s the NOCs could be understood only as part of the public policy of the producer governments and not as actors with independent aims and interests. Other producing countries also reserved a large share of the upstream sector for national oil companies, as was the case with Mexico (PEMEX), the United Kingdom (BP), and Norway (Statoil). Some of the NOCs control enormous oil reserves. For instance, the Saudi Arabian company Aramco holds ten times the reserves of Exxon, the world's largest private oil company. The NOCs of Venezuela, Iran, and Iraq have been important actors in the international oil industry for more than three decades. Many European consuming countries also established national oil companies with the objective of controlling the downstream segment of their national oil industry. Some of these consumer NOCs also engaged in upstream activities in other countries, such as Italy's ENI. Some producer NOCs, such as the Norwegian Statoil, have also been engaged in exploration and production outside the home country for a few decades, but the main picture has been that NOCs are confined to forming an essential part of public administration in the domestic oil industry, and thus don't have strong international ambitions.

In the 1980s and 1990s the international oil market changed character once again. In particular, the price fall of 1986 changed the market. With oil prices in the range of \$15–\$25/barrel neither companies nor countries could hope to reap super profits. Oil became a commodity like any other. Without the super profit in exploration and production of oil, the fiscal reason for state-owned companies disappeared. The low price from the mid-1980s put pressure on profit and created the need for cost-efficiency all over the oil industry. This coincided with "the general complexion of the interface between national governments and TNCs [shifting] from being predominantly adversarial and confrontational to being non-adversarial and cooperative" (Dunning, 1998, p. 281). Many developed countries privatized their state-owned companies in a number of sectors, a shift in policy initiated by Margaret Thatcher in the UK. A number of developing countries followed suit. The oil sector was an exception to this trend, but broad political support for state-owned companies, both domestically and internationally, was gone.

The price increase in the 2000s again raised the stakes in the oil market. Most producing countries and some newly important consuming countries (especially China) vitalized the role of their NOCs. Some analysts drew pessimistic conclusions based on the renewed market power of the NOCs:

> If an increasing proportion of global oil and gas resources are under the control of NOCs, it is reasonable to expect that an increasing majority of oil and gas developments will be driven with political objectives in mind. Relative to a commercial outcome, this will result in inefficiencies in the production of revenues, which can manifest through lower levels of production and higher prices than would otherwise occur. (Eller, Hartley, and Medlock, 2007, pp. 33–34)

The private oil companies are generally regarded as more efficient than state-owned oil companies (Victor, 2007). Private and state-owned oil companies are hard to compare. There are a number of factors influencing the conditions for their respective performance. A fundamental difference is that the goal of a private oil company is profit and profit alone. The business strategies of private firms can vary, and so can their horizon regarding short-term versus long-term profit. But, in the end, a private company losing money cannot sustain operations for many years. State-owned companies have a much wider set of goals. Tordo (2011) analyzes the performance of NOCs within a model of value creation, suggesting a broad definition of value. One of her key findings is the importance of the structure and organization of ownership of NOCs. "In general, NOCs that are wholly owned by the state tend to have large national missions objectives and fewer incentives to improve efficiency than partly privatized NOCs. All other things being equal, internal governance mechanisms – the procedure and processes that govern the functioning of the institutional structure of governance – are more critical for value creation than external governance mechanisms" (Tordo, 2011, p. 102). Wolf (2009) has a similar approach, but a more narrow focus on profit, and makes an explicit comparison between private and state-owned oil companies. He outlines an oil and gas profit chain, including a set of structural factors at the firm, country and market level, in order to control for exogenous factors in the comparison of private and state-owned oil companies. His findings are "generally supportive of the hypothesis that 'ownership matters' in the sense that private ownership encourages better performance and greater efficiency than state ownership does" (Wolf, 2009, p. 2650). If performance differs, so do profit margins. Although governments can be less profit-oriented, and thus more patient – compared to private investors – toward companies losing money, they still will find it hard to subsidize state-owned E&P companies in the end, in particular if it becomes obvious that private companies could perform better, and produce a net profit for the resource owner. As indicated by the brief recent historical account above, the role of the NOCs has expanded in periods with high oil prices, and contracted in periods with low oil prices. This makes Victor (2013, p. 458) conclude that "the world oil price is probably the single largest factor to watch when the future for NOCs is assessed."

Victor, Hults, and Thurber (2012) find weaknesses with both statistical quantitative approaches and detailed historical case studies in the study of NOCs. In order to capture the complexity of the explanations for variations in NOCs' performance, and still be able to make generalizable inferences, they take a hybrid approach comprising structured case studies of 15 NOCs. In their voluminous book, they combine detailed cases of all 15 companies and provide cross-cutting studies and comparative analysis. In their conclusion they make several interesting observations regarding common explanations for the existence of NOCs and their performance. Even before the establishment of many NOCs the governments had "already figured out ways to rectify the imbalance of information and power [of the IOCs] and squeeze out more of the revenues for themselves, such as changing tax and royalty rules, without needing to resort to state ownership" (Victor et al., 2012, p. 891). Thus securing control of the income from oil production seems redundant as an argument for the creation of an NOC. Their findings also seem to support the logic of the Obsolescing Bargaining Model, as the NOCs, "were largely created after the riskiest part of the oil industry – the initial exploration of virgin territory – was already completed" (Victor et al., 2012, p. 893). Another often-cited rationale for creating and sustaining NOCs is their role as an integrated contributor to the nation's industrial base, and the national economy at large. Of the 15 cases studied, only Statoil of Norway is found to perform such a role (Victor et al., 2012, p. 894). In line with the observations above, they also find it "extremely difficult" to measure NOCs' performance. However, in contrast to the authors cited above who emphasize the oil price as the key factor, they conclude that the "single most important factor in explaining the performance of NOCs is the goals that governments set for them" (Victor et al., 2012, p. 900).

The nature, behavior, and roles of NOCs are very different today from the situation in the 1970s. First, the NOCs of the 1970s were almost completely oriented toward the domestic oil industry, while several of today's NOCs operate in other countries. There they face other NOCs on the opposite side of the negotiating table. Marcel (2006, p. 218) finds that Middle East NOCs distrust other NOCs and do not find them attractive partners, as IOCs complement their own strengths and assets to a greater degree. Nevertheless various alliances between NOCs are emerging. One illustration is how "Sonatrach, Statoil, Petrobras and Saudi Aramco are active participants and organizers of the NOC Forum, which ... has brought CEOs of national oil companies [together] to share ideas on how to develop NOCs' core competences" (Marcel, 2006, p. 220). The oil industry has also become more fragmented during the last three decades, as oil companies have outsourced several engineering and technological services. Thus, NOCs can acquire technology from sources other than the IOCs (UNCTAD, 2007, p. 118). However, various forms of contractual relations between oil-producing governments and IOCs have emerged (Likosky, 2009). Consequently, the IOCs have re-entered exploration and production in many of the countries that they were kicked out of in the 1970s. In general a wide variety of alliances between NOCs and IOCs has become the order of the day. This will potentially influence the operations and behavior of NOCs in a commercial direction. Marcel (2006, p. 209) observes "an increased blurring of differences between NOCs and IOCs." The set of influential actors in the oil industry has increased, and the structure has become more and more complex. These aspects will be discussed further in Chapter 4.

2.5 THREE CASES OF PRODUCTION GOVERNANCE

In this chapter and the next, three countries, Venezuela, Saudi Arabia and Norway, have been singled out to provide a more detailed exposition of how the general arguments of the chapters have played out in reality. In this chapter as a historical account of the development of government control over the oil sector in the three countries. In the next chapter the cases are related to how the three countries have handled the challenges of the so-called resource curse.

2.5.1 Venezuela

The first discoveries

The first serious oil discovery in Venezuela was made in 1912. The president, Juan Vincent Gomez, took it upon himself to hand out the concessions to explore, produce, and refine oil. They were granted mostly to his friends, and then redistributed to the international oil companies (IOC). From 1914 to 1917, several more oil fields were discovered. This coincided with the break-up of Standard Oil in the US. The subsidiaries of Standard Oil were eager to redirect their interest to oil provinces outside the US (cf. Chapter 5). In addition, the use of oil products in transportation was increasing rapidly. Together these factors created a great interest in exploration in Venezuela among the IOCs. In 1918, Venezuela became a net exporter of oil, and by 1928 Venezuela was the largest oil exporter in the world. In common with most new oil-producing countries, the government of Venezuela was unprepared for this rapid development, but it also had other weaknesses. Karl (1997, p. 76) notes that Gomez "inherited a simple and underdeveloped administrative apparatus that relied on personal authority, capricious and informal justice, and clientelist forms of recruitment. The state's jurisdiction was extremely limited." Combined with a corrupt president for whom oil represented an instrument of private enrichment for himself and his friends, the ineffectual Venezuelan government did not at this stage represent a challenge for the companies. Nevertheless, Gomez started building administrative capacity and tried to take advantage of the competition among the IOCs when negotiating concessions. An Office of Mines was created in 1909, and legislative processes "culminating in the Petroleum Law of 1922, were especially critical to reshaping the minimalist state" (Karl, 1997, p. 78). A fiscal regime for the oil industry was set up with an exploration period of three years, signature bonuses and surface taxes (Mommer, 2002, pp. 110–111). By the end of the 1930s, Creole Petroleum Corporation (acquired by Standard Oil of New Jersey in 1928) controlled 50 percent of Venezuelan oil production, while 35 percent was controlled by Royal Dutch Shell and 14 percent by Mene Grande, a subsidiary of Gulf Oil.

The Hydrocarbon Law of 1943

The Second World War precipitated an economic crisis in Venezuela. A short-term fall in oil production, reduction of exports in general, and wartime disruption created a large deficit in the state budget. The crisis exposed the risk of relying on exports of a single commodity and strengthened the argument for more control over the operations of oil companies. The result was The Hydrocarbons Law of 1943. It was, according to Karl (1997, p. 85), "perhaps the most important piece of legislation in the history of Venezuela [as it] ushered in the final stages in the consolidation of the petro-state." The companies accepted an increase in governmental royalties from 9 to 16.67 percent, and agreed to develop refineries in Venezuela. The taxation system was reformed, introducing an income tax. The law also ended concession trading, as only producing companies could acquire new concessions. Mommer (2002, pp. 113–114) concludes that "the Venezuelan state, as sovereign and as natural resource owner, was put on the same level, in its rights and in its obligations, as the state on federal lands in the Unites States." Furthermore, the principle of a fifty-fifty division of profits between the companies and the state was introduced. The IOCs fought this principle, but it was implemented in all of Venezuela's oil contracts in 1948 (Maugeri, 2006, p. 57). The law had an immediate effect on the state tax collection from the oil industry. From the fiscal year 1942–1943 to the fiscal year 1944–1945, total revenues more than doubled (Karl, 1997, p. 86). The Hydrocarbons Law of 1943 was the first major political step taken toward gaining more government control over the Venezuelan oil industry. It remained the basis for regulation and taxation of the oil industry in the South American country for more than 30 years.

Nationalization in 1976
Venezuela played a key role in the establishment of OPEC in 1960 and in the negotiations with the companies in the early 1970s (cf. Chapter 6). By then, the epicenter of oil production had moved to the Middle East. Cooperation inside the Organization of the Petroleum Exporting Countries strengthened the oil-producing states also regarding the development of their governance of the internal oil sector. In line with the trend among the Middle East oil producers, Venezuela nationalized its oil industry in 1976. A state-owned petroleum company, Petróleos de Venezuela S.A. (PDVSA), was established. All foreign oil companies were replaced by Venezuelan companies. "Each of the former concessionaires was simply substituted by a new 'national' oil company, which maintained the structures and functions of its multi-national corporation (MNC)-predecessor" (Bye, 1979, p. 67). However, the IOCs continued to provide technical services to the national oil companies, and even more importantly, to dominate the sales of Venezuelan oil. Nevertheless:

> It is clear that the power relation between the MNCs and the state has changed over the 60 years of the Venezuelan oil economy. Up to 1935, the companies got

92% of the incomes produced in the industry, and the state only 8%. The two last years prior to nationalization, the relation was a contrary one: 94 % went to the state and 6% to the companies. (Bye, 1979, p. 75)

Both OPEC's increased market power and the wave of nationalization of the oil companies, created an enormous optimism in the oil-producing countries regarding their new found power and thus potential prosperity. It was to be short-lived as predicted by Venezuelan oil minister and OPEC co-founder Juan Pablo Pérez Alfonzo in 1976: "Ten years from now, twenty years from now, you will see, oil will bring us ruin . . . It is the devil's excrement" (Useem, 2003). Following the nationalization in 1976, PDVSA "began a massive programme of investment in oil exploration and development operations whose economic impact spread throughout the whole economy" (Rutledge, 2006, p. 86). During this period, the oil price increased dramatically, creating an overvaluation of the national currency. This stimulated excess consumption of imported goods, while the other sectors of the economy suffered, thus making Venezuela possibly the most prominent example of the resource curse (cf. Chapter 3).

The aperture strategy of the 1990s
In the 1990s, PDVSA initiated a strategy of foreign downstream investments, focused in particular on refineries in the US. These were to be fed by increased crude exports. "Between 1991 and 1997 Venezuelan oil production increased by 33 percent, from 2.5 to 3.3 million b/d (barrels per day). At the same time, Venezuelan oil exports to the USA rose from around 1 million b/d in 1991 to 1.8 million b/d in 1997" (Rutledge, 2006, p. 87). The *aperture* ('opening') strategy in the 1990s gave PDVSA incentives to internationalize its operations. "It then started to transfer to Venezuela, on a massive scale, costs incurred in its ventures abroad, thus increasing the profits deemed to have accrued outside the country. The benefits to the company were obvious, as it is subject to a 67.7 percent income tax in Venezuela compared with a rate of 34 percent in the United States" (Mommer, 2001). It also achieved a reduction in revenues from 16.67 percent to 1 percent for four joint ventures with foreign companies in the Orinoco Belt, and used its foreign affiliates to 'export' profits through transfer pricing (Mommer, 2001). The Venezuelan case is striking, as the share of PDVSA income that was transferred as revenue to the government between 1976 and 1992, varied between 64 percent and 81 percent, averaging 71 percent. Between 1993 and 2000, the proportion varied from between 28 percent and 50 percent, with an average of 36 percent (Mommer, 2001). "PDVSA sought to attract large infusions of

foreign capital through joint ventures and operating agreements. . . . Hand in glove with this strategy was a policy of 'internationalization'" (Hellinger, 2006, pp. 58–59). This illustrates the general observation that "private sector involvement may increase the size of total revenues but reduce that of the government take" (Sarbu, 2014, p. 27). The private involvement in the Venezuelan case came through the foreign alliances of PDVSA. However, the retraction to government control was not going to be a success either.

The Chávez era

Hugo Chávez took office as President of Venezuela in February 1999. The new constitution prohibits privatization of PDVSA, but "the new oil regime continues to allow joint ventures, shared risk partnerships, and service and operating agreements" (Hellinger, 2006, p. 63). The joint ventures were made subject to higher royalties and increased taxes. The increase in oil prices during the 2000s made the re-nationalization easier to swallow for PDVSA and its foreign partners. Nevertheless, the so-called 'oil war' broke out in 2001, with massive demonstrations in Caracas. In late 2002 another strike almost shut down PDVSA's oil operations (Vivoda, 2008, p. 101). After over two months 12,000 PDVSA employees were fired, and replaced by workers loyal to Chávez. This caused a setback in the operative efficiency of the company. The main challenge for PDVSA and Venezuelan economy, in general, is not necessarily the re-nationalization of the oil industry, but how Chávez's policies disrupted Venezuela's oil industry through lack of investment, corruption and cash shortages. The financial resources of PDVSA were spent on social programs, creating a governmental overspending followed by increasing inflation:

> There is no question that Venezuela under Chávez came to experience one of the worst cases of Dutch Disease in the world. The Chávez government deliberately maintained an overvalued exchange rate during the oil boom that began at the end of 2003 . . . Because of this persistent overvaluation, Venezuela's trading sector became increasingly distorted. Exports of fuels boomed, but, by 2008, exports of everything else had collapsed. (Corrales, 2013)

Chávez's successor, Nicolás Maduro, has continued many of the same policies. Maduro has directly printed more currency, resulting in inflation as high as 700 percent. The continuous fall in oil production and the oil price fall in 2014 have further worsened the economic situation in Venezuela.

In 2015, PDVSA tried to sell Citgo Petroleum Corporation (CITGO), the company that owns the Venezuelan refineries in the US, but was unable to find a buyer. In December 2016, a restructuring of PDVSA debt offered a 50.1 percent stake in CITGO as a guarantee in case of default. The Russian oil company, Rosneft, is supposedly holding an option to pick up CITGO if PDVSA fails, and thus place Rosneft in charge of 750,000 barrels per day, representing 4 percent of total US refining capacity as well as 4,000 employees, three pipelines and 48 petroleum terminals. In August 2017, PDVSA struggled to repay $725 million of debt, part of a total $5 billion owed, despite the fact Venezuelan citizens are experiencing ongoing famine. Fearing loss of their stake and high position in the oil industry, Venezuela is rushing to pay back their investors to forestall requests for oil reserves as collateral.

We will return to the Venezuelan case in the next chapter, focusing on the resource curse. Regarding the governance of the Venezuelan oil sector and economy in general, the conclusion of professor Javier Corrales (2015) is crystal clear:

> All oil-based economies have suffered from the decline in oil prices since June 2014. But Venezuela's economy has essentially collapsed, ravaged by what we might call RIDDS: recession, inflation, dwindling foreign reserves, debt, and shortages. Despite Maduro's claims, Venezuela's RIDDS is not the result of external shocks, or even the local bourgeoisie's "economic warfare." It's not the result of oil dependence, either. Neither does it have much to do with the economic incompetence of the country's leaders, conspicuous as that factor may be. Venezuela's economic woes started long before the current downturn in oil prices and the start of Maduro's administration. Rather, the blame for Venezuela's RIDDS must be laid on the nature of the country's regime, which disincentivized its leaders from competently managing the oil boom, and is now crippling the government's ability to respond to the downturn.

2.5.2 Saudi Arabia

First discoveries
The early days of the Kingdom of Saudi Arabia coincide with the early days of Arabian oil. The key political figure in the formation of the Saudi state was Abd al-Aziz ibn Saud. In 1902 he led the recapture of Riyadh and developed alliances with the tribal forces of the Ikhwan to capture Al-Asha from the Ottomans in 1913. The Middle East theatre of the First World War was dominated by the war between Britain and the Ottoman Empire, the latter in alliance with Germany. The British encouraged the so-called Arab Revolt from 1916 to 1918. The revolt was rooted in an Arab nationalism which had been growing since the mid-1800s. During the Great War the aim was enhanced into seeking independence from the

Ottoman Turks. Ibn Saud avoided involvement in the revolt, which failed in its ambition of independence. The end of the First World War nevertheless saw the end of the Ottoman Empire. In the aftermath of the war Ibn Saud seized the opportunity to gain control over more territories of the Arab Peninsula. By 1927, he had declared himself ruler of both Hejaz and Nejd. The alliance with the Ikhwan forces broke up as the Ikhwan sought to expand into the British protectorate of Transjordan, while Ibn Saud sought to avoid confrontation with the British. The Kingdom of Saudi Arabia was declared in September 1932. The economic situation was poor as the "main sources of income were pastoral agriculture in the interior, trade (pearl fisheries, export of Arabian horses to India, agricultural products from Asir and al-Hasa) and the Hajj (levies on pilgrimage to Makkah and Madinah)" (Sarbu, 2014, p. 114). A key figure in the development of oil in Saudi Arabia was a New Zealand engineer, Major Frank Holmes. "He was convinced that the Arabian coast would be a fabulous source of petroleum, and he pursued his dream with unswerving stamina" (Yergin, 1991, p. 280).[3] Already in 1923 Ibn Saud had granted Holmes a concession to explore for oil in the Eastern part of the peninsula. Holmes also operated in Bahrain and the Neutral Zone between Saudi Arabia and Kuwait. He also challenged the Turkish Petroleum Company in Iraq (Yergin, 1991, p. 281). Holmes' concessions were later picked up by Standard Oil of California (Socal). In 1932 oil was found in Bahrain. This increased the interest in Saudi Arabian oil concessions.

In May 1933, Socal was granted a 60-year concession for oil exploration and production covering an area of 93,000 square kilometers of land in eastern Saudi Arabia. The company paid £35,000 in gold up-front, of which £30,000 was a loan and £5,000 advanced royalty payment. The loan was to be repaid solely with royalty income from oil discoveries. Standard Oil could deduct the loan from future governmental revenues from possible oil production. Socal's operations in Saudi Arabia were organized through a subsidiary company called the California Arabian Standard Oil Company (Casoc). In 1938, oil was discovered in Saudi Arabia. The discovery released another loan of £100,000 in gold. The cash payments were crucial to Ibn-Saud's financial position. Although the number of pilgrims picked up during the late 1930s, the Second World War completely halted this source of income. The Second World War also constrained the oil production in Saudi Arabia.

Middle East oil rents
In the 19th-century oil industry in the United States, the standard royalty rate to the landowners was 12.5 percent, but this was based on the oil company covering all costs. "Experience shows that a one-eighth [12.5 percent] royalty takes about half of the profits in the average case" (Mommer, 2002, p. 51). As the oil industry internationalized in the first half of the 20th century, revenues, royalties and profit sharing became hot topics, in particular since the companies operating outside of the US faced governments on the opposite side of the negotiating table, rather than individual landowners as in the US. US oil companies operating abroad could also deduct foreign income tax from their US income tax, but fixed payments, such as operating costs and royalties, could not be deducted. (Yergin, 1991, p. 446). Thus, if the host countries increased the income tax for a company paying tax in the US, it would not cost the company a dime, but would only transfer money from the Treasury of the US to the Treasury of the host country. In 1943, Venezuela became the first of the non-US oil states to introduce the principle of a fifty-fifty share in oil production.

In 1950, the Saudi Arabian government and the US oil companies operating in Saudi Arabia as the Arabian-American Oil Company (Aramco), agreed to a fifty-fifty deal, with an income tax component. It made a big difference. Before the deal, in 1949, the Saudi Arabia Treasury collected $39 million in royalties and the US Treasury $43 million, from Aramco. In 1951, after the deal was agreed, Saudi Arabia collected $110 million and the US $6 million. Aramco sought to depress the companies' taxable income, but the government's revenue nevertheless rose "from around 28 cents a barrel in 1951 (while the posted price for Gulf exports was $1.75 per barrel) to around 80 cents per barrel in 1956 (posted price $1.93)" (Evans, 1990, p. 342). The fifty-fifty principle rapidly spread to other oil-producing countries in the Middle East (Yergin, 1991, pp. 447–448).

The oil from the Middle East competed with US produced oil in the US market. However, US oil was more costly to produce. "For example, in the late 1940s, oil was selling for around $2.50 a barrel. Some grizzled stripper-well operator in Texas might only make a 10 cent profit on his oil. But in the Middle East it only cost 25 cents a barrel to produce oil" (Yergin, 1991, p. 432). Thus, the potential profit was much larger in the Middle East than in the US.

Saudi ARAMCO – the accidental NOC[4]
In 1948 Socal (later Chevron) and Texaco, which held the Saudi Arabian concessions, agreed to include Standard Oil of New Jersey (later Exxon) and Socony-Vacuum (later Mobil) as additional shareholders in their daughter company conducting the oil production in Saudi Arabia. The

company had changed its name in 1944 to the Arabian American Oil Company – Aramco. In 1952, the headquarters of the company moved from New York to Dhahran in Saudi Arabia. From 1968 the strategy of the Saudi Arabian government changed from profit-sharing to seeking state participation in Aramco's upstream operations. Threats of new legislation unless the government was included in Aramco led to the 1973 agreement in which the state received a 25 percent ownership stake of the company's upstream producing assets. The government put strong pressure on Aramco's partners, achieving a majority share of 60 percent of the company by late 1974. In 1980, the government purchased 100 percent of Aramco, with retroactive financial effect back to 1976. In 1988, the company was taken over by a new national oil company – the Saudi Arabian Oil Company, known as Saudi Aramco. In 2016, the company had amassed crude oil and condensate reserves of 260.8 billion barrels, with a production of 10.5 million barrels per day.

As the outline shows, Saudi Aramco did not follow the abrupt nationalization strategy of other Middle East oil-producing countries in the early 1970s (cf. section 2.4.2 above). "Saudi Aramco was never intended to be the national oil company (NOC) of Saudi Arabia. Instead, that outcome was an accident of history" (Stevens, 2012, p.173). The wave of nationalizations in the early 1970s made it politically impossible for the Saudi Arabian government not to follow suit. But it did so gradually – by increasing state participation in Aramco, taking 25 percent in 1972 with the intention of waiting until 1982 before taking a 51 percent share (Stevens, 2012, p.181). Although the formal ownership changed, the professional operative functions did not. Saudi Aramco is run by technocrats with high standards insulated from political interference, although a thorough scrutiny of the company is hard to execute as its operations are conducted under a veil of secrecy (Stevens, 2012, p.174). Also, the share size of the company, its production level and its assets makes it seem profitable and efficient by itself.

State control
Saudi Arabia is an Absolute Monarchy where the King has unrestricted supreme authority, including legislative, executive and judicial power. The King is prime minister and presides over the Consultative Assembly of Saudi Arabia called the *Majlis*, an advisory body formed in 1926 by Ibn Saud. It has 150 members, all appointed by the King, with limited political power to propose legislation and interpret existing legislation. Sarbu (2014, p.116) observes that several institutions of consultation and dialogue has been created since the early 1990s, but "these institutions are not guided by the logic of representation but still of co-optation . . .

Despite some efforts at modernizing the Saudi politics, no actual steps have been taken towards democratization." The public administration of the petroleum sector was, until 2015, headed by the Supreme Council on Petroleum and Mineral Affairs. In 2015, the Supreme Council of the Saudi Arabian Oil Company (Saudi Aramco) replaced this body. At the same time the company was separated from the Ministry of Oil.[5] The Crown Prince heads the new Council. The Supreme Council oversees the operating and investment plans of the company and approves its annual reports and account. The Minister of Energy, Industry and Mineral Resources is head of the board of directors of Aramco, which also includes the President/CEO (Chief Executive Officer) of the company. This is a closed public administrative system, characterized by close links between the royal family and the company. Describing the system before the 2015 reform, Stevens (2012, p. 188) concludes that in practice, "Saudi Aramco is virtually self-regulating and [the Supreme Council] provides only light supervision, largely endorsing decisions taken by Saudi Aramco." The reform, at least in theory, opens up for more political interventions in the running of the company and thus, the public administration and industrial operation of the Saudi Arabian oil sector. Saudi Arabian oil production constituted 13.4 percent of total world production in 2016 (BP, 2017). The high production level, combined with low production costs, gives the state (read: the royal family), large direct incomes. "Instead of a government living off taxes collected from the population . . . the King as the custodian of the national wealth distributes some share of the oil money to the population. Allocation and cooptation often pave the way to consensus" (Sarbu, 2014, p. 123).

Market hegemony

Saudi Arabia's large market share also makes the Kingdom's oil policy, administration and operations vital to the global oil market. It follows that Saudi Arabian decisions have greater strategic implications, both economically and politically, than is the case for most other oil-producing countries. The overall level of production, decisions to increase production capacity, and potential market interventions are determined at the political level. Therefore the country's dominant market position has implications, in turn, for Saudi Arabian oil politics and oil-related public administration.

Saudi Arabian oil production grew rapidly through the 1970s, reaching 10 million barrels per day (mbd) in 1980. In the 1980s, Saudi Arabia took on the role as swing producer inside OPEC, trying to support the oil price set by the organization, cutting its own production to less than 4 mbd in 1985. The country then turned the global oil market around, by changing its market strategy. When Iraqi oil production collapsed after the outbreak of the Iraq–Kuwait war in 1990, Saudi Arabia almost regained its previous market share, producing about 9 mbd in 1991. The Kingdom has increased the production level slowly, reaching about 12 mbd in 2015, disproving claims that Saudi oil reserves were deteriorating (Simmons, 2005), and sustaining a share of world production of 12–13 percent from 1990 until today. The Kingdom's production level and its ability to adjust production in large quantities, has given Saudi Arabia a singular position in the oil market. Claes (2001, pp. 201–238) characterizes Saudi Arabia as a hegemonic power, both inside OPEC and in the oil market in general. First, as an incapable hegemon from 1973 to 1981, unsuccessfully trying to limit the price increases agreed in OPEC, then as a benevolent hegemon, taking a disproportionate burden of the costs of providing a collective good for the oil producers – a high oil price. Finally as a coercive hegemon since 1985, flooding the market in 1986 and demanding contributions from others before contributing to producer cooperation by cutting its own production. The latest example of this role was the market policy of the Kingdom following the oil price fall in the autumn of 2014. Saudi Arabia is the only actor in the oil market that can be characterized as a true *price-maker*. Thus the country is in a unique position for governing its own petroleum sector and pursuing an oil policy designed to serve its national economic interests.

2.5.3   Norway

The first discoveries
In 1962, the Norwegian government was approached by the American oil company Phillips Petroleum with a request to acquire "an oil and gas concession covering the lands lying beneath the territorial waters of Norway plus that portion of the Continental Shelf lying beneath the North Sea which may now or in the future be under the jurisdiction of Norway."[6] Two prior events facilitated this request. First, the North Sea had been subject to maritime delimitation between the UK, Denmark and Norway (cf. Section 1.4), with the implication that the continental shelves in the North Sea came under defined jurisdiction. Second, a huge gas field, the Groningen, had been discovered in the Netherlands in 1959. Phillips Petroleum was of the opinion that the geological structures containing the Groningen field might indicate deposits of hydrocarbons in the North Sea as well. The Norwegian Geological Investigation, on the other hand, stated that the possibility of hydrocarbons on the Norwegian Continental Shelf could safely be ruled out.[7]

Granting Phillips Petroleum the sole right to exploration and production would obviously give the company a dominant position and sideline the government. This contradicted the Norwegian tradition of an active governmental role in most economic sectors, although in combination with private actors. On the other hand, the Norwegian bureaucracy was somewhat reluctant to enter into unknown industrial adventures following the so-called Kings Bay affair.[8] The onus for handling the oil issues was passed to an independent entity called The Government's Oil Council (Statens Oljeråd). A handful of people were given the entire administrative responsibility including drafting the necessary legislation, negotiating with foreign companies, coordinating with other governmental entities and, last but not least, preparing the licensing procedure. The aim of the Oil Council was to have a rapid exploration of large parts of the Shelf in order to determine whether or not there were any commercially viable oil resources. The first licensing round in 1965 is still one of the largest rounds ever announced. The Oil Council openly discouraged Norwegian industrial and shipping interests from entering the oil industry at this time, due to the uncertainty and high risk to invested capital.[9] The capital, know-how, and technical experience of the international oil companies (IOCs), was used in developing a general legislative framework to ensure governmental control over the resources, but gave the foreign companies the responsibility for exploration and the operative activity on the Continental Shelf. In the first licensing round in 1965, 22 production licenses were awarded for 78 blocks. The first well was drilled in 1966. It was dry. By 1969, 16 exploration wells had been drilled and only one had proved to contain a substantial amount of hydrocarbons. The international oil companies had spent $41 million. The optimism was gone, and the IOCs tried unsuccessfully to get out of their drilling obligations (Hanisch, 1992, pp. 119–121). In August 1969, the oil rig 'Ocean Viking' started drilling in block 2/4. The rig drilled two wells only 1,000 meters apart, both with substantial traces of hydrocarbons. In June 1971, oil production commenced on the now named Ekofisk-field.[10]

State control

The discovery boosted the exploration activity. A number of major discoveries were made in the early 1970s. At the same time, the OPEC members, in their negotiations with the IOCs, announced they would include a clause ensuring state participation (cf. Chapter 2). The international climate was changing. After the second licensing round was announced, the government included a clause of state participation with "carried interest" until commercial discoveries were made. Furthermore, only individual applications were allowed, thus the companies submitted competing analyses of the fields. This effectively increased the information and know-how in the Norwegian oil bureaucracy (Andersen and

Austvik, 2000, p. 35). During the 1970s, the concessions increasingly came to include non-economic or technical conditions such as encouraging Norwegian partners, placing orders with Norwegian industry, creating jobs in Norway, and so on (Noreng, 1980, p. 126). In a famous report to Parliament the Norwegian government discussed the consequences of the oil discoveries for the Norwegian society at large.[11] The report emphasized the importance of democratic control and state engagement in all parts of the petroleum industry, the aim of using the oil revenues to achieve greater equality in living standards and prevention of social problems, and finally the ambition of developing a national oil industry.

In 1971 the so-called "10 oil commandments" were agreed in Parliament. Among these were ambitions to ensure: (a) national governance and control of all activities on the Continental Shelf, (b) that the petroleum resources contributed to the development of new industrial activities in Norway, (c) that oil and gas should be piped to Norway, (d) that the state engaged in all aspects of the petroleum activities where appropriate, and (e) that a state oil company should be established. In 1972 the administrative structure was split into three parts: the Ministry of Industry handled principles, legislation, and concessions; the Oil Directorate handled daily administration, exploration, and control; and a state oil company was put in charge of the government's commercial interests. This is usually referred to in the literature as the 'Norwegian Model'. The Norwegian oil sector regulations became a legislative framework giving the state the ultimate control over the resources, a politically governed concession system, and a strong element of direct state participation through the state oil company – Statoil. The Norwegian model had certain peculiarities, but was in line with the changes in the state–company relations in the OPEC countries. Preferences were given to the Norwegian firms, Statoil in particular. This reduced the position of the IOCs developed in the initial phase before the first discovery, much in line with the perspective of the obsolescing bargaining theory of Raymond Vernon (1971) outlined in Section 2.4.1. Statoil was set to be the key institution for implementing the government's petroleum policy.[12] The long-term perspective was that the IOCs active on the Norwegian Shelf should become primarily consultants, entrepreneurs, and possibly minority shareholders.[13]

After Statoil was created in 1972, the state participation agreements with the IOCs were amended to include a 50 percent direct share to be granted to Statoil in every block, in addition to the carried interest clause. Statoil thus was exempted from incurring expenses during the exploration phase. In 1974, a new "sliding scale" was devised, which enabled Statoil to claim an additional share of 30 percent of a given field after profitable discoveries were made. At the Gullfaks field Statoil was awarded an 85 percent share. The carried interest concept enabled the state to combine a risk-averse posture with a very high direct state ownership share. Since the voting rights were based on a company's ownership share, Statoil had a veto over all production leases and field development decisions that were made after 1973. At the Gullfaks field, Statoil could take all these decisions alone. Statoil was given the right to acquire the operator responsibility at the large Statfjord field from Mobil within 10 years. Statoil could use expertise and information acquired by the private companies, select its own partners in a handful of promising concessions, and exercise a role as key advisor to the ministry. The preferential rights granted to Statoil gave the company a dominant position in the petroleum sector.

A state within the state?
The petroleum sector's share of Norwegian gross domestic product (GDP) increased from 6.8 percent in 1978 to 16 percent in 1981. In the same period the oil sector's contribution to the state income increased from 3.8 billion to 27.8 billion Norwegian Kroner. The Norwegian economy had been transformed into an oil-based economy. Statoil accumulated a substantial part of the proceeds. The accumulation of income in one company raised concern about the division of the economic rent between Statoil and the public treasury. The income gave the company a strong incentive to increase its activity in order to prevent the transfer of capital to its owner – the Norwegian state (Richardson, 1981, p.44). The larger the share of capital the company could retain, the higher was its growth potential. Statoil's high capitalization also enable the company to develop relations with industrial actors involved in the oil and gas activities.[14] Richardson (1981, p.45) notes that "Statoil's relationship to the rest of Norwegian industry could provide it with a degree of autonomy not envisaged by central policy-makers." The high degree of administrative discretion in the concession system enabled the government to select those oil companies that favored the use of Norwegian goods and services. From 1979 onward, the state participation agreements included special regulations about the purchase of Norwegian goods and services. Statoil participated in the negotiations with private industry actors even when the company itself did not act as an operator of a field.[15] Statoil's strong integration into the overall regulatory structure created a need for reform of the concession system.

The election in 1981 paved the way for a new Conservative–Centre coalition government, with the aim of reducing the power of Statoil, a company born out of the Social Democratic era from the Second World War until 1981. In 1983 a government commission proposed a division of funds between Statoil and the public treasury, and thus split the company's operative industrial functions and the flow of income from the petroleum sector at large. Furthermore, the Commission noted that the wide range of preferences granted to the company gave it sweeping leverage to influence the actions of all business actors in the petroleum sector (Selvig, 1983, p. 15). The split of ownership in the oil fields between Statoil and the State itself, was agreed in the so-called "Statoil compromise," between the Conservative–Centre government and the opposition Labor party in 1984. The state's direct share of the fields became known as the State's Direct Financial Interest (SDFI). Statoil continued to 'operate' the direct shares of the government. "While the main tendency in Norway since 1945 has been to integrate organized interests, and thus social conflicts, into the administrative apparatus, the key argument of the conservative-center program was that the state, in order to govern, needed a certain distance and independence from the various interests" (March and Olsen, 1989, p. 100). The chosen model in the petroleum sector – a direct state share of field ownership in addition to the share of the state oil company – was a Norwegian innovation, but the Conservative-Centre government was inspired by the new ideologies espoused by British Prime Minister Thatcher and US President Reagan. In its general economic policy, the Norwegian administration liberalized the financial markets, abandoned regulations in the housing market, and pursued a market-oriented industrial policy. The policy of constraining the power and wealth of Statoil was in line with this, but was hardly a case of liberalization in itself, as it implied an increased direct role of the state in the oil sector. As the then-Prime Minister, Kåre Willoch, later reflected in his memoirs, "The aim was to prevent Statoil from growing beyond reasonable limits and exercise disproportionate influence" (Willoch, 1990, p. 289). A classic principal–agent dilemma.

Privatization and internationalization
In 2001, Statoil was privatized and made a public limited company, listed both on the stock exchanges in Oslo and New York. The government has retained a large share of stocks in the company. In 2017, the government share of the company was 67 percent. With the privatization, the SDFI was transformed into a state holding company named Petoro (Moses and Letnes, 2017, p. 83). With the privatization, Statoil is under standard legislation and regulation of public listed companies, executed by the Norwegian government; and as listed at the New York Stock Exchange, the US Securities and Exchange Commission. This obviously restrains governmental interference in the day-to-day operations of the company. As majority owner, the state can exercise its influence at the shareholders' meeting, but "the Norwegian government is reluctant to use its majority shareholder position to affect [Statoil's] policy decisions, for fear of threatening its market value" (Moses and Letnes, 2017, p. 83). The government

can still impose legislation regulating Statoil and other companies operations in Norway.

The relationship between the government and Statoil was also challenged when the company initiated an internationalization strategy in the 1990s through an alliance with British Petroleum, primarily covering joint exploration and production (E&P) projects in areas like the former Soviet republics, China, Vietnam and West Africa. The alliance lasted until 1999. In retrospect, it seems fair to conclude that the alliance boosted the internationalization of Statoil. The alliance made it easier for the company to reshape itself from a state-owned national oil company with obligations as an extended arm of the Norwegian government, to an international oil company (IOC), as similar to the private IOCs as possible, given a state ownership of 67 percent. Today Statoil has activities in more than 30 countries, and in 2015, almost 40 percent of total equity production of oil and gas came from activities outside of Norway. In 2018, Statoil changed its name to Equinor.

NOTES

1. WSJ News Graphics, April 15, 2016, http://graphics.wsj.com/oil-barrel-breakdown/ (accessed June 19, 2018). Based on Rystad Energy.
2. These aspects will be fully developed in section II of this book, but as part of gaining more influence over price setting in the oil market, the producing countries also gained bargaining power toward the oil companies concerning the conditions for their operations in the member countries of OPEC.
3. Yergin (1991, pp. 280–302) devotes a chapter to the Arabian oil concession with the telling sub-title: "The World That Frank Holmes Made."
4. The title is taken from Stevens (2012, p. 175).
5. "Saudi Aramco gets new supreme council headed by deputy crown prince." *Reuters*, May 1, 2015. https://www.reuters.com/article/saudi-oil-aramco/saudi-aramco-gets-new-supreme-council-headed-by-deputy-crown-prince-statement-idUSL5N0XS0LR20150501 (accessed January 5, 2017).
6. Letter from W. Dunn, head of the Paris office of Phillips Petroleum, to Trygve Lie, October 29, 1962, quoted in Hanisch (1992, p. 12).
7. See facsimile of the letter in Helle (1984, p. 13).
8. In November 1962 a gas explosion in a coalmine on Svalbard had killed 21 people. The investigators' report showed culpability on the part of the Minister of Industry at the time, Kjell Holler. A majority in the Parliament supported a no-confidence vote based on charges of withholding information to the Parliament about the situation prior to the accident. The Labor party government, led by Einar Gerhardsen, was forced to resign.
9. *Report to Parliament*, no. 11 (1968–1969), pp. 6–7.
10. Today (2017) production is maintained at a high level through continuous water injection and the drilling of new production and injection wells. Production in 2016 was about 120,000 barrels per day.
11. Report to Parliament no. 25 (1973–1974). English edition, http://www.regjeringen.no/upload/FIN/okonomiavdelingen/Stmeld_25_1973–74.pdf (accessed June 19, 2018).
12. *Report to Parliament*, no. 25 (1973–1974), p. 9.

13. *Report to Parliament*, no. 25 (1973–1974), p. 13.
14. In 1983, Statoil purchased Norwegian goods and services for a total sum of NOK 9.3 billion. See *Report to Parliament*, no. 35 (1984–1985), p. 106.
15. *Official Report to the Government* (NOU) no. 16, February 1983, p. 34.

3. Oil income – blessing or curse?

With Mads Motrøen

3.1 WHAT IS A RESOURCE CURSE?

3.1.1 Background

Oil discoveries can turn out to be a curse rather than a blessing. Following the oil boom of the early 1970s, oil-producing states became wealthy practically overnight. This was the largest transfer of wealth between states ever to happen short of wars (Karl, 1997, p. xv), but correlated with severe negative consequences for many of the producer countries. These consequences related to the sudden shift in financial status probably constitute the most intensely studied part of the relationship between oil and politics.

In the decades following the oil boom, many oil states suffered serious financial difficulties and political deterioration (Karl, 1997). This was certainly the case for the developing countries. Their non-oil counterparts, by contrast, generally saw steady political and economic development from 1980 to 2006 (Ross, 2012, pp. 1–2). The oil-producing developing countries, however, experienced lagging economic growth and no political development in the same period. In this period, per capita income fell 6 percent in Venezuela, 45 percent in Gabon and 85 percent in Iraq. The OPEC countries saw their combined GDP decrease by 1.3 percent each year between 1965 and 1998 (Gylfason, 2001). Other oil producers, such as Algeria, Angola, Colombia, Nigeria and Iraq, underwent widespread political instability and civil wars (Ross, 2012).

The oil states in question remain stuck at the same level of economic development 30 years after gaining the extra income from oil, in addition to suffer from deteriorating political development; should not the oil income have given them a head start? Taken together, these observations suggest that oil had a paradoxical effect on the states, causing lagging growth and political instability. These negative outcomes were labeled the 'resource curse', a term coined by Auty (1993).

This 'curse' is a new phenomenon, as it is not reported in the historical data from oil states. The negative effects seem to start with the advent of booming oil prices in the 1970s, and became even more pronounced after 1980. Prior to this decade most oil-states experienced above average levels of economic growth; it was only after oil prices quadrupled in nominal terms (Karl, 1997, p. 119) that the negative effects are observed.

Political development also remained static in most of these newly rich oil countries, while many comparable countries underwent democratic transitions. Before the oil boom, there were few differences in regime type between producers and non-producers. During what became known as the 'third wave' of democratization, however, the oil-producing non-democracies were left behind in the political development seen in other parts of the world (Ross, 2012, p. 63).

How can wealth be detrimental to societal development? Does oil wealth really hamper growth and damage political institutions? This chapter will present several mechanisms encompassing what the research community take to be the negative effects of oil wealth.

3.1.2 Four Aspects of the Resource Curse Debate

We can sort the various aspects of the resource curse discussion into four parts:

The first part will focus on the direct economic effects of large governmental oil revenues. The direct effects are related to the revenue generated by macro-economic indicators, specifically the monetary impact of an external positive income shock to the economy of an oil state. This section refers to the economic literature concerning the concept of the 'Dutch Disease', which is a component of the economic side of the resource curse.

The second part of the chapter concerns the economic challenges facing governments of oil states and the macro-economic instruments they use to combat the resource curse and turn it into a blessing. We call this section 'Fiscal Policy', and this relates to how the state tackles negative economic consequences caused by Dutch Disease.

The third part will cover the political side of the resource curse. We focus on how governments of oil states use oil wealth for political purposes, and the implications of these policy choices. We also investigate how oil wealth creates incentives for specific behavior for both the rulers and the ruled, and how these effects are thought to produce negative effects both for the political system and the economy.

Finally, we present the research suggesting that the resource curse is illusory and relies on mistaken assumptions, measurement errors and other factors. We end the chapter with a discussion of how convincing the body of research actually is, and whether windfalls of oil profit are a curse or a blessing.

3.2 DIRECT ECONOMIC EFFECTS – THE DUTCH DISEASE

Numerous economic effects follow from increased oil production. Some relate to oil exports and some to the governmental income in itself. Various authors attribute different mechanisms to the phenomenon called the 'Dutch Disease'. In essence, the Dutch Disease refers to the negative economic impacts of a sudden inflow of foreign currency.[1] We start with this narrow definition of the Dutch Disease, before expanding the set of implications. We assume that the oil-producing country is not the only producer, but rather a small producer relative to the world market for these goods, and is thus unable to influence the world market price.

3.2.1 Exchange Rate Appreciation

Let us consider a country discovering oil for the first time. It soon starts producing and exporting oil, selling on the world market in US dollars. The oil companies' expenses are mostly paid in the national currency and the government receives taxes in the national currency. Thus, the oil exports create an added demand for the national currency compared with the situation before the income from oil export started. Increased demand for the national currency will, all other things being equal, increase the exchange rate.

There is also a 'monetary effect' as the conversion of foreign currency into local currency increases the overall supply of money and thus raises domestic prices. Again, the 'real' exchange rate appreciates: one unit of foreign currency now buys fewer services in the domestic economy than it did before. Both of these effects are 'automatic', as they will happen unless someone intervenes in order to stop them. An increased exchange rate has immediate consequences for trade, as exported goods become more expensive in foreign markets, while imported goods become cheaper in the domestic market.

It follows, then, that both exporting industries and domestic import-competing industries will lose competitiveness because of the overvalued currency. This negative effect is one of the most robust empirical relationships in international economics (Gylfason, 2011, p. 15). This isolated exchange rate effect can hardly be avoided and will happen regardless of whether the income from oil exports is domestically spent or saved. However, the oil income could potentially compensate for this isolated exchange rate effect, and in fact more than offset the isolated loss. Most often, and for most oil producers, the oil price will provide the economy with large net export earnings. However, the oil producers might be inclined to spend some of these earnings in the domestic economy. Then, more severe macro-economic effects could ensue.

In order to understand these effects, we need to develop an understanding of the economy as divided into two sectors – the traded and non-traded sectors. The traded sector represents goods and services that are – or at least can be – produced in other countries. This includes most kinds of merchandise, industrial goods and some services such as shipping and financial services.

The non-traded sector comprises products that must be consumed in the same country as they are produced, due to physical or economic conditions. Examples here are food products that are hard to transport or conserve, and local services like hairdressing and childcare. Public services obviously fall into this category as well. The distinction with the traded sector is not always clear-cut, as individual consumers can choose to purchase non-traded goods in a foreign country, but hardly on a large scale.

Increased spending falls on both traded and non-traded goods, but the effects are somewhat different. The increased demand for traded goods can be met by increased imports. The increase in demand for non-traded goods must be met by increased local production. Since domestic resources (labor in particular) are used to meet the increased demand for non-traded goods, there are less resources available to meet the increased demand for traded goods, so the production of traded goods is reduced. The demand for traded goods must be met by increased imports. The oil boom thus creates a trade deficit for non-oil traded goods. As demand for non-traded goods increases, we can assume that the price also rises. However, the price of the traded goods is set on the world market, and is thus unaffected. This rise in relative prices of non-traded goods is called a real exchange rate appreciation (Sachs, 2007, pp. 181–182).

Spending the oil income in the domestic economy shifts production from traded to non-traded goods and services. This shift in economic activity can have costly effects on the economy, as workers need to develop new skills in order to acquire new jobs. This must happen in either the oil sector or in the non-traded sector, and capital needs to be redirected. As Sachs writes, these adjustments cannot be called a 'disease' per se – rather, this rise in non-traded production is the only way the economy can enjoy more of both traded and non-traded goods (Sachs, 2007, p. 183).

These mechanisms suggest that the increased demand for non-tradable goods can only be met by increased domestic production. This effect multiplies as the increased demand will cause wages in the non-traded sector to rise, and thus feeds into the tradable sector as companies in this sector have to increase wages in order to hold on to workers. The non-oil tradable sector is doubly hit by a higher exchange rate and the pressure to boost wages, making their products more expensive both in foreign markets and in import-competing domestic markets. Through this mechanism, the growth of the oil export sector undermines the competitiveness of other sectors of the economy.

As a result, many oil-producing countries find it hard to sustain a diversified economy.[2] One might question the reason for adhering to diversification as an isolated goal, as the oil sector in many cases represents a strong comparative advantage for the oil-exporting country (Gelb, 2011, pp. 59–62). It is not obvious that economic growth in the oil-rich countries would have been stronger with a more diversified economy, although empirical findings suggest that diversified economies perform better in the long term. This relative lag in performance is usually attributed to the reduction of the tradable-goods sector, which makes the real exchange rate more volatile and hence lowers investment in the non-traded sector. Diversified economies are also found to make adjustments with much smaller costs (Hausmann & Rigobon, 2003, p. 31).

The most serious challenge, however, emerges if the existing income from oil exports is strongly reduced or disappears. In this case, consumption levels need to be reduced and production moved from non-traded goods to traded goods. In the traded sector, companies can only adjust the quantity they produce, as prices are set on the world market. In order to increase production in the traded sector, wages will have to come down, so that the companies can hire more people in order to augment the quantity produced. The workers will usually resist this. The risk is that a reduction or cessation of oil income results in unemployment and, in fact, a lower level of consumption than before the oil income appeared. Usually, some form of governmental involvement is necessary to handle these macroeconomic effects of the oil income.

3.2.2 The Role of the Exchange Rate Regime

It is important to note that oil income represents a severe challenge to any country. It is popular to refer to a lack of solid political and economic institutions as an explanation for the resource curse. However, even developed countries with strong and sound political and economic institutions, such as the Netherlands (in the case of gas), Norway and Canada, have all faced severe challenges in implementing adequate and flexible policy responses to the economic effects of booming income from exports of oil and gas.

We will start out by examining the immediate challenges related to the macro-economic policies of the oil state. We address two different situations: (1) where the government wants to be proactive and avoid the negative effects of oil income, or (2) where the oil income is already disappearing and the government wants to avoid having to deal with the negative effects.

Since we have focused on the real exchange rate appreciation as the key mechanism producing the Dutch Disease, it seems reasonable to discuss the possible role of the exchange rate regime of the oil state. There are two main categories of regimes for determining the exchange rates between countries: a floating system, where market forces (i.e. the relationship between supply and foreign demand for the currencies in question) set the exchange rate; and a fixed system, where the exchange rates are fixed and governments are determined to uphold the exchange rate.

The latter can be the result of an individual act of a single country 'pegging' its currency to another currency – usually a major currency like the US dollar or the euro. A fixed regime can also be established through cooperation among several countries. The euro itself is an extreme version of a fixed system, under which the national currencies are abandoned. The previous European exchange rate systems, and the global system in the Bretton Woods era, were cases of countries agreeing on fixed exchange rates, with various mechanisms for adjustments.

With a floating exchange rate, the oil income will increase the nominal exchange rate against other currencies like US dollar or euro. This creates a downward pressure on prices of non-oil traded goods in the local currency, which leads to a fall in the price of traded goods relative to non-traded goods. If the currency is fixed, or pegged to the dollar or euro, the domestic spending of the oil income leads to an increase in the prices of non-traded goods, while the prices of traded goods are kept constant due to the fixed nominal exchange rate (Sachs, 2007, pp. 186–188). The floating exchange rate creates a somewhat more 'automatic' adjustment of the economy. However, Sachs (2007, p. 187) suggests that an adjustable pegged exchange rate regime is probably preferable for "small countries facing large structural transformations, instability in the demand for the local currency, and . . . uncertainties of oil and capital flows."

If we turn to the situation where the oil income starts to fall or disappear, the pegged or fixed exchange rate leaves the responsibility of adaptation to the production costs in the traded sector, in particular to the reduction of wages. With a floating exchange rate regime, the deterioration of the economy due to the reduction in oil income will usually lead to a depreciation of the exchange rate, which increases the price of imported products. As prices in the non-traded sector are unaffected by the depreciation of the exchange rate, the competitiveness of non-oil traded goods in foreign markets is enhanced. Thus, weaker oil prices or reduced oil exports can improve the non-oil traded sectors of the economy. While it might be better to have a fixed exchange rate regime during an oil boom, the floating regime seems better when the tide turns and the oil income starts to fall.

Table 3.1   Average annual growth in per capita GDP at purchasing power prices

Country group	1960–1998	1960–1980	1980–1998	Number of countries
All developing	1.7	3	0.2	115
Oil exporters	1.1	5.2	−2.1	15
Others	1.8	2.7	0.5	100

Source: Hausmann and Rigobon (2003, p. 6).

3.2.3   Empirical Support for the Dutch Disease

Above we have described the mechanism of the Dutch Disease, and discussed differences between periods when the oil income rises and periods when the oil income declines. Hausmann and Rigobon (2003, p. 5) show that the "oil-exporting countries grew faster in the period of rising oil prices and volumes between 1960 and 1980 relative to other developing countries and collapsed when oil revenues declined after 1980. If the Dutch Disease story was right, the post-1980 story should have been one of greater growth. Hence, the story as such does not fit the facts" (cf. Table 3.1).

Although the theoretical economics of the Dutch Disease might be correct, in real life the negative economic effects do not necessarily appear. Furthermore, a one-sided focus on the possible downsides of oil income is misguided "whatever bad effects specializing in natural resources might generate they have to be compared with the benefits of owning large natural resources" (Hausmann & Rigobon, 2003, p. 6). Furthermore, temporality can be important in evaluating the effects of oil income. If revenues are intrinsically temporary, the Dutch Disease would indeed be present. However, for countries that have remained primary commodity exporters for decades, this is not necessarily the case (Cavalcanti, Mohaddes, & Raissi, 2014). These issues will be discussed further when we return to the general discussion of the relationship between oil income and economic growth below.

3.3   FISCAL POLICY

So far, we have considered the somewhat unavoidable macro-economic effects of the income from oil exports. However, oil has a wide array of other effects working through the actors and institutions in the political system at large. The immediate question is how the oil income should be handled in terms of the fiscal policy of the government of the oil state. The recommendation seems to be straightforward: Do not spend the money! While consumption creates an immediate positive economic effect, investments or savings are instruments for creating a sustainable positive economic effect from the windfall profit. Atkinson and Hamilton (2003, p. 1,804) hypothesized that the curse could be a manifestation of governments' inability to manage large resource revenues in a sustainable manner. They conclude that while some evidence suggests resource revenues constitute an ailment when directed toward public investment, there is even stronger evidence for a resource curse when the revenues are consumed. The 1973 oil price shock sparked tremendous interest in all aspects of the oil market and its macro-economic effects. Economists started discussing how the oil producers could turn windfall profits into enduring economic prosperity. This endeavor involves a number of both economic and political factors, but the immediate answer relates to a prudent fiscal policy.

3.3.1 Sustainability

The debate among economists in the early 1970s over the issue of resource rents was in fact rooted in the ethical question of intergenerational equity in consumption and the use of existing resources. Rawls (1971, pp. 284–293) finds that "the question of justice between generations . . . subjects any ethical theory to severe if not impossible tests . . . I believe that it is not possible, at present anyway, to define precise limits at what the rate of savings should be." This impossible task is further complicated in cases where the present generation is extracting exhaustible resources, since these resources will be depleted and made unavailable to future generations. Obviously inspired by Rawls' fundamental critique of the utilitarian approach to social choice, Solow (1974) set out to develop an economic model of intergenerational equity including the case of exhaustible resources. He concluded that earlier generations were entitled to consume the finite resources so long as they added to the stock of reproducible capital.

Hartwick (1977) formulated the argument more precisely and formulated a rule related to sustainable development with exhaustible resources. 'Hartwick's Rule' states that the resource owner should instantly invest the resource rents in reproducible capital, goods or assets, and then spend only the rent from the reproducible capital or assets in order to sustain consumption. To some extent, this fiscal rule is parallel with, and compatible to, the extraction rule of Harold Hotelling discussed in the previous chapter. The economic literature on this issue has been extended and further developed over the years, particularly with reference to what is called the Dasgupta–Heal–Solow–Stiglitz model. Two more recent contributions, which provide elaborations and more general propositions with fewer or weaker conditions, are those of Benchekroun and Withagen (2011) and Mitra et al. (2013). This elaborated economic literature suggests an apparently simple rule of thumb for the fiscal policy of governments of oil-rich nations: invest the rents in other assets. However, putting this rule into practice is not so easy. Hamilton and Ley (2011, pp. 136–137) suggest this is dependent on four aspects of the fiscal system functioning efficiently and effectively:[3]

- The government needs to be able to capture the rent from the resource extraction, and to do so in an effective manner. This is particularly important if private firms are responsible for the exploitation of the resources (cf. the discussion of state-company relations in Section 2.4.).
- The government needs to establish and enforce strict fiscal rules in order to avoid or limit discretionary use of the resource rents. This implies the need for sound economic and political institutions (we will discuss this aspect further in section 3.4.).
- The government needs to establish and operate a natural resource fund (or a so-called Sovereign Wealth Fund, see section 3.3.3.).
- The government or the fund must be able to manage the public investment program effectively and profitably.

In line with the various forms of licensing contracts developed in Section 1.3, the government has at its disposal different ways of capturing the resource rent. Taxation is an obvious form of governmental rent-capturing. This could take the form of income tax, indirect taxes (like tariffs and value-added tax), or taxes designed to capture the super-normal profits of resource extraction. The exact level of this super-profit is volatile and hard to determine, as it is subject to fluctuations in the oil price. Furthermore, there are information asymmetries between the companies operating the oil fields and the government. As the government does not want to jeopardize production, it needs to avoid suppressing after-tax company profits. The tax system thus needs to be consistent in order to provide the companies with predictability when they make their investment decisions. It also needs to be flexible enough to provide the companies with profit, but not too much profit.

3.3.2 Volatility

An important part of the resource curse debate has centered around the effect of volatility in income from the extraction of natural resources.

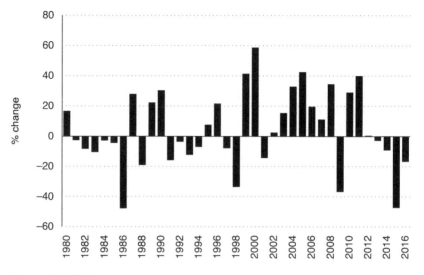

Source: BP (2017).

Figure 3.1   Oil price – percent annual change 1980–2016

Figure 3.1 shows the annual percentage change in the oil price from 1980 to 2016. We can safely conclude that the oil price is volatile.

The volatility of prices is not in doubt, but the question is how this volatility manifests in volatile income or economic growth. The recent history of oil clearly illustrates the economic challenges that ensue following a fall in the oil price. From 2012 to 2016, the oil price fell from over $111 per barrel to less than $44 per barrel. Table 3.2 shows the implication for the role of the oil exports as share of GDP of the OPEC countries. For a key country like Saudi Arabia, the values of the oil exports fell from $337 billion to $134 billion.

The question then arises – how does this volatility create problems for the economies of oil-producing states? If the oil income increases at a steady rate, or at least is sustained in real terms, the economy of the oil state would derive a persistent positive stimulus. However, unpredictable changes in income mean the economy has to expand and contract at short notice. As discussed in section 3.2 on the Dutch Disease, a fall in oil income implies that the level of consumption has to be reduced too, and production moved from the non-traded to the traded goods sector in order to sustain economic growth and welfare levels.

In the traded sector, the companies are only able to adjust the quantity produced, as prices are set on the world market. In order to increase

Table 3.2   Petroleum exports as share of GDP, OPEC countries, 2012 vs.
2016

	2012	2016	Diff.
Algeria	23.10	11.57	−11.53
Angola	60.65	27.07	−33.58
Ecuador	15.69	5.63	−10.06
Gabon	51.93	29.41	−22.52
IR Iran	17.28	10.03	−7.25
Iraq	43.15	26.31	−16.84
Kuwait	62.35	37.50	−24.86
Libya	67.44	28.09	−39.36
Nigeria	20.72	6.94	−13.78
Qatar	34.92	15.05	−19.87
Saudi Arabia	45.85	21.01	−24.85
UAE	23.03	12.27	−10.77
Venezuela	28.23	8.75	−19.48
OPEC avg.	32.98	15.16	−17.82

Source: OPEC (2017).

production, wages will have to come down if the quantity produced is to increase. The workers will usually resist this, the traded sector will lose competitiveness and the result will be unemployment. In a welfare state, an increased level of unemployment will be met with economic compensation by the state, and thus will further curtail the state budget in addition to the reduction in direct state income from oil production. This is the effect of the *reduction* in oil income, not the *volatility* as such. However, the ebb and flow of oil income creates an on–off trigger of the Dutch Disease mechanism and continuous changes in the relative growth of the traded and non-traded sector. Addressing the resource curse in general, van der Ploeg and Poelhekke (2009) estimate both a growth equation and an equation for the unanticipated variance of growth in GDP per capita. They suggest that the volatility of commodity prices trumps the level of natural resources as the key explanation for the lack of growth in resource-rich countries. Above we focused on the negative effect of an increase in the real exchange rate, the core of the Dutch Disease mechanism. Here, the point is that uncertainty regarding the real exchange rate "exacerbates the negative effects of domestic credit markets constraints, and thus curbs economic growth" (van der Ploeg & Poelhekke, 2009, p. 735).

Furthermore, tight credit constraints can make investments pro-cyclical and thus amplify volatility. Well-developed financial institutions should be able to curb such effects. In countries with weak financial institutions, however, the macroeconomic effects can turn into spirals of increasing volatility, with dire consequences for economic stability and growth. Uncertainty is detrimental for private investors as the risk premium increases. In particular, Foreign Direct Investments could easily dry up in such a situation. With increased uncertainty the risk of firms making planning errors increases (Ramey & Ramey, 1991). van der Ploeg and Poelhekke (2009, p. 736) summarize the role of volatility as "bad for growth, investments, income distribution, poverty, and educational attainment." (see also Ramey and Ramey (1995)). The recommendation is for the government to save the resource income and thus stabilize the economy. Preferably also to improve the efficiency of financial markets and diversify the economy, through which the "shocks to non-traded demand can be accommodated through changes in the structure of production rather than expenditure switching . . . Unfortunately, resource-rich economies are often specialized in production of natural resources and thus tend to be more volatile" (van der Ploeg & Poelhekke, 2009, p. 736).

3.3.3   How to Save the Income?

Having put the ball in the government's court, the question is what options are available for an oil-rich government to curb volatility and sustain oil-generated wealth? As indicated above, the easy answer is do not spend the money. But the next question is *how* to save it?

Luciani (2011) makes some innovative suggestions for oil-producing states, including the use of the futures market as an instrument to hedge against the volatility of oil prices and thus reduce risks and limit the negative economic impact of fluctuating prices. Except for Mexico, he finds few examples of countries pursuing this strategy. Among the international oil companies, activity in the futures market varies. The trick with hedging is that one needs a counterpart with an opposite risk profile in order to make the deal. If the major oil-producing states entered the futures market for oil, financial institutions could provide some insurance instruments, but would most likely not be able to balance fully the hedging positions of the producing countries. Such deals would more likely work if they were made between producer and consumer countries with perfectly opposite interests and risk profiles (Luciani, 2011, p. 217).

Another idea of Luciani is for the oil-producing country to peg its national currency to the world market price of oil. "By pegging the currency to the commodity . . . the government can isolate its finances from the vagaries of the commodity prices . . . by passing the buck to all income earners in the national currency who then see their international purchasing power fluctuating in concert with commodity prices" (Luciani, 2011, p. 218). However, protecting the state finances by exposing citizens and firms to the risk of income volatility could be a risky strategy for political reasons, even in non-democratic states. The state could also abdicate from the task of stabilizing the economy and simply hand out the windfall profit to the country's citizens.

It is hard to see how this would have any effect on curbing the resource curse – the individual recipients of the oil money would have very little incentive to act responsibly and save the money[4] – although the government could avoid the blame. We thus need to resort to more traditional ways of combating volatility and achieving sustainability, in line with the economic arguments about the sustainability of resources. In this respect, Hartwick's Rule – which recommends that the government invests all profits or rents from exhaustible resources in reproducible capital – is particularly relevant.

The definition of reproducible capital is somewhat elusive. The essence is that the investment produces a positive future return, preferably over the long term. Most investments do this, directly or indirectly, albeit with various risks. Investment in infrastructure is often regarded as particularly valuable as it should benefit large segments of the society, and thus could potentially increase activity and subsequently growth across various sectors of the economy. The investment decisions can be politicized, as projects are selected for political purposes.

The principal purpose of oil funds is to secure the oil wealth for future generations (accumulation funds) and/or compensate for the fluctuation in oil prices (stabilization funds). The same fund can of course serve both goals. However, when oil prices fall the goal of sustainability can contradict the goal of stabilization. Furthermore, the exact amount of government intervention necessary to stabilize the economy is hard to determine in advance. The two purposes are also connected in another way – as the fund, in order to balance wide fluctuations in oil prices, will have to maintain a substantial capital base.

There are wide variations regarding the amount of money saved in sovereign wealth funds in oil-rich countries. As mentioned above, Saudi Arabia has most of its savings in the Central Bank, not in its sovereign wealth fund. Norway has a sovereign wealth fund as an entity within the Central Bank, although the report from a government commission in 2017 suggested a separation of the two. The amount of money saved also differs. Saudi Arabia is not very transparent regarding state finances, but given the sustained high production level and low production costs over the last twenty years, the country accumulated large public savings, but the oil price drop from late 2014 has made annual budgets turn into deficit.

Venezuela has produced more than twice as much oil as Norway. The present economic situation in Venezuela is deplorable, while the Norwegian Sovereign Wealth Fund, the largest in the world, just passed the one trillion dollar threshold (cf. section 3.5).

It is appropriate to subscribe to the conclusion of Hamilton and Ley (2011, p. 144): "While the Hartwick rule is easy to state, it is complex to implement, and it requires fiscal discipline." In his detailed analysis of the OPEC countries performance in managing the oil wealth from 1974 to 1994, Amuzegar (1999, pp. 218–221) provides a number of concluding observations supporting the resource curse hypothesis among the OPEC members:

> The hasty expenditure of oil windfalls on a multitude of poorly planned and even more poorly coordinated public projects resulted in a feverish rate of development . . . [T]he elaborated and physical infrastructure put in place facilitated industrial and agricultural expansion but increased the state's maintenance burden, often beyond budgetary capabilities or tolerance . . . At the institutional level, oil windfalls encouraged profligate spending and wasteful outlays . . . Fiscal discipline was gradually relaxed and in some cases broke down totally. Domestic taxation was either spared or kept at minimal levels . . . No members except Indonesia developed substitute export goods large enough to finance its import needs . . . [T]he members' miscalculations and mismanagement were aggravated by global oil market volatility . . . The magnitude of rent-seeking activities was, in turn, directly related to the size of per capita oil windfall and the quality of governance. . . . [T]he windfalls failed to ensure rapid growth in most group members and probably even stifled it in a few.

He also finds some positive effects, as suggesting that "most of the people in most of these countries became better fed, healthier, more educated, more comfortably housed and better prepared to face the challenges of the twenty-first century" (Amuzegar, 1999, p. 221). In particular, the Gulf monarchies have turned almost overnight from relying on small farming and fishing to enjoying the highest living standards in the world. Nevertheless, his overall conclusion is that the "real pity is that despite all such unavoidable negatives, most members were still not on a secure path toward sustained growth and prosperity, even after 20 years of effort" (Amuzegar, 1999, p. 222).

3.4 THE POLITICAL RESOURCE CURSE – THE RENTIER STATES

While the Dutch Disease literature focuses solely on economic factors and the problems that arise prior to any political interference, the term 'resource curse' covers the effects on societal actors as well. The resource curse is thought to be especially contagious to states that derive a significant proportion of their income from rents, making them what Mahdavy (1970) called 'rentier states.' In his study of the political effects of oil wealth in Iran, Mahdavy argued that the extra income yielded large political benefits for the Shah, even though it led to sub-optimal economic development. The rent income is thought to produce political deterioration and muted economic growth by altering the incentives of state actors. We will call this effect the 'political resource curse', even though it produces both political and economic consequences. Several scholars have broadened Mahdavy's investigation of Iran, and suggested that this effect is universal.

The first wave of rentier state/resource curse literature was convinced that oil discoveries spurred increasingly authoritarian political systems (Gelb, 1988; Karl, 1997; Mahdavy, 1970; Ross, 2001; Tsui, 2011) and declining economic growth (Sachs & Warner, 1995, 2001; Auty, 1993, 2001). As Karl claims, oil-dependent countries "consistently demonstrate perverse linkages between economic performance, poverty, bad governance, injustice and conflict" (Karl, 2004, p. 37).

In a follow-up article to their seminal work, Sachs and Warner (2001) summed up the evidence six years after their initial paper. They concluded that the link between natural resources and slow growth was "not bulletproof, but quite strong." The main cause, they claimed, was a lack of openness to international trade and investment and poor bureaucratic capacity. Repeated cross-country regressions (e.g. Sachs & Warner, 1995; Doppelhofer, Miller, & Sala-i-Martin, 2000; Ross, 1999; Sala-i-Martin, 1997) consistently produced evidence backing up Sachs and Warner's initial claim, concluding that the curse was a reasonably solid fact (Sachs & Warner, 1995).

However, in recent years this insight has been modified (e.g. Ross, 2012). A study by Haber and Menaldo (2011) suggested that there was even *no correlation at all* between oil and autocracy. The study used a statistically strict methodology to test long-run relationships between resource wealth and regime type in the period between 1800 and 2006. Reassessing this claim, Andersen and Ross (2014) agree that the long-term effects might be weak, but that the most pronounced political resource curse appeared after 1970. As Ross writes, while many countries developed accountable and democratic institutions in the period from 1980 to 2006 and saw steady economic growth, this was only true for non-oil countries (Ross, 2012, p. 1).

Today, most scholars seem to agree that oil wealth hampers political development and economic growth to some degree, due to the effects on the political system itself. While earlier studies argued that resource wealth fueled both authoritarianism and the withering of political institutions, others found little evidence of any great changes in the political regime type. On the contrary, oil wealth has been found to have stabilizing effects throughout different types of initial regime configuration (Cuaresma, Oberhofer, & Raschky, 2011; Morrison, 2015; Smith, 2004). Wright, Frantz, and Geddes (2013) find that this also applies to the rate of leadership transitions in autocratic countries – the turnover is lower in resource-rich countries. Ulfelder (2007) shows how oil-rich autocracies in particular are typically more durable, and finds that energy resource income is significantly linked to regime survival. Such stability might also depend on mediating factors. Bjorvatn and Farzanegan (2015) find that differences in the political stability of resource-rich countries depend on the power of the incumbent.

There is now a much wider recognition of the complexities of the resource curse phenomenon, and studies from the last two decades incorporate context-specific explanations. These explanations hinge on the relative importance of resources in the economy, macroeconomic trends and conditions, the interaction with socio-political institutions, and so on (Papyrakis, 2016, p. 176).

The theoretical focus is usually on how resource wealth influences the nature and structuring of incentives and policy choices in political systems. These are hypothesized to reduce growth (Auty, 2001; Sachs & Warner, 1995; Sala-i-martin, 1997), limit the opportunity for potential democratization (Ross, 2012, p. 108) and, due to the perversion of incentives for politicians, lead to severe misallocation of capital in the economy at large (Robinson, Torvik, & Verdier, 2006). It is also thought to induce authoritarianism (Karl, 1997), increase the level of repression (Ross, 2001), rent seeking (Torvik, 2002) and corruption (Brollo, Nannicini, Perotti, & Tabellini, 2013). Skocpol (1983) suggests that oil rents help governing elites ensure the loyalty of key allies, by increasing their economic benefits. Increasing public spending may also placate the citizenry. Alternatively the resource wealth can be used for more effective suppression (Selvik & Utvik, 2016).

Thus, many social scientists trace the resource curse to the governmental level, but as Ross points out, they agree on little else (2012, p. 5). The numerous pathways between oil income and sub-optimal outcomes must also interact with each other. In order to shed some light on the bigger picture of the resource curse in a political setting, we will examine the most important mechanisms in turn.

3.4.1 Taxation

The scale of oil revenues has a huge impact on government income, allowing countries to abandon taxation as their main source of revenue. Tax income as a percentage of government revenue is significantly lower for oil producers compared to other (especially low-income) countries (below $5000 GDP per capita) (Ross, 2012, p. 31).

This is one of the most important mechanisms proposed by rentier state theorists. High revenues generated by petroleum products can leave the state autonomous vis-à-vis the society, without the need for taxation to fund the typical expenses of a state. When levels of taxation decrease, the government becomes dependent on highly volatile oil income, which brings with it a diverse set of problems.

Morrison (2015) shows how the average effect of increased non-tax revenues has a very strong and significant impact on both levels of taxation and government spending. With windfalls of oil revenue, the extractive capacity of states (i.e. their ability to collect taxes from their citizens more efficiently) tends to wither (Morrison, 2015, p. 48). The rents become the new main source of income. With expanding budgets, the government no longer needs to be held accountable for the allocation of what used to be scarce resources. With increased oil revenue, the economic interactions between the government and its citizens thus will weaken (Smith, 2004, p. 233). This depletion of authority eventually transforms the government from an extractive state into a distributive one. The government loses both authority and jurisdiction (Karl, 1997, pp. 58–64), as well as a valuable source of information generated by the tax bureaucracy (Smith, 2004, p. 233). The citizens, meanwhile, might experience the government as increasingly opaque, since the tax/expenditure connection is lost (Ross, 2012).

However, long-term stability requires a steady income in order to keep taxes low. Once a government moves away from tax as the main source of income, they place this stability at risk. In addition, taxation involves more than merely collecting financial resources from citizens. A tax-dependent state must decide which groups should benefit from redistribution and which groups should be taxed higher. Taxation also has the potential to increase transparency, as the citizens are concerned with how their taxed resources are put to use.

This is one of the proposed reasons for why some oil states tend to develop unaccountable institutions, and why democratic transitions could face severe difficulties. Many scholars have pointed out the importance of taxation for democratic development. Bates and Lien (1985, p. 59) argue that in order for a government to increase taxes, it will need to cede political power. In other words, taxation leads to representation, and even more so if the citizens do not receive commensurate benefits (Ross, 2012, p. 247). Taxation is also found by Acemoglu and Robinson (2006) to be integral to democratic transitions. They argue that a concession of political power is one of the few credible commitments that rulers might make in order to 'exchange' power for tax income.

In this view, the short-term benefit of decreasing the tax burden is obvious, as the citizens will perceive this as a huge benefit. In dictatorships, this might relieve tensions and calls for democratic reforms. By increasing the ratio of benefits to taxes, the political leadership will not be subject to the same demands for political representation. For example, in the case of Saudi Arabia, the country did collect taxes in the wake of the oil boom, but the tax bureaucracy was disassembled as the rents started to flow (Chaudry, 1997, p. 143).

Without the need for taxation, Ross argues, the need for representation in order to grant citizens political power is no longer present (2012, p. 66). Or as Luciani puts it: "The absence of taxation mutes the rationale for accountability and establishes an essential paternalistic relationship between the state – personified by the ruler – and the people" (Luciani, 2011, p. 220). This is thought to influence political development.

3.4.2 Government Spending

We have seen how political leaders often reduce the level of taxation in order to stay in power. This frequently happens – quite unsurprisingly – in the months before elections (Karl, 1997, pp. 179–181; Ross, 2012, p. 69). While a big tax cut makes for political popularity, other benefits might also do the trick. Where taxation is found to sharply decrease with increasing oil wealth, the increase of public spending is even sharper, according to Morrison (2015).

An immediate effect of the oil boom in the 1970s was an unprecedented increase in public spending for most oil countries. Venezuela, for instance, embarked on expensive state-financed projects to boost industrialization. They also subsidized consumer goods and increased employment through public-sector jobs (Karl, 1997, p. 27). The same tendency was seen across the other OPEC countries as well, where the governments took a modernizing and industrializing role by allocating large sums of oil income to create and expand everything from infrastructure, education and healthcare, to establish or enlarge key industries (Amuzegar, 1999, p. 49).

This spending spree had both positive and negative consequences. Investments in infrastructure, education, healthcare and social services will have a weaker effect on overall consumption in the economy compared to direct subsidies, lower taxation or state consumption of goods and services. This is because such investments usually stimulate economic growth. As we saw in section 3.3, it is better to invest than consume this wealth. The positive effects of increased public investments can outweigh the negative consequences of real exchange rate appreciation, but such investments will still generate adjustment costs in the economy. As Sachs writes, "The optimum response is to spread the investments over time, to maximize the benefits of the investments net of the adjustments costs themselves" (2007, p. 186). In other words, the real danger is when the government spends its oil revenue on consumption rather than investment.

As a result, oil rents often end up funding a disproportionately large part of the state budget in oil-producing countries (Ross, 2012, p. 31). In 1980, major oil exporters had a ratio of oil exports to total exports that was far higher than other primary non-oil commodity exporters (82.5 percent versus 50.7 percent) (Karl, 1997, p. 47). No matter what the consumption/ investment ratio is, this makes for a serious dependency on continued oil income in the future.

In the midst of this bazaar of popular policy choices, the occasional politician could probably stop and think about saving some of the oil rents for later. However, they would then find themselves in a classical political predicament called 'the prisoner's dilemma'. Imagine leading a government that is convinced of the virtues of prudent spending and retaining the level of taxation. This might be possible if you can make sure that everyone else plays by the same rules. If, however, your government is without practical means to enforce such rules, you will assume that the opposition will campaign on increasing the general welfare should you choose to be the voice of moderation. Thus, even if one government desists from widespread increases in public spending for a period, this is no guarantee that the next government will be similarly restrained.

As a result, the 'petro-status quo' is often maintained, as certainly was the case in most of the states with oil reserves in the decades after the oil price boom. The levels of public spending and taxation shifted drastically in favor of the citizens. The temptation to follow this spending scheme is obvious when we make the rather uncontroversial assumption that political leaders want to stay in power.

Lack of investments

As we have already discussed, there is a significant difference between consuming and investing the oil resources. However, we often observe the governments allocating too much towards consumption in order to receive political support. This is found by several empirical studies to have negative consequences on both political systems and economic growth.

Papyrakis and Gerlagh (2004) examine the effect of natural resources on corruption, investment, trade, schooling, and then indirectly on economic growth. They find a particularly strong effect through the investment channel. Their analyses show that 41 percent of the indirect negative impact of natural resources on growth stems from the negative effect on investments. They explain this in terms of the altered incentives of governments in natural resource-rich countries, where windfalls decrease the need for savings and investment.

This fact is also highlighted by Gylfason and Zoega (2001). They find that investment in capital is inversely related to the share of natural capital in national wealth and directly related to the development of the financial system. Specifically, they show how the few resource-rich countries that have enjoyed rapid growth have had much higher rates of gross saving and investment since 1965 than the majority with negligible growth. They also show that economic growth is inversely related to natural resource abundance, as well as to initial income. In addition, they find growth to be directly related to the level of education and investment.

Patronage

Tax cuts and increased public spending follow almost universally from a windfall of petroleum dollars, and might seem to be two sides of the same coin. In the political sphere, the role of public spending used as *patronage* is usually thought to be the most effective way to translate oil wealth into political support. 'Patronage' refers to spending money to placate different actors in society – either the citizens or other powerful groups and individuals – in order to gain political advantage (Robinson et al., 2006, p. 449). This effect is hypothesized to increase the stability of the incumbent regime, or to encourage authoritarian tendencies with severe effects on the accountability of institutions.

There is no clearer example of the excessive use of patronage than in the Gulf countries following the Arab Spring. The richest oil states were quite resilient to the wave of uprisings and subsequent challenges to the incumbent regimes, with the exception of Libya. The governments of major Arab oil producers – Algeria, Kuwait, Saudi Arabia, Qatar, the United Arab Emirates and Oman – emerged from their troubles relatively unharmed. One of the reasons for this was their ability to use oil wealth to dampen calls for political reform (we discuss the case of Saudi Arabia in section 3.5).

Robinson et al. (2006) put the notion of patronage to the test on a larger scale, by examining a proposed mechanism explaining why political leaders engage in inefficient redistribution. First, they claim political leaders over-extract the natural resources in order to get rich now rather than in the future. After all, next year they might not be in power anymore. Since this increases the value of staying in power, they distribute resources so that the probability of re-election is maximized (2006, p. 466). The reason many oil-rich governments choose employment rather than income or single-payments – like tax cuts – is that the latter is not a credible offer in the long run, while employment is far more politically costly to reverse. It is thus more efficient to buy votes through employment. Since only the incumbent can determine the level of employment, this often leads to the political status quo being preserved (2006, p. 450). When the country in question suffers from bad and unaccountable institutions, this way of distributing wealth results in inefficient and slow growth.

3.4.3 Institutions

It is further suggested that the negative effects of oil rents are usually found in cases where the political institutions are already poor, in contrast to high quality institutions that might "ameliorate the perverse political incentives created by resource booms" (Robinson et al., 2006, p. 450) and promote accountability (2006, p. 447). In other words, the character of the institutions has a strong mediating effect, and is suggested to 'decide' whether the resource curse manifests in the political systems.

There has been increasing interest in the role of institutions in political economy, and this is no less true in discussions about the resource curse. Mehlum, Moene, and Torvik (2006) assert that the heterogeneous growth performance among resource-rich countries is primarily due to how resource rents are distributed via institutions. They also distinguish between 'good' and 'bad' institutions:

1. Producer-friendly institutions
   a. Rent seeking and production are complementary
   b. Resource abundance attracts entrepreneurs into production, implying higher growth
2. Grabber-friendly institutions
   a. Rent seeking and production are competing
   b. Resource abundance attracts scarce entrepreneurial resources out of production and into unproductive activities.

Here, the authors explain the gains from unproductive activities as a result of weak institutions, for instance due to a weak rule of law, malfunctioning bureaucracy and/or corruption. This approach contrasts with the rent seeking explanation of Sachs and Warner (1995), who dismissed this interpretation as empirically unimportant, and rather favored the Dutch Disease explanation. Mehlum et al. (2006) argue that institutions come before any such explanation in the causal chain by (partly) determining how natural resources affect growth, regardless of whether resource abundance has any discernible effect on institutional development. Their main claim is that natural resources put institutions to the test. Where the natural resources produce inferior results is usually where the political institutions are weak, or 'grabber-friendly'. The notion of the resource curse is thus conditional on the quality of existing institutions (2006, p. 3).

3.4.4 Corruption and Rent Seeking

When the government becomes the prime source of capital, two other central – and closely related – problems emerge: *corruption* and *rent seeking*. Rent seeking might be viewed as a special case of corruption pertaining to the public sector. As Lambsdorff puts it, rent seeking is the "various forms of seeking preferential treatment by public decision makers, for example [through] competitive lobbying and corruption" (2002, p. 98).

In the case of resource-rich economies, the problem arises when the state becomes the prime supplier of capital. As Knutsen et al. (2017) state, "natural resources introduce 'high-rent activities' which [increase] the bribes that involved economic actors can possibly pay while still reaping profits, and thereby incentivizing bureaucrats to request bribes." They further argue that political corruption increases since the economic costs of accepting corruption are lower in economies dominated by natural resource extraction.

Some cross-country studies find support for a link between natural resources and corruption (e.g. Leite & Weidmann, 1999), but it is hard to separate from the institutional framework. Countries with 'grabber-friendly' institutions are often more corrupt to begin with. Leite and Weidmann also take this under consideration, as resource wealth could affect the levels of corruption contingent on government policies and (lack of) bureaucratic power. Indeed, another cross-country study by Alexeev and Conrad (2009) finds only weak support for their initial findings.

While cross-country studies will have a hard time discerning the mechanisms that cause resource wealth to induce corruption, there are other ways to highlight this problem. One example is the aforementioned study by Knutsen et al. (2017), which uses local data on mining to investigate levels of corruption. While not tackling the role of oil endowments specifically, it shows the local effects of resource extraction and finds that opening of new mines strongly increases bribe payments to local officials and the local police.

Another 'meso-level' approach is found in Brollo et al. (2013), which finds oil wealth to increase political corruption and the quality of politicians. Their theory suggests that larger budgets encourage the rent-grabbing predilections of incumbent politicians "without disappointing rational but imperfectly informed voters" (2013, p. 1760). Through empirical observations of municipalities in Brazil, they find that larger transfers to municipal governments increase the observed corruption, as well as reducing the average education of mayors.

This supports what Karl (1997) suggests is a major problem for oil-rich countries – namely that actors throughout the society will gear toward extracting parts of the state's oil revenue for personal gains when this is the most easily accessible capital (1997, p. 178). In her study of Venezuela, she focuses on the rent-seeking activities of larger actors, including organizations, branches of public office, and even banks. She finds rent seeking to distort their incentives and that it shifts the focus from potentially productive goals to a myopic concentration on extracting rents from the state coffers.

Rent seeking is also found to be the cause of detrimental political development and economic growth in larger samples. Robinson et al. (2006) found increased misallocation of capital to increase after resource booms, and they link this to the fact that politicians use the rents to influence the outcome of elections because of the increased value of being in power.

Baland and Francois (2000) point out that while rent-seeking behavior is well documented in developing countries, it does not happen in every oil state. Several other contributions have investigated how rent seekers prey on the productive sector and entrepreneurs, lowering the returns to both rent seekers and their 'prey'. When resource income is booming, this activity should increase. This also might lead to a decline in overall production. Baland and Francois find that the initial equilibrium, i.e. starting position, determines how correlated rent seeking and exogenous increases in resources are. They argue that when a large part of the population is already engaged in productive behavior, such as entrepreneurship, the effects are smaller. If the population is engaged in rent seeking already, this will multiply in tandem with the increase in income (2000, p. 529). Since rent seeking is seen as especially problematic for healthy growth, this might explain why some oil states fare better than others.

3.5 THREE CASES OF BLESSING AND CURSE

3.5.1 Venezuela

Probably the most prominent example of a rentier state suffering both a political and economic resource curse is Venezuela. Many of the discussed problems relating to a sudden increase in oil wealth can be observed here over the last 50 years. Their problems reach up to the time of writing, as Venezuela under President Maduro is slowly turning into a failed state. The country did not diversify its economy at all during the first decades of the oil boom, and has continued to buy most necessities from abroad, even food. In 2018, Venezuela is left with a starving population after the oil price fall of 2014. The story of Venezuela is worth detailing, because it is the best example of a curse that follows a large influx of oil wealth. Granted, not all of their problems can be explained by this simple fact, but there are compelling cases to be made that oil is the source of many of the country's most serious problems.

The perils of being a rentier state can be compared with winning the lottery. If an average person won millions of dollars in the lottery, he or she might lose the incentive to work. They can live off the lottery prize for years to come. This scenario will often result in increased spending, maybe on a new house, cars, and more expensive habits. The problem arises when the money runs short, and the lottery winner is stuck with their habits and expenses. Without any lasting investments in future profits, they will have to radically decrease spending, rid themselves of the expensive habits, and find new sources of income by going back to work. For the sake of this comparison, we might imagine that the person 'forgets' the skills that previously gave them income, that is, their profession. They would have to restart their job training and maybe get more education, at the same time as the money is running out.

The oil price increase in the early 1970s was such a lottery prize for many oil producers, including Venezuela. Venezuela embarked on an expensive oil-rent driven expansion of the state. Many prestigious state-backed projects commenced, which rapidly resulted in new jobs and a general increase of welfare levels. Consequently, the government could also afford to reduce the taxes on wealth and income. This, of course, made the voters happy and the governments popular. So, while expenses went up, the taxes went down.

However, these effects did not only stem from self-preserving politicians wanting to stay in power. According to Karl, they also originated from a 'domestic contradiction' facing all oil producers, but that some tackle better than others (1997, pp. 50–51). This contradiction consists of oil wealth being an engine of growth, but without generating links to the economy at large. Oil as a commodity generates a *fiscal link* when it is sold on the world market, that is, it links into the stream of income. However, the nature of oil and oil discovery might make it hard for the commodity to generate links into ideal production and consumption patterns, and this tendency is most prominent in developing countries, like Venezuela.

On the consumption side, collecting huge amounts of oil rent provide the means to buy abroad. This reduces incentives to buy at home, since the products are readily available on foreign markets. This is the same effect as outlined in section 3.2, as the demand for tradable goods increases. As mentioned above, this is particularly harmful for foodstuffs. For developing countries, the tradable products now available for import usually come in more sophisticated variants than what is produced domestically. When importing consumables, there is also a negative effect on the level and rate of production. When the country imports what it needs and wants, it supports foreign industries rather than developing home-grown enterprises.

So far, this is a potential problem for all kinds of wealth. It could be argued that parts of the Western world also face this problem, as industrialized countries increasingly buy their labor-intensive goods from East Asia, leaving their own manufacturing sectors barren. With oil, however, there is also an intrinsic problem for developing countries with regard to the missing links to the economy.

The initial input requirements of oil production are usually not satisfied by domestic sources, especially not in developing countries. From the start, these countries are dependent on both technology and expertise from more developed countries. In addition, when the extraction and production chain is in place, oil does not create adjacent industries compatible with lower levels of technological and economic development. In the absence of strong interests arguing for a more diversified economic model, such as existing manufacture or agricultural organizations, most politicians will favor the continuation of a narrow and resource-led industrialization.

Compare this to the production of coffee. The export of coffee requires domestic transportation, processing and packaging – all potential boosters to regional development and job creation. Oil, on the other hand, is extracted with existing, often foreign, high technology, moved in pipelines, and (at least up to the late 1990s) usually shipped to refineries in advanced industrialized countries. According to Karl, this is why oil lacks the ability to create lateral links to the rest of the economy, and why oil production locked the development trajectory of Venezuela into an unfortunate track. Once in this position, it is very hard for any country to turn it around. According to Karl, arguing for alternative fiscal bases through taxation was impossible in Venezuela at this point – the oil-based social forces with a vested interest in the continuation of oil-led development were already in place (1997, p. 57).

3.5.2 Saudi Arabia

While Venezuela is a good example of a rentier state suffering under severe political and economic instability, it is still a scholarly debate over the «true» influence of oil on Venezuela's poor institutions and unstable political history (see for example Dunning, 2008).

In Saudi Arabia, however, the *stabilizing* force of oil wealth is unambiguous, and it is probably the most prominent example of a functioning rentier state that derives its power directly from the oil income. Since the oil booms of the 1970s, the Saudi Arabian monarchy has strengthened its claim to power through its widespread distribution of wealth. The oil booms gave many countries the ability to fast-track projects related to defense, national security, education, health, social security and infrastructure (Luciani, 1990, p. 90), as we also saw in Venezuela.

While such projects are seen in many rentier states, the beneficiary role of the state is taken to its extremes in Saudi Arabia where contracts issued by the state is given as an expression of royal gratitude (Luciani, 1990, p. 91). As should be noted, the main difference between Venezuela and Saudi Arabia is the political system. Saudi Arabia is a strong, authoritarian monarchy whereas Venezuela holds elections. The monarchy has arguably allowed Saudi Arabia to better control the national wealth without as many contenders to the political power.

The beneficiary role is also clearly in place towards the general population, and is usually seen as the most effective way to maintain the political stability. As Smith (2004) argues, oil states are generally found to be more politically stable. This stability is of course contingent on many other factors, but the fact that much societal tensions stem from resource scarcity allows the rentier state to bypass the most serious political challenges.

The political economy of Saudi Arabia is characterized by the dominant role of the state, which has marginalized the private sector as well as the formation of other societal groupings (Selvik & Utvik, 2016, p. 72). While the distributional system was in place already in the 1950s, it was vastly accelerated with the oil windfalls in the 1970s. This allowed the Saudi state to grant massive distributions to its populace. (Selvik & Utvik, 2016, p. 72).

Oil wealth has provided Saudi Arabia with a bulwark against pressures for political representation and protests. In one way, the credo of 'no taxation without representation' is turned against the population: there is no taxes, so there is neither any grounds for claiming representation. The question, of course, is how long the Saudi Arabian monarchy can keep this up.

One of the main problem for the monarchs is that there has been no ideologized economic nationalization process (Luciani, 1990, p. 53). Thus, the only viable social contract between rulers and the ruled is the continuing promise of the monarch to provide for the citizens. It is, in other words, an oil-based social contract (Selvik & Utvik, 2016, p. 3). While the Saudi Arabian citizens are provided access to free education, secure jobs, housing and subsidized goods, the cost of this is ever-increasing. At the same time, the private sector is further marginalized and the salary levels are much higher in the over-employed public sector (Selvik & Utvik, 2016, p. 75).

These distributing schemes can work wonders in the face of unrest. When the international protests during the Arab Spring in 2011 broke loose, the Saudi Arabian state used its distributing prowess to placate any potential protests with a 'stick and carrot'-approach. While new laws against civil disobedience were put in place, the security apparatus infiltrated social media groups and plans for protests were effectively disrupted. At the same time, massive distributing schemes – totaling $130 billion – were announced (Selvik & Utvik, 2016, p. 21), more than the total national budget in 2007 (Selvik & Utvik, 2016, p. 71).

Overnight, the monarchy authorized a 15 percent increase in public-sector salaries along with a grant of two months' salary to every state employee. They introduced a massive affordable housing plan, a two-month stipend bonus for all students, as well as new unemployment benefits and the repayment of housing loans for hardship families. The regime further promised new employment opportunities in the near future, and created 60,000 new jobs in the Ministry of the Interior (Selvik & Utvik, 2016, p. 21).

The effect on the citizens was to a large extent successful. Among the youths aged 18–25, 76 percent said that the country is going in the right direction in 2012. This was an increase of 16 percentage points in one year (Selvik & Utvik, 2016, p. 71). Nevertheless, the demographics of Saudi Arabia pose a future problem to the rulers, as there is a large youth population without the same prospects of secure jobs in the near future. Youth unemployment is rising, as the coveted public sector jobs employ citizens from an ever increasing 'waiting list'. In the meantime, the unemployment benefits are only 15 percent lower than the minimum salary in the public sector, providing a strong disincentive to take employment in the private sector (Selvik & Utvik, 2016, p. 74).

There are other downsides to these schemes as well, and some scholars note the changing tides in the Saudi public in spite of the high levels of welfare. As Steffen Hertog writes, the post-Arab Spring period marks a return to the distributing schemes of the 1970s (Selvik & Utvik, 2016, p. 73). While there was some alleviation in public spending through the 1990s and 2000s, it has now reached unprecedented levels. At the same time, the citizens are more preoccupied with social and political issues than before, and this might lead to future problems that might not be as easily solved by simply increasing public spending.

One of the main preoccupations of the wider Saudi public is the level of corruption in the government, which is increasingly reported by the press (Selvik & Utvik, 2016, p. 87). The citizens also hold the state to higher standards of quality in services, and Saudis are frequently mobilizing for consumer rights, and several universities have held protests against corruption and mismanagement of public funds (Selvik & Utvik, 2016, p. 87). These themes might be more explosive than previously thought, especially after the Arab Spring, as they could spill over into wider political demands for representation.

In Venezuela, some of the government's current troubles could be solved with increased oil income. In combination with an increasingly educated public and increasing levels of unemployed youths with high expectations of material well-being, the Saudi Arabian monarchy faces future problems that even oil wealth might not solve (Selvik & Utvik, 2016, pp. 88–89). However, as we saw in Section 2.5.1, Saudi Arabia still has plenty of unexploited oil fields and huge reserves, and thus the possibility of keeping a rentier peace in many years to come.

3.5.3   Norway

Until the 1990s, the Norwegian government either consumed or reinvested into the oil sector all state income from oil and gas production. In the early 1980s, the income was used to pay off foreign debt, and thus solidified the Norwegian economy. There are two main sources of oil income for the Norwegian government: Petroleum taxes and revenue from the government's direct share of ownership (cf. Section 2.5.3.). As Figure 3.2 illustrates, the net cash flow to the government increased strongly after 2000.

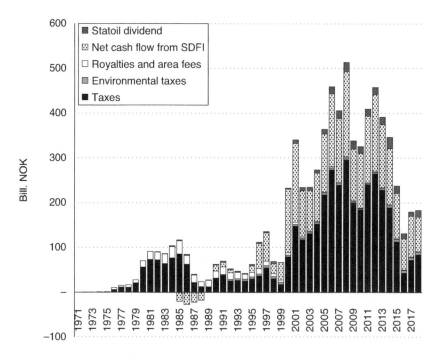

Source: http://www.norskpetroleum.no/en/economy/governments-revenues/ (accessed January 6, 2018).

Figure 3.2   The net government cash flow from petroleum activities

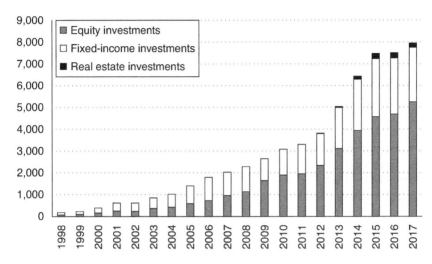

Source: https://www.nbim.no/en/the-fund/market-value/ (accessed January 6, 2018).

*Figure 3.3   Market value of the Norwegian fund 1998–2017, in Norwegian
kroner (billions)*

In 1990, before significant net profit was available, the Norwegian government set up an oil fund. The system was designed so that all governmental
income from the oil sector was put into a fund managed by a special
branch of the Central Bank, which invested the money in foreign government bonds and shares on world stock exchanges, later also real property.
The Ministry of Finance made the first transfer to the fund in 1996. Figure
3.3 shows the increased value of the fund. The fund has a value of one
trillion US dollars, equal to about 240 percent of the Norwegian GDP.

The Fund is supposed to serve several purposes (Mestad, 2015). First,
to avoid more money into the Norwegian economy than it can absorb.
Second, to serve as a 'rainy-day' buffer, facilitating a Keynesian economic
policy of increased governmental spending when the economy was in
a downward cycle. Third, the fund was supposed to save the oil wealth
for future generations, in the shape of financial assets. As pointed out in
Section 2.1, the value of oil in the ground is not to be regarded as income,
but as a wealth. The aim of the owner should be to preserve or increase
the value of the wealth, either as oil in ground or in another form. With
a sovereign wealth fund receiving the income from oil sales, the wealth is
preserved, albeit in the shape of financial assets.

With broad parliamentary support, the Norwegian government in 2001
introduced a budgetary rule that the government is permitted to use the

fund to balance the annual budget, but only by extracting a maximum 4 percent of the fund's value, unless an exceptional economic situation arises. The 4 percent threshold was set according to what was assumed to be the long-term return on the fund's investments. After the financial crisis the current threshold has been debated. Many Norwegian economists believe that the approximated return of 4 percent is too high, and unsustainable in the long term. They have therefore suggested lowering the threshold to 3 percent.

The counter-argument is that the political agreement behind the fund has no constitutional or legal basis outside the parliament's decision. The only way to make it harder for future governments and politicians to change the threshold is to act as if it is written in stone. Lowering it now will make it easier for future 'irresponsible' leaders to raise it. So far, the rule of action has a very solid standing among leading Norwegian politicians. All parties in the parliament, with the exception of the Progress Party, initially agreed to this rule and various governments have generally kept to the rule of action with a few deviations, one case being the financial crisis in 2008.

In the short term, this system gives the government some latitude for exercising a Keynesian adjustment policy to expand the budget in times of slowdown in the economy and contract it in times of high pressure in the national economy. When the Norwegian economy has been sound, various governments have used less money from the fund than the rule allows. The budget proposal for 2014 – both from the outgoing and incoming governments – used approximately 2.9 percent of the fund's value. In 2017, the government reduced the threshold in the 'rule of action' from 4 to 3 percent of the value of the fund, thus restricting its ability to spend money from the fund. This was in line with recommendations from economists, based on the observation that, given global economic conditions, the long-term real return on the fund's investments was unlikely to exceed 3 percent.

The Norwegian long-term strategy is to preserve the value of the wealth, slowly introduce the income from the oil activity into the wider economy, whilst at the same time avoiding the implications of the Dutch Disease. Obviously, as the fund grows, so does the absolute value of 3 percent. Subsequently, every government will usually have a bit more oil money available to the budget every year. It also decouples fluctuating oil income from the budgetary spending of the same money.

3.6   CRITIQUE OF THE LITERATURE

So far, we have discussed the negative effects of oil wealth on the economy and the political system, as well as how the country cases highlight some of the details of governance in oil-rich countries. We now turn to the critical side of the story, where we investigate the literature that modifies, or even denies, the resource curse.

Several of the studies critical to the resource curse highlight the endogeneity of measurements, which might result in biased or non-definitive results. Brunnschweiler and Bulte (2008) critically evaluate the empirical basis for the resource curse finding that the apparent paradox may be a 'red herring'. This is mainly because the measures used when presenting the evidence are endogenous to the underlying structural factors.

By separating resource *abundance* and *dependence*, Brunnschweiler and Bulte find that abundance, constitutions and institutions all determine the degree of dependence. This means that when measuring a country's dependence on resources, this measure might be related to the resource curse itself. For example, in a country with a heavy and corrupt bureaucracy, the economic growth could suffer. However, the level of bureaucratic effectiveness could also affect the resource dependence, through the ease of starting new businesses. The bureaucracy will then affect both the dependence and the growth. Thus, they argue that abundance and dependence are separate phenomena, something much of the research literature does not consider. As we have seen, the researchers are familiar with the conditional effects of institutions, as shown by Mehlum et al. (2006). However, if the most often used measurement of resource dependence is the problem, then this contention is much more serious than the research merely hinting at conditional explanations. Brunnschweiler and Bulte (2008) further claim that resource dependence does not directly affect growth at all, following from their disentanglement of abundance and dependence. What is left, then, is abundance, which they find to exert a *positive* effect on both economic growth and institutional quality.

Smith (2015b) highlights several other problems with the natural resource export revenue/GDP-ratio measurement of dependence. For instance, if you compare a large country like Nigeria with 175 million citizens with Equatorial Guinea of one million, there is a huge difference in the state's coercive capacity even if both countries rely on oil exports for 50 percent of their exports. Poorer countries will also have a larger export ratio than richer countries, since richer countries consume more of the natural resources domestically (Smith, 2015, p. 601).

In the mentioned study, Brunnschweiler and Bulte (2008) therefore argue that the total resource stock is a better measure of resource abundance, as opposed to current economic flows deriving from these stocks, because this 'passes' the oil export revenues/GDP ratio's endogeneity problem concerning institutions.

Wright and Czelusta (2004) find that countries with certain institutional designs may fail to industrialize, and that failing to develop significant non-resource sectors may make them dependent on primary sector extraction. This would again suggest that the negative effects of dependence are correlated with pre-existing institutions.

Stijns (2005) presents evidence against the robustness of Sachs and Warner's (1995) statistical results, by applying the measurement of natural resource reserves/stock and shows that its effect on growth is at best unclear. Stijns finds that their results are not robust to changes in natural resource abundance from trade-flows to reserves or production. There are several reasons for substituting Sachs and Warner's data on primary export intensity. First, a resource-rich country may export few natural resources if the manufacturing sector intensively uses its natural resources. Second, as Wright (2001) argues, if countries fail to build on their resource base productively, then the measures of dependence may be a proxy for development failure for reasons that have little to do with the character of the resources.

In addition, Stijns claims that one of the reasons natural resources are not significant determinants of economic growth is because they can, simultaneously, exert both negative and positive effects on the economy (see also Papyrakis & Gerlagh, 2004). For example, Stijns finds some evidence that oil and gas reserves are associated with better education, more market-oriented economic policy, and more favorable investment-saving characteristics, but that they do also produce some Dutch Disease symptoms, causing slower growth in non-resource sectors.

James (2015) proposes another, and elegantly simple, explanation for why resource abundance is often tied to slow growth: a slow-growing resource sector. If the resource sector is slow, this sluggishness is disproportionately represented in the data of resource-dependent countries. James finds little evidence to back up the claim that growth in non-resource sectors is hampered by natural resources. Rather, he finds that resource-dependent countries grow slowly during certain periods (the 1980s), but relatively quickly in others (the 1970s), and explains this by pointing toward the average sector-growth heterogeneity which is caused by variations in the resource price. James also demonstrates that much of the observed growth heterogeneity in resource-abundant countries can be attributed to the types of industry that a particular country specializes in.

Alexeev and Conrad (2009) also call into question the resource curse hypothesis, and the negative effects of oil and mineral wealth on countries' institutions. It is usually suggested that large endowments of natural resources lead to phenomenon X, where X can be the Dutch Disease, involving the neglect of human capital development, rent seeking, a decline in saving and investment, the deterioration of institutions or increases in income inequality. Alexeev and Conrad argue that all these correlations are due to the misinterpretation of available data. They follow several earlier studies (Easterly & Levine, 2003; Hall & Jones, 1999; Rodrik, Subramanian, & Trebbi, 2004), in measuring long-term growth via GDP per capita levels rather than by calculating growth rates over a given period of time, because the 'whole' process from discovery to depletion often starts well before the period usually investigated (generally 1970). They find that most of the major oil exporters began commercial exploitation of their oil wealth well before 1950. Therefore, even if the existing empirical literature is correct, it is possible that a large oil endowment results in high growth rates in the early stages of extraction and slower rates when the oil deposits mature.

Alexeev and Conrad (2009) also use measures of natural resources that are not expressed in terms of GDP, because of the problems associated with this measure (namely, that it incorporates other parts of the economy that might influence the ratio without having an effect on natural resources, see Smith (2015) for a discussion of these measures). According to Alexeev and Conrad, institutions have not deteriorated in resource-rich countries – they simply have not improved. This is in agreement with Ross' (2012) conundrum, that the real paradox is why these states did not grow faster than they did. They claim these earlier results are obtained by controlling for initial GDP income. Because the quality of institutions is correlated with GDP in non-resource countries, and because resources increase GDP, regressions on institutional quality in conditions of resource wealth bias the result toward a negative effect. According to their GDP-based calculations, resource-rich countries should have high quality institutions, but they are often poor relative to industrialized countries with the same GDP levels. This is, indeed, a negative aspect of natural resource wealth, in that it halts institutional development, but it is in line with the results found in Acemoglu, Johnson, and Robinson (2001), and Rodrik et al. (2004): Institutions affect growth, but not the other way around.

3.7 CURSE OR BLESSING – AND HOW DO WE KNOW?

As we have seen, this field of research has been – and still is – rife with controversy, especially in later years. Closer scrutiny and improved statistical methods have uncovered several problems with the most ardent and monolithic hypotheses regarding the political and economic effects of oil income. As a result, serious scholars in the quantitative field no longer believe that there is a deterministic relationship between petroleum and a political or economic resource curse, no matter the conditions.

Concerning solely the economic effects, there is even less agreement on whether the resource curse is real at all. According to one meta-study, 40 percent of the empirical studies on long-term economic growth in resource-rich countries find a negative effect, while another 40 percent find no effect. The last 20 percent of these studies report a positive effect from resource abundance (Havranek, Horvath, & Zeynalov, 2016). The authors of this meta-study add that when method heterogeneity and potential publication bias are taken into account, the overall hypothesis of the resource curse is weak. Other scholars have also noted the lack of certainty. As van der Ploeg and Poelhekke (2016, p. 213) lament in another meta-study: "The answer to the question whether the resource curse exists thus depends on what type of data set is used and what question is asked."

In light of this, we think there are two main challenges that stand out. These are the large heterogeneity in (and indeed disagreement on) measurements of oil dependency, and the lacking focus on causal mechanisms.

The articles discussed in this chapter show the plethora of approaches taken by scholars, without any agreement on how to measure the effect of oil wealth. As seen in the quote by van der Ploeg and Poelhekke, this has led to different questions being asked. The result is that the contributions differ in what they investigate, thus not leading towards any agreement on what the resource curse is or what the effects are.

But how does one correctly measure the concept of oil dependency? It could be argued that the larger part of the economy driven by oil income, the greater is the dependency. This is usually measured by dividing the oil export revenues as a proportion of GDP. Unfortunately, using this measure introduces significant variation in the fiscal impact of oil, relative to the size of population. As Benjamin Smith (2015, p. 601) argued, the substantial difference between Nigeria and Equatorial Guinea with respect to their coercive capabilities and rentier capacity are masked when they have the same level of oil exports as share of GDP. In addition, each of these come with their own endogeneity problems.

As touched upon in section 3.6, other authors have suggested a difference between abundance and dependence, and that one does not necessarily imply the other (Brunnschweiler & Bulte, 2008). This further problematizes how to correctly measure the impact of oil. If a country is wealthy because of their petroleum resources, it does not automatically follow that it will become *dependent* on oil income. Upon receiving windfalls of oil wealth, the country in question will most likely have unprecedented means at their disposal and should not be labeled as *dependent*. Over time, the spending might make them dependent on future oil income by not having any viable options to extract income, for example, from taxation. Thus, the way the money is spent might make them dependent, not the oil wealth in itself. Dependence might appear over time, maybe decades, and if the country handles the wealth with adequate measures, they might escape dependence altogether.

Moreover, it should be clear by now that quite a lot of other factors influence the variables of interest, like political stability or corruption. For example, oil wealth could very well alter the incentives for policy makers, but it will by no means make these incentives uniform regardless of their previous state. Having an oil export/GDP ratio of 50 percent does not imply that two countries are equal in any other respect.

However, the overarching problem of measurement heterogeneity is that results are seldom reproducible. Many scholars develop and adopt their own operationalization of oil dependency, and as we have seen, others contest that measurements of dependence are the right way to investigate this problem to begin with.

From the initial focus on taxation and spending levels, previous insights into societal actors' incentives were adopted to the resource curse literature. Even prior to suggesting the potential effect of oil through these channels, neither levels of taxation nor public spending are bulletproof indicators of future political actions. Taxation and public spending are two of the mechanisms proposed to link oil income with political outcomes. The characteristics of the rentier state, with its focus on incentives for societal actors, is another way to understand how the malign effects occur. The problem with these, and other, explanations is that they are often hypothesized to apply to every oil-rich country, regardless of culture, institutions and even level of income. A more fine-grained approach with regard to mechanisms is needed, in which Knutsen et al. (2017) and Brollo et al. (2013) are good examples.

Even though these problems persist today, there are some carefully considered stylized facts remaining. These facts are marked by a reasonably careful scope regarding the effect of oil, and is easier to accept than the most deterministic conclusions. According to Ross (2015), the scientific community studying the political effects of oil wealth has produced solid evidence for three of the numerous hypotheses put forward over the last 30 years: Petroleum makes authoritarian governments more durable by increasing the available means to placate the citizens (as seen in Saudi Arabia), it increases corruption (as seen in Brazil), and it *helps* trigger conflict in low and middle-income countries when located among marginalized groups (as seen in Congo-Brazzaville and Sudan) (2015, p. 240).

NOTES

1. The origin of the phrase is the economic crisis in the Netherlands in the 1960s that followed the discovery of natural gas in the North Sea.
2. Among the OPEC countries, the value of petroleum exports as a share of GDP was on average 15 percent in 2016, down from 40 percent in 2008 OPEC (2017).
3. The list has been slightly elaborated.
4. There are other good arguments for giving the oil income to the citizens, in one form or another. Alaska has such a system, but the hand out is based on the dividend of a presumably permanent investment fund.

PART II

Market control

4. Institutional governance

4.1 PERSPECTIVES ON INTERNATIONAL INSTITUTIONS

Over the last decade 'global energy governance' has emerged as a new field in the study of the politics of international energy (van de Graaf and Colgan, 2016). Some scholars take a very programmatic approach, asserting the need for overarching political governance of all aspects related to the coming energy transition, in particular the close relationship between energy and climate change (Heubaum and Biermann, 2015; Wenger, 2009). The aim of this chapter is far less ambitious. We are only concerned about a single primary energy source, albeit the most important one – oil. Furthermore, we are only interested in the governance of the international *market* for oil. The relationship between oil and climate change will be discussed in Chapter 10. Nevertheless, there are important insights about the market aspects from the studies of international institutions in general, and the new focus on energy governance in particular.

The role of institutions in human life and society can hardly be over-stated. Douglass C. North defines institutions as the "rules of the game in a society or, more formally . . . humanly devised constraints that shape human interaction. In consequence, they structure incentives in human exchange, whether political, social or economic. Institutional change shapes the way societies evolve through time and hence is the key to understanding historical change" (North, 1990, p. 3). In the study of international relations we find a similar definition of institutions as "persistent and connected sets of rules (formal and informal) that prescribe behavioral roles, constrain activity, and shape expectations" (Keohane, 1989, p. 3). International institutions are important as they influence states' incentives, and the costs and benefits related to possible state acts, although the underlying interests of the state is determined autonomously. Furthermore, institutions can facilitate actions by the states that would have been hard to perform for any state on its own (Keohane, 1989, pp. 5–6).

The concept of institutions will thus be used as a general term encompassing both formal and informal rules and the regulation of actors' behavior. The main focus, however, will be on formal organizations, networks, and interactions between actors for the purpose of governing the oil market. This is in line with Colgan, Keohane, and van der Graaf (2012, p. 122), where changes in the energy regime complex are understood as "institutional innovation defined as significant organizational changes."

One challenge with these approaches is that they tend to regard international energy policy as a sub-field of international relations, adequately captured through the lenses of geopolitical and/or international institutional perspectives. Without disregarding the merits of these approaches, when the focus is on market governance, as it is here, the independent power of commercial actors, oil companies in particular, plays a vital role in any attempt to govern the oil market. The major international private oil companies are among the very largest companies in the world. In addition, new national oil companies have entered the oil industry over the last decades. In sum, these corporations possess tremendous economic power, even though states have taken more control over the oil market compared to the days of the Seven Sisters (cf. Chapter 5). It follows that these economic actors also have considerable political influence. To map out the institutional structure of oil market governance, we thus have to combine the roles of both governments and companies. Therefore, a perspective derived from the state-focused discipline of International Relations (IR), or public policy, is not sufficient. The perspectives of International Political Economy (IPE) provide an important and necessary supplement. Susan Strange (1988, p. 191) found the mutual influence between politics and markets as vital, and the field of energy studies in need of "some analytical framework for relating the impact of states' actions on the markets for various sources of energy, with the impact of these markets on the policies and actions, and indeed the economic development and national security of the states."

Section 4.3 is an attempt to follow-up on the request of Strange, developing a framework for understanding the interrelationship between governments and companies in the global oil market. First, Section 4.2 will discuss the role of key formal international institutions in the field of energy, with a primary concern for their impact in the governance of the oil market. The Organization of the Petroleum Exporting Countries (OPEC) is a special story, told in Chapter 6.

4.2 INTERNATIONAL GOVERNMENTAL ORGANIZATIONS (IGOs)

4.2.1 GATT/WTO

At certain crucial moments in history, it is possible to re-design political structures and institutions. The fall of the Berlin Wall in 1989 signaled the end of the Cold War, and the end of the bilateral superpower order of the US and Soviet Union. It is still unclear what shape the new security order of the world will take. Regarding international political economy, a crucial meeting took place at the Hotel Mount Washington, in the little town of Bretton Woods in New Hampshire, US in 1944. Forty-four countries, with an impending world war victory at hand, met to draw up the future world economic order. One thing was certain – the history of the world economy between the two world wars was not to be repeated. In particular, since they all agreed that the economic weaknesses had made a strong contribution to the rise of fascism, and thus to the Second World War. The principles and institutions of a new system for the governance of world economy had to be drawn from scratch.

The increasing protectionism aimed at reducing imports and increasing exports through competitive devaluations during the inter-war period was regarded as particularly destructive to the global economic welfare – and thus important contributing factors behind the depression of the 1930s. Both the US and UK delegation were committed to the connection between free trade, peace and prosperity. The traditional idea that the national economy could regulate itself had lost all credibility. In line with the ideas of the British economist John M. Keynes, who incidentally led the British delegation to Bretton Woods, governments had to intervene to correct market failures, and should take an active part to ensure full employment and an appropriate level of activity in the domestic economy. For the individual governments to be able to do this, they would need some kind of protection against competitive pressures in the international economy. What emerged from Bretton Woods was a post-war system encompassing free trade, but also fixed exchange rates and restrictions on capital movements across borders. Thus, governments could adjust the domestic economy through variable interest rates, taxes or governmental spending, without the risk of inflation and the outflow of capital. Two institutions – the World Bank and the International Monetary Fund (IMF) – were set up to govern the monetary part of the system, aside from subsequent negotiations on trade liberalization within the framework of the General Agreement on Tariffs and Trade (GATT). John Ruggie has characterized the system as 'embedded liberalism' (Ruggie, 1982).

The question, in our context, is how this overarching international economic system affected the governance of the oil market. The importance of the oil market to the global economy suggests a very high attention to oil in general trade negotiations. Llewelyn Hughes refers to estimates suggesting that spending on crude oil reached more than 4 percent of global GDP in 2007 (Hughes, 2014, p. 17). Nevertheless, he concludes that while "there is no explicit exemption for crude oil in the trade regime, governments have failed to reach agreement on how to treat natural resources within it" (Hughes, 2014, p. 6). He points to the fact that the US became a net importer of oil at the same time as the trade regime, and the historical perception of oil as a strategic resource, emerged. Thus, oil came under the GATT exclusion clause for reasons of national security (Hughes, 2014). Timothy Meyer clearly demonstrates the absence of any specific reference to energy products in the GATT negotiations, although the GATT regulations still can be legally relevant for energy-related products (Meyer, 2016, pp. 144–145). However, the liberalization of energy trade was not a political priority at the inception of the international trade regime after the Second World War. As described in Chapter 5, the global oil industry was controlled by the Seven Sisters, backed by the Western Great Powers, almost as a 'private government of oil' (Engler, 1961, pp. 34–64). Attempts to supersede this with free trade regulations based on the GATT regime would diminish the role of the Sisters, and thus the interests of their home governments, most prominently the US, UK and France.

This attitude changed when the governance of the oil market changed hands in the 1970s – from the multinational oil companies to the oil producers. Few oil producers were members of GATT at that time, and thus were not subject to the GATT regulations – although the US unsuccessfully tried to address export restrictions and dual pricing by the oil producers in the Tokyo-round of GATT negotiations (Meyer, 2016, p. 145).[1] OPEC has been a thorn in the side of major oil-consuming countries since the embargo of 1973 (cf. Chapter 6), particularly in the side of the US. In his memoirs, Secretary of State Henry Kissinger, quotes his briefing of the newly elected President Gerald Ford on the subject: "We have to find a way to break the cartel . . . It is intolerable that countries of 40 million can blackmail 800 million people in the industrial world" (Kissinger, 1999, p. 669). The main political instrument to limit the power of OPEC was the establishment of the International Energy Agency (IEA) (cf. Section 4.2.2). As more OPEC members have joined WTO (World Trade Organization), the possibility of using a judicial instrument under the GATT/WTO regulations to reduce the market power of OPEC, has emerged. At face value, the cartel-like behavior of the OPEC members seems to violate the free trade ideals of the WTO, but on closer inspection, this is not so obvious.

In his 2003 article, Melaku Geboye Desta, found that OPEC's establishment of production quotas represented a violation of GATT Article XI:1, which prohibits the imposition of quantitative restrictions on both imports and exports by its members, whether done individually or in concert with others (Desta, 2003, pp. 534–535). However, the GATT Article XX(g) provides an exception as it states "nothing in this Agreement shall be construed to prevent the adoption or enforcement by any contracting party of measures . . . relating to the conservation of exhaustible natural resources if such measures are made effective in conjunction with restrictions on domestic production or consumption."[2] In his 2010 article, Desta rejected the idea that the OPEC measures fall within Article XI, as this article relates to export restrictions, not restrictions on production: "the [OPEC] quotas apply to a natural resource which becomes a tradable product only after the actual production process has taken place. Until that point, there is no product whose export to restrict . . ." (Desta, 2010, p. 450). He concludes: "This author is of the view that it is unlikely a WTO claim will be brought against an OPEC country challenging its production management practices, and if one were to be brought, it is unlikely to succeed" (Desta, 2010, p. 463).

The key countries behind the formation of GATT/WTO did not consider the oil market as suitable for trade liberalization. This was partly due to the security content of oil in the aftermath of the Second World War, partly because of the experienced need for regulation of the industry, and also a consequence of the fact that the oil market regulators in the 1940s were multinational companies of the Great Powers themselves.

When the tides shifted, and the oil-producing countries took control of the market, the Western consuming countries were taken by surprise: "No crisis of the second half of the twentieth century fell on a world less prepared for it than the one triggered by the quadrupling of oil prices in the fall of 1973" (Kissinger, 1999, p. 664). Although the shift in market power from the companies to the oil-producing states had started in 1971, it was not until the oil shock in 1973 that the economic and political implications became obvious to the governments of the consumer countries. Not least because the embargo had such explicit political overtones related to the war between Israel and the Arab countries (cf. Chapter 6). For the institutional aspects of oil market governance, it triggered the establishment of an oil-consumer institution.

4.2.2   IEA

In 1974, the US Secretary of State, Henry Kissinger convened a conference in Washington with the aim of creating an anti-OPEC organization to counter the market power of OPEC. The idea was that the strengthened solidarity of the OPEC members should be met with increased solidarity among the consumer countries. The instrument for regaining control over the oil market was to establish a program for emergency burden sharing, the conservation of energy, the development of alternative energy sources and the creation of a financial safety net (Kissinger, 1999, p. 669). The European consumer countries and Japan were more vulnerable to oil supply interruption from the Arab oil exporters, and thus resisted the anti-OPEC profile advocated by the US (Lesage, van der Graaf, and Westphal, 2010, p. 59). France did not join the IEA until 1992. The emerging non-OPEC producer – Norway – joined the organization, but only by an associate agreement, excluding it from the emergency distribution of oil.[3] As discussed above, the US policy itself was somewhat incoherent. The coordination and cooperation among the consumers in their response to the price increase was, in fact, uncoordinated and competitive: "Some pressured the oil companies into giving them preferential treatment. Others imposed restrictions on the export of petroleum. Larger countries' companies bid up oil prices on the spot market. European countries sought to distance themselves from the Dutch and appease the Arabs" (Lesage et al., 2010, p. 59). In order to balance the various positions among the consumer countries, IEA was established as an agency under the Organisation for Economic Co-operation and Development (OECD), with broader and less explicitly anti-OPEC aims. The initial core aim of the IEA was to handle supply disruptions using an emergency oil crisis management system, originally triggered by a 7 percent reduction in daily oil supplies. The 1979 oil crisis demonstrated that the 7 percent threshold was too restrictive and a more flexible system of crisis cooperation was adopted. The original crisis system was never activated.

The idea that the response mechanisms should be 'automatic' was also unattainable, as countries preserved their sovereign control over established oil stocks. Furthermore, the system for building emergency oil stocks varied among the IEA member countries, as some made the oil companies responsible for having sufficient commercial stocks, while others developed public stocks under direct governmental control. In 1984 a more flexible consultation procedure was established, called the 'Coordinated Emergency Response Measures' (CERM). This system has been applied in relation to the 1991 Gulf War and to Hurricane Katrina in 2005.

The organizational structure of having the IEA as a sub-entity under the OECD has become a problematic restriction as new large oil consumers have emerged outside the OECD, in particular countries like China, India and Brazil. The IEA has tried to bypass this restriction by establishing various forms of cooperation with non-member consumer countries. In the case of China, the IEA website describes the cooperation as follows: "The IEA has established in-depth bilateral co-operation with China in a wide range of topics including energy security, energy statistics, energy markets (coal, oil, gas, renewables, and energy efficiency), the IEA Technology Collaboration Programmes, energy technology in cleaner coal and CCS [carbon capture shortage], industry, buildings, and transportation."[4] At the IEA Ministerial meeting in 2015, China became one of the first countries to activate Association status with the Agency.

The IEA has become a vital institution for providing information on international energy, and its agenda-setting role has increased in recent years. However, as a market-governing institution it is safe to conclude that the IEA "has limited authority in rule creation and enforcement" (Kohl, 2010, p. 198), although the organization might contribute to coordinated consumer behavior by other means, such as information on the market situation and proposals for joint action by member states. "Apart from crisis planning, the IEA essentially remains an agency for compiling data and making forecasts on energy markets" (Noreng, 2002, p. 48). However, over the last two decades, the scope of IEA has been extended to encompass almost all energy sources and topics related to energy markets and politics. The importance of providing reliable data and information for business and political decision-makers should not be underestimated.

4.2.3   IEF

Although the IEA did not acquire an explicit anti-OPEC profile, the fact that OPEC organized net exporters, and IEA consumers, gave the two organizations an antagonistic relationship. Without any overarching institutional framework, the two bodies lived separate lives without much interaction during the 1970s and 1980s, although some attempts were made to create a producer–consumer dialogue.

In 1991 ministers from oil-producing and oil-consuming, countries met in Paris. Such meetings have continued every two years and morphed into an organization called the International Energy Forum (IEF), which, since 2003, has had a permanent secretariat in Riyadh (Lesage et al., 2010, pp. 61–63). Discussions at the first meetings were somewhat amputated as the key factor of the price of crude oil was off the agenda. However, over the years, the bi-annual meetings have led to several joint projects tapping the common interests of both producers and consumers. In particular, the Joint Oil Data Initiative (JODI) aiming to provide reliable data and statistics related to the oil market and the oil industry in general, has been rather successful. The 72 member countries include all OPEC and IEA members, but also a number of non-OPEC producers, non-IEA consumers, and transit countries. IEF has the potential to develop into an overarching organization for governmental dialogue, information exchange and cooperation related to all aspects of the oil market and industry. So far, however, it lacks effective instruments for governance of the market. It is hard to see that the leading countries among the producers or consumers will develop an interest in turning the IEF into such a powerful common intergovernmental organization. From the perspective of Saudi Arabia, on the producer side, a potent IEF would reduce the ability of the Kingdom to determine market interventions, both in terms of deliberations inside OPEC and its independent market policy. On the consumer side, the dominant actor still is the US, although China has taken over the role as the largest oil importer. However, the US has a long-standing tradition of being very reluctant to commit itself to international treaties on issues regarded as politically sensitive to US security or economic interests. Moreover, Saudi Arabia and the US have a long history of bilateral dialogue and cooperation on oil-related issues (cf. Chapter 7). Adding seventy other countries into their special relationship could hardly be assumed to serve their respective national interests.

Although the confrontation of 1973 is long gone, its passing has not led to the emergence of an overall global energy regime complex (Colgan et al., 2012, pp. 130–131). Since the overall economic institutions seem inadequate for the purposes of international governance of the field of energy, it is most likely that this government will continue as a patchwork of bargains, agreements and cooperation by sub-groups with common interests, partly or entirely in conflict with other sub-groups. Even with the issue of climate change influencing the energy sector, it is fair to assume that the lack of a global encompassing energy governing institution will prevail.

4.3 THE POLITICAL ECONOMY OF OIL MARKET GOVERNANCE

The international governance system relating to oil might seem chaotic, but some traces of structure can be identified. As pointed out in the introduction, this requires the inclusion of the economic actors in the equation. In this respect, perspectives on the governance of the oil market derived from the field of International Political Economy (IPE) tend to have more dynamic models which encompass interactions and bargaining among both political and economic actors.

Susan Strange and John Stopford have developed a model for the dynamic interaction between governments and companies. Their starting point was how the:

upheavals of the international political economy during the last decade have altered, irreversibly we believe, the relationship among states and multinational enterprises . . . As a result, firms have become more involved with governments and governments have come to recognize their increased dependence on the scarce resources controlled by firms. (Stopford and Strange 1991, p. 1)

A core element of their approach is what they call *the triangular diplomacy*, implying the existence of a dynamic interaction between three different relationships: (1) between governments; (2) between companies; and (3) between governments and companies. In addition, cooperation and conflicts in the oil industry play themselves out in both a vertical and a horizontal market structure (cf. Chapter 5).

The history of the international oil market suggests that different actors have dominated the market at various times, based on market power resources, but also on patterns of collusion among market actors. Claes (2011, pp. 294–307) shows how many of the key historic cases of governance, cooperation or institutionalization can be interpreted along Stopford and Strange's three dimensions, like the Red Line Agreement in 1928, the role of the Seven sisters, the Tehran and Tripoli agreements of 1971, and the establishment and role of OPEC. However, in order to fully capture the role of the companies, we need to see the oil industry along both the horizontal and the vertical dimensions of the market.

4.3.1 The Role of the Vertical Market Dimension

Even though the OPEC countries dominated the upstream segment, exploration and production, from the 1970s, the IOCs continued to control the downstream segment of the market, such as refineries, marketing, and product sales. From the early 1980s some of the major oil exporting countries started to make downstream investments in Western Europe and the United States, gaining partial or total control over companies that could refine and distribute part of the exporters' crude oil exports in the main consuming countries. The aim was to secure sales outlets and thereby more stable revenues in an increasingly volatile market. These exporters also bought tankers, harbor and storage facilities, and petrochemical plants in consuming countries. Among the largest downstream investors were Kuwait, Venezuela, Saudi Arabia, Libya, and Norway. By 1990, Kuwait and Venezuela had refining capacity (domestic and foreign) covering 90–100 percent of their production capacity; the corresponding figure for Saudi Arabia was about 50 percent (Finon, 1991, p. 264), The pace of downstream integration slowed during the 1990s (Hamm, 1994, p. 186). This might be explained by the weakened financial position of several oil producers as the price fell. With the OPEC countries taking control over crude production, the IOCs tried to develop alternatives to OPEC's crude, in places such as Alaska and the North Sea.

The decline in refining and distribution margins in the late 1970s and early 1980s led to a wave of closures, modernizations, and takeovers, especially in the United States. During this period of painful restructuring, independents and majors were competing for a limited volume of known reserves – a scarcity that more than tripled the median transaction value for reserves in place in the United States (Smith, 1986). Much of this wave of reserve purchases and oil company mergers and acquisitions was financed through debt. Thus it came as no surprise that, as soon as spot prices began to show the first indications of decline, companies with financial difficulties tried to resell the same reserves bought some years earlier. Numerous properties changed hands repeatedly in a short period. In a similar way, refiners who had upgraded their facilities at high cost in the late 1970s became caught in an economic squeeze in the mid-1980s. Refinery upgrades were based on the belief that the wide price spread between heavy and light crudes that had existed in the 1970s would continue. It actually narrowed – from $8.50 per barrel in 1982, to $4 per barrel in 1984. Costly revamping to feed heavy crude proved to be a bad investment for a business already beset by marginal economies. In several cases banks helped companies resist selling upstream and downstream properties by restructuring loans and advancing some loan forgiveness, but a further price decline in 1986 forced many companies to divest in order to fulfill debt obligations. This reduced the number of oil companies and improved the position of those that were able to react quickly to changes in crude supply and product demand.

In the upstream segment of the market there were similar problems. Between 1985 and 1987 the seven largest majors replaced only 40 percent of the oil consumed in the United States through new discoveries, extensions, and improved recovery rates in existing fields. For oil consumed outside the United States the figure was 59 percent. When revisions of oil reserves and purchases are taken into account, the majors' replacement was still 11 percent short of production. The majors – primarily Exxon, Shell, and BP – purchased reserves from smaller companies that were either cutting back their oil activity or dropping out of the industry altogether. But the majors were still 'crude short', even if they were better off in this regard than some of their smaller competitors. The companies seemed to be preparing for a more competitive environment, in which increased size was perceived as necessary for taking higher risks in upstream investments. For the OPEC countries the key problem was the ability, or rather lack of ability, to finance the necessary investments in their existing production facilities, on their own. As most OPEC countries produced close to capacity, any increase in production capacity implied new investments. The financial reserves of the OPEC countries were no longer what they were in the heyday of high oil prices. By 1990 virtually all OPEC countries were in need of more financing, more technology, and more organization (Finon, 1991, p. 263). Many OPEC countries revised their policies and opened up for production-sharing agreements with foreign firms.

During the 1990s a new order emerged in the international oil market, based on a convergence of interests between the international oil companies, who provided technology and financial resources for exploration and production, and the producing countries who controlled access to the resources. The large oil exporters were searching for secure outlets for their crude oil in order to protect themselves against future market volatility. Downstream integration – in one way or another – was an expression of a risk-averse attitude on the part of the oil exporters, understandable given their experience in the oil market during the 1980s. Companies in financial difficulties need new investments – for example in their refineries – whereas crude-short companies are interested in arrangements that enhance their access to oil reserves. For the majors, joint ventures with NOCs from the OPEC countries provided protection against future scarcity, which was the companies' nightmare of the 1970s. This opened the way for the companies' return to the upstream market, which has subsequently partially reversed the structural change of the 1970s. The interaction between producer government and the IOCs, that had been an essential issue in the horizontal dimension of the market, was re-created in the horizontal dimension.

4.3.2   New Actors[5]

A new type of actor has entered the global energy scene. During the last decade, new NOCs from China, India, Malaysia, Brazil, and Russia have entered the international oil industry, competing with the IOCs for upstream contracts. This has made the category of NOCs more heterogeneous. Modifying the typology suggested in Quilès and Gullet (2006), Claes and Hveem (2009, pp. 4–5) identify three different types of state-controlled oil companies according to two dimensions – the type and extent of state control of the company and the company strategy:

1.   National companies under total state control, producing mostly at home and thus being mostly export oriented in their strategy; examples are ARAMCO (Saudi Arabia), PDVSA (Venezuela), IOC (Iran), and PEMEX (Mexico);

2.   National companies under state control, but with a strategy of increasing foreign production as they represent import-dependent countries; key examples are the Chinese companies Sinopec, CNOOC, and CNPC;

3. State-controlled companies that primarily follow a commercial and global strategy whether as exporters or importers; examples are ONGC (India), Petrobras (Brazil), Petronas (Malaysia), and Statoil (Norway).

Many of these companies have grown quickly in terms of turnover – they invest aggressively in expansion, particularly abroad. And as in most cases their home base is a BRIC country (Brazil, Russia, India and China), they are also perceived as being associated with the emerging geopolitical powers of the world and pushing a new world order. They are thus called 'Emerging National Oil Companies' (ENOCs). The ENOCs are regarded as less efficient than the IOCs:

> Many of these companies have been found to be inefficient, with relatively low investments rates. They tend to exploit oil reserves for short-term gain, possibly damaging oilfields, reducing the longer term production potential. The potential supply constraint related to the inefficient operations of the national oil companies may be a destabilizing factor in the world oil market. (Pirog, 2007 summary)

Furthermore, it is argued that the behavior of the ENOCs is infused with politics: "At worst, the business of pumping and selling oil is entirely subsumed by politics."[6] This creates an unfair competitive situation for the IOCs: "International companies face intense pressure from shareholders to maximize profits. National oil companies, however, often do not have the same profit needs and in some cases [have] been willing to plunk down more money and accept lower returns."[7]

In particular, the increased international operations of the Chinese oil companies have attracted public attention in the West. In 2005 the CNOOC bid for Unocal, a California-based exploring and marketing company, had high level political ramifications. Following a vote in the US House of Representatives, the bid was referred to President George W. Bush in order to review its implications for national security. In response, CNOOC withdrew its bid. It did, however, succeed in making fairly large investments in Australia and Canada, in addition to investments in several transition or developing countries. In particular, Chinese oil company investments in Africa have created political ripples. Compared with the commercial asset value of investments in Africa, Chinese ENOC investments comprise just 8 percent of the combined value of IOC investments, and only 3 percent of all companies' investments in African oil (Downs, 2007, p. 44). In 2006, the production of the Chinese ENOCs in Africa was about 267,000 barrels per day, compared with the 4.1 million barrels per day produced by Algeria's Sonatrach, the biggest company in Africa (in volume terms).

Sudan is the most important operating country for the Chinese ENOCs in Africa; 81 percent of the 267,000 barrels per day are produced in Sudan. CNPC's investments in upstream activities in Sudan are the company's largest overseas investment (UNCTAD, 2007, p. 118). In 2006, less than half of this production reached China; most of it was sold on the international market. This was probably a result of the high price in the international market (Downs, 2007, p. 45), and indicates that the Chinese ENOCs may be making market decisions based on commercial motives. Kong (2010, p. 158) concludes that "Chinese NOCs will be run like a commercial international oil company that follows market principles." However, as the commercial logic of the Chinese companies is not focused on short-term returns and shareholder value, they are able to pursue long-term industrial interests. Without reference to shareholders' alternative investment options, the companies can also enter into projects that IOCs would regard as too risky. If this is the case, the role of the Chinese companies could be regarded as serving the interests of consuming countries, bringing to the market oil that would otherwise not be produced and marketed.

In Russia, Vladimir Putin increased state control over the petroleum sector, pushing a merger of gas and oil producers and exercising effective management control over companies in which the state is the principal shareholder, as in the case of Gazprom, or actively supporting companies, as in the case of Lukoil (Boussena and Locatelli, 2006). The Russian state has also introduced a tougher tax regime for foreign companies operating Russian petroleum resources. Venezuela, under President Hugo Chávez, and Bolivia, are two other cases that have followed the same pattern. Bolivia nationalized its gas industry and Venezuela reduced the agreed share of foreign companies in the development of the oilfields in the Orinoco Basin. Rejecting the new conditions, the two US companies, ExxonMobil and ConocoPhillips, abandoned their operations. ConocoPhillips was particularly negatively affected as its Venezuelan investments constituted approximately a tenth of its total reserve holdings.

The IEA World Energy Outlook of 2008 painted a rather bleak picture regarding the future for long-term oil supplies following the role of the ENOCs:

> The national oil companies in the leading resource-holding countries are increasingly taking on the task of developing new fields themselves ... The increasing ambitions of the national companies reflect a trend in emerging economies towards greater direct state control over natural resources, a phenomenon commonly referred to as "resource nationalism". There are concerns that the national companies may, in general, be less willing than the international companies to develop and produce remaining oil and gas reserves on the scale required to meet global demand. (IEA, 2008, p. 334)

Although there are some cases of renationalization in the oil industry, one should, for several reasons, be cautious in interpreting this as a general new trend. First, one could question the idea that NOCs are less willing to develop and produce oil than IOCs. Why should state-owned companies be less interested in making money than private firms? Also, governments benefit from richness, possibly even more so than private shareholders, as a government's very existence can depend on income from oil production (Crystal, 1990; Selvik and Stenslie, 2011). Second, "resource nationalism has not challenged the free international trade in crude oil: in fact, it has diversified the crude market and made it more competitive . . . than during the period of control by the 'Seven sisters'" (Mitchell, 2007, p. 85). Third, one could argue that rather than being a new trend it is a correction of a previous anomaly: "In all these cases, the terms for foreign companies were negotiated in the 1990s during a period when the host countries' governments were politically and economically exceptionally weak. One could argue that the terms granted then were unsustainably good for the foreign investors during the current period of high oil and gas prices" (Mitchell, 2007, p. 93). Fourth, the rules of the WTO apply, at least in principle. to the oil and gas trade; China, India, Saudi Arabia, the Gulf States, and all the other OPEC members, with the exception of Iran and Algeria, are members of the WTO. Finally, the international oil industry has become increasingly technology driven. The IOCs are still the technological spearheads of the industry. World investments in exploration doubled from 1995 to 2005 to reach US$225 billion. The Big Five[8] among the private companies contributed 22 percent, OPEC national companies 7 percent, and the other national and state companies of producer countries 24 percent of this total (Quilès and Gullet, 2006, p. 79). This is another indication that the NOCs represent a dynamic source of investments in the industry, besides the Big Five and 'junior' companies (which account for the remaining 47 percent of exploration investments).

4.4   THE NEW INSTITUTIONAL OIL REGIME COMPLEX

Taking the vertical market dimension into account, and including the new oil companies in consumer nations, the set of actors becomes more complex. The number of agreements and cooperative arrangements among different types of countries and companies have increased dramatically. We are facing a new and far more complex oil industry structure. In their review article on global energy governance, van de Graaf and Colgan (2016, p. 5) list a number of studies of energy governance arrangements and institutions. Some of them are relevant for the governance of the oil market. IEA and OPEC in particular have attracted much attention from scholars of global energy governance. Neither of these organizations has been able to elevate itself into a kind of World Energy Organization. This is primarily because they only serve the interests of either consumers or producers. The joint efforts of producers and consumers in establishing the IEF, was an attempt to cultivate their common interests, such as price stability, transparency and predictability. However, the IEF has even weaker regulatory power than IEA and OPEC. No overarching oil market governance institution is in sight. The same holds for broader global energy governance. The field is characterized as "fragmented, and dispersed into a patchwork of various overlapping and sometimes overtly competing organizations" (Lesage et al., 2010, p. 51). Van de Graaf and Zelli go even further and claim that:

> If one ought to describe the global political economy – the 'who gets what when and how' – of energy in a single word, 'fragmentation' would be an appropriate term. The pursuit of wealth and power in energy is driven by a hugely diverse set of actors and institutions, operating across different political scales, geographical spaces, energy sources and market segments. They are also constantly in motion, molded by global shifts in technology, politics, the environment and the economy. (van de Graaf and Zelli, 2016, p. 47)

Traditionally the structure of the international oil industry has been defined as a *trilateral oligopoly* capturing the pattern of interaction between three groups of actors:

- oil-consuming countries;
- international private oil firms – both upstream and downstream; and
- oil-producing countries, including their state-controlled producing firms.

The changes in relative market power among these groups have been the result of a combination of internal cohesion in the individual groups and changes in cooperative and conflictual relations among them (Adelman, 1977; Roncaglia, 1985).

Inside the three groups, we find attempts to coordinate behavior. The main reason for such cooperation is to strengthen the group's position in relation to the other actors in the market. One reason for establishing cooperation between the international oil companies (IOCs), was to ensure the strength of the individual company in relation to the authority exercised by the governments of the producing countries. The producers' main reason for establishing OPEC was to counter the market power of the major oil companies, and for some OPEC member states the geopolitical power of the majors' home states. The consumer countries established the International Energy Agency (IEA) to counter the market power of OPEC. The relations between the three groups of actors in the trilateral oligopoly are both cooperative and conflictual. The main *conflictual aspects* of the relations in the trilateral oligopoly are many. Obviously, there are pure economic conflicts between producers and consumers. This is beyond the scope of this study. The conflicts between producer governments and international oil companies (IOC) were discussed in Chapter 2. However, the consumer-producer relations have also had prominent a political-ideological dimension, as many key oil producers are former colonies of the key consumer countries, US excepted. The main conflict between producers and consumers has been connected with supply disruptions following political conflicts in the Middle East, and the ideological attacks on OPEC for being a cartel disrupting the international free trade liberalism advocated particularly by the United States.

Theoretically, IOC cooperation with the producers *or* the consumers would respectively increase or decrease world oil prices. The IOCs have been attacked by the producers for siding with the consumers. As OPEC gained strength in the early 1970s, its first goal was to reduce IOC influence on the price policy. On the other hand, in the Congressional hearing before the Subcommittee on Multinational Corporations in 1974–1975, the so-called 'Church Commission', representatives of the IOCs met senators who were highly critical of the role of the companies, suggesting that the companies cooperated among themselves and with the producing countries to drive prices up and thus increase their own profits at the expense of the American consumer (Church, 1974).

The *cooperative aspects* of the inter-group relations follows the assumption that there can be aspects of the political relations between actors in the various groups that are mutually beneficial. Saudi Arabia, a key producer for a long time, has sought military support from Western consuming countries, in particular the United States, in exchange for a more consumer-friendly oil policy. Another example of how geopolitical considerations enter the calculus, but do not trump economic factors, is that Saudi Arabia uses its dependence on the income from oil exports to finance domestic redistribution as a way of maintaining internal political stability (Cappelen and Chaudhury, 2004). The exchange between producing countries and the IOC do have mutually beneficial features, as the obsolescing bargaining theory of Raymond Vernon (1971) suggests. The relationship between the consumer countries and the IOC was more important in the 1950s and 1960s than it is today. But this relationship also had cooperative aspects. The IOCs benefited to a certain extent from the political backing of consumer countries in their operations in the

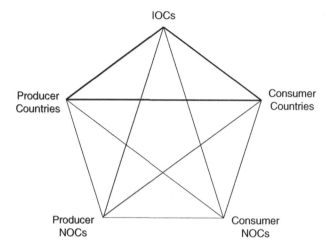

Source: Author, based on Claes (2011, p. 309).

Figure 4.1   *The new complex oil market structure, old structure in bold*
lines

producing countries, and the consumer countries could use the IOCs as a spearhead to establish political ties with strategically important countries in the Middle East, for purposes outside of their interest in cheap oil.

Today the structure of the global oil industry can be described as a pentangle of interrelated actors cutting across the government-company and IOC-NOC dimensions (Figure 4.1).

At face value, this increased complexity implies weaker governance and increased instability, which potentially can result in increased conflict among both companies and countries. To avoid this "policy-makers need to adapt and strengthen the institutional architecture of international oil and gas relations" (Goldthau and Witte, 2009, p. 390). Since oil trade has become globalized and the interdependence among the actors has increased, political institutions should also be renewed. Neglecting the role of commercial actors in the governance structures of the oil market would be a great mistake. As pointed out by Keohane and Underdal (2011, p. 51), one essential feature of international governance today is that "many of the most important institutions . . . are not built around formal organizations but constitute networks with regular patterns of interaction." This, indeed, applies to the international oil market. These patterns of interaction cut across the NOC–IOC divide, and include both governments and companies. The network and pattern of interaction in the global oil market is outlined in Table 4.1.

Table 4.1   Patterns of network interaction in oil market governance

	IOCs	Producer countries	Consumer countries	Producer NOCs	Consumer NOCs
IOCs	Seven Sisters[b]	Concessions for exploration and production (E&P)	Private downstream activities in refining and product sales	Production sharing agreements (PSAs)	Companies' alliances in upstream investments abroad
Producer countries		OPEC[a]	IEF[a]	State ownership of E&P in domestic oil provinces, e.g. NOCs in OPEC countries	Consumer NOCs E&P abroad, e.g. Chinese companies in Sudan
Consumer countries			IEA[a]	Foreign NOCs' downstream investments abroad, e.g. Kuwait's investments in U.S. refining	State ownership of domestic downstream activities, e.g. ENI in Italy
Producer NOCs				The NOC Forum[b]	Companies' alliances in upstream investments abroad
Consumer NOCs					Minimal activity

Notes:
a)   Formal international governmental organizations.
b)   Informal among companies alliances.

Source: Author, based on Claes (2011, p. 210).

Although several international governmental organizations address energy issues (Lesage et al., 2010), analysts of global energy industries should not repeat the mistakes of the past, pointed out more than 30 years ago: "The tendency to overlook or underestimate the interests and influence of the large transnational corporations and 'their' home governments has been strong, not only in the case of crude oil, but in the case of primary commodities and raw materials in general" (Hveem, 1978, p. 11).

Thus, the next chapter will address the market governing efforts of the multinational oil corporations, known by the acronym IOC (International Oil Companies), although the historical part will begin by tracing the role of Standard Oil in the US in the 19th century. Economic theories of producer cooperation is based on cooperation among companies, not states, although states have interfered in the oil market from its inception. The most prominent case of state-based oil producer cooperation is of course the Organization of Oil Exporting Countries (OPEC). This organization will be the subject of Chapter 6.

NOTES

1. The OPEC members, Kuwait, Nigeria and Venezuela joined the WTO in 1995. Angola, Ecuador, Qatar and UAE joined in 1996 and Saudi Arabia in 2005. The rest of the OPEC members, Algeria, Iran, Iraq and Libya, are in the process of negotiating their accessions. A major oil producer outside OPEC – Russia – joined the WTO in 2012.
2. https://www.wto.org/english/res_e/booksp_e/analytic_index_e/gatt1994_07_e.htm#article 20 (accessed July 22, 2017).
3. The Norwegian considerations demonstrate the interrelationship between economic and political factors related to the effects of the 1973 oil crisis. "Decisive for the Government's viewpoint however, have been considerations of a foreign policy nature," said Norwegian Foreign Minister Knut Frydenlund in Parliament on May 28, 1976 "In this connection it is a matter of cooperating with countries with whom we cooperate also in virtually all other areas." His remarks are referred to in Sydnes (1985, p. 125).
4. https://www.iea.org/countries/non-membercountries/chinapeoplesrepublicof/ (accessed July 24, 2017).
5. This section is based on Claes and Hveem (2009).
6. Leader in *The Economist* August 10, 2006.
7. Justin Blum in *The Washington Post* August 3, 2005.
8. *Financial Times*, March 11, 2007. The original Seven Sisters have in fact been reduced to four: Exxon/Mobil, Royal Dutch Shell, BP/Amoco/ARCO (now BP), and Chevron Texaco. The fifth among todays Big Five is Total, a merger of three companies, Total, Elf (both French) and Petrofina (Belgian), none of which were regarded as part of the Seven Sisters in 1971.

5. Producer governance

5.1 THE ECONOMICS OF PRODUCER COOPERATION

In Part I of the book, we established the state's sovereignty over oil resources, the government's role in the extraction of oil and control over the income from this extraction. In this part, the attention is on the marketplace for oil trade, specifically the value of the extracted oil, that is, the oil price. Although the governments of oil-producing states can own the resources and control the extraction, the value of the oil is determined by the market price. Thus, ownership and state control or nationalization of the industry in itself does not determine the level of income from the resource extraction. Governments of oil-producing states also seek to control, or at least influence, the oil price. In this endeavor, legal instruments are not available. To set the market price politically is tempting, but it potentially has some economic repercussion. In this part, we are exploring the heartland of interaction between politics and market economics. We thus need to start with some basic economic concepts.

5.1.1 Market Structure

The concept of market structure generally refers to "certain stable attributes of the market that influence the firm's conduct in the marketplace" (Caves, 1980). A more specific definition relevant for this chapter is "the number and size distribution of suppliers and the degree of vertical integration" (Adelman, 1972). Changes in the structure of the international oil market are supposed to constrain the market actors' behavior, but also make some paths of action more feasible than others.

The market structure has both a vertical and a horizontal dimension. The horizontal structure refers to the number and size distribution of companies in each stage of the production chain, while the vertical dimension refers to the degree of integration across the various stages of the production chain. Both dimensions are important as the effect, for instance, of forming a monopoly in one stage depends on the concentration in the previous or following stage. Market concentration in crude oil production will form the basis for the discussion of OPEC in the next chapter. Here, the vertical dimension is developed as a basis for illuminating the historical cases of Standard Oil and the Seven Sisters.

In the oil industry, five stages of the value chain are usually identified:

1. Exploration
2. Production
3. Transportation
4. Refining
5. Distribution and sales.

Concentration in the first two stages, called the *upstream sectors*, is somewhat geologically predetermined as exploration and production (E&P) can only happen at the location of the actual oil deposits. Although some advantage can be gained by technology and know-how regarding the discovery and determination of oil fields, the location of oil deposits is the first determinant of the structure of the oil market. Offshore drilling increases costs compared with onshore activity. Alaskan or Siberian oil drilling, for instance, takes place in a far more difficult climate than drilling in the Saudi Arabian desert. Furthermore, there are different crude qualities, as well as differences in the location of deposits and their quantity and quality, which will determine the costs of extraction from individual oil deposits. Over the last decades, new drilling techniques, such as horizontal drilling and injections programs, have increased the rate of extraction and reduced production costs.

The last three stages of the product chain are the *downstream sectors*. The transportation of oil can take place both before and after refining. Most oil transportation today is done by tankers, except for short distance transportation from producing wells to shipping terminals. The location of the refineries will determine the distribution of the content of transportation between crude and products. Since this stage of the production chain is possible to locate either near the oil fields or near the consumers, it is sensitive to the economic interests of states' national industrial policies. Therefore, arguments regarding employment, national control over resources, and national economic and industrial development and growth become important political factors in the location and running of the refinery industry.

The last stage, distribution and sales, has to take place where the customers are. It is therefore impossible for activities at this stage of the production chain to escape national jurisdiction and control. An international oil company can locate its activities at other stages more or less in a country of its own choice, but this is not so with distribution and sales. Thus, these aspects of the oil market are more influenced by particularities of national markets and various regulations in consumer countries.

For the purposes of this chapter, the different stages of the production chain represent different conditions for the relationship between the actors in the oil market. The main focus of this study is on the crude oil market (i.e. the production stage). However, actors tend to use their power at other stages to influence developments in the crude oil market. We thus need to connect the concept of market structure with the concept of market power.

5.1.2 Market Power

Market power is defined as "the ability of a single, or group, of buyer(s) or seller(s) to influence the price of the product or service in which it is trading. A perfectly competitive market in equilibrium, ensures the complete absence of market power" (Pearce, 1983).

All the factors discussed in the previous section concerning market structure are important in determining the market power of the sellers. The vertical structure gives rise to actors' strategic positions in controlling other actors' oil outlets or access to crude oil reserves. Market concentration is the basis for coherent action by groups of actors leading to the realization of monopoly profit. Barriers to entry protect this profit against outsiders. And, finally, if demand is inelastic, consumers will continue to buy the product although the price may increase due to the sellers collecting a monopoly profit.

Given the assumption that groups of actors securing market power in the crude oil market will set the price to their own benefit, the distribution of market power implies the distribution of monopoly profit. The possible existence of monopoly profit in the industry follows from the definition of market power, as the competitive market is defined as a market without any group of actors having market power. The loss of market power by a group of actors could mean one of two things – either the market has become more competitive or another group of actors has increased its market power. Market actors can hold tangible power resources such as physical control over oil resources or production facilities; ownership of distribution channels or marketing facilities; and concessions to conduct business at the different stages of the production chain where such concessions are necessary. Actors might also hold intangible power resources as well. These can take the form of information about reserve deposits, production methods, or trading instruments. This variety demonstrates that market power is exercised in both the vertical and the horizontal market structure.

An understanding of changes in the distribution of market power is key to understanding changes in the international oil market. This calls for some comments. Given the definition of market power, there is, in a sense, a fixed amount of power at every stage of the vertical production chain. At each step, the market actors are in a zero-sum game over the ability to determine the price of the traded oil. It follows that the same must be true for all the stages taken together. One actor's exercising of market power at one stage thus constrains other actors' exercising of their market power at other stages of the production chain.

At any given stage, market power is a relative concept. The higher the concentration is on the seller side, then the lower it is at the same time on the buyer side. The higher the sellers' market power, the lower the market power of buyers – and vice versa. If there is low concentration on both sides, market power is also low for all actors (see Pearce, 1983, p. 274). With a high concentration on both the seller and the buyer side, as for instance in a situation where a monopoly is selling to a monopsony (i.e. only one buyer), the monopolist has the advantage if the buyer experiences inelastic demand.

5.1.3   Monopoly Theory

The essence of economics is "how societies use scarce resources to produce valuable commodities and distribute them among different groups" (Samuelson, 1988). The challenge is how to allocate scarce resources between different valuable uses. "Such allocations are typically done either by the private sector through markets or by the government. Economists tend to favor the private sector . . . when the market is perfectly competitive, property rights are well defined, externalities are few, and the subject industry does not have decreasing costs as production increases" (Dahl, 2004).

Given these conditions, a perfectly competitive market with many small buyers and sellers taking the market price as given is efficient because it maximizes the economic welfare of both consumers and producers. The oil market has resembled this ideal of an efficient competitive market only for brief periods. To the contrary, the history of oil is characterized by various attempts to form monopolies. For most economists, a monopoly implies inefficiency. Economic arguments are usually expressed through mathematical models and graphs. The verbal argument regarding the economic consequences of market concentration can, however, be expressed as follows:

There are three essential characteristics of a monopoly: there is only one seller, the consumers cannot easily substitute the product with something else, and there are high barriers for other producers to enter the market. In a competitive market, the individual sellers have no influence on the price of the product in the marketplace. Economists call them 'price-takers', while a monopolist is a 'price-searcher'. Because of their unique status as the only supplier of the product, monopolists have some ability to control the price of the product they sell. However, even monopolists have to obey the falling demand curve, as consumers buy less of a product if the price increases. Thus, if the monopolist wants to sell more they must lower the price and if the monopolist wants to impose a higher price they must reduce the quantity sold. Lowering the price of additional units of the product will lower the price of all units sold.[1] Thus, the marginal revenue will fall more rapidly than the price. It follows that the monopolist's marginal revenue (MR) curve will, after the first unit of output is sold, always lie below the demand curve.[2] In the competitive market mentioned above, an optimal quantity is produced when the marginal revenue equals the price. This implies that on the last item sold, the producer only covers their marginal costs. In the case of monopoly, the optimal produced volume is where marginal costs equal marginal revenue. The monopolist will charge the highest price per unit at which that quantity can be sold, and the price, also on the last unit, will be above the marginal costs and marginal revenue. This implies that that the monopolist produces a lower quantity of goods and sells them at a higher price compared to the producers in a competitive market. This creates an extra profit for the monopolist above the profit of competitive firms, and is called 'monopoly profit'. This is a deviation from economic efficiency.[3] It thus reduces the welfare to society in general (cf. Figure 5.1).

This very brief exposition of monopoly theory presupposes that there is one, and only one, producer who is able to dominate the entire marketplace. This is seldom the case, although one of the historic cases presented in this chapter is exactly such a case. The other cases are characterized by the attempt by groups of producers to gain dominance over the oil market. Although the producer group tries to behave as one, and reap the same benefits as the single monopolist, the relationship between them has caught the interest of economists.

5.1.4   Cartel Theory

A cartel can broadly be defined as "an explicit arrangement among, or on behalf of, enterprises in the same line of business that is designed to limit competition among them" (Stocking, 1948), cited in (Greer, 1984). A more precise and specific oil-related definition is presented by Mead (Mead, 1986). He advances a "professional definition of the cartel term" as "a single seller or a group of sellers operating in unison to reduce output below competitive levels in order to obtain a price above competitive levels." The structural conditions for the possibility and importance

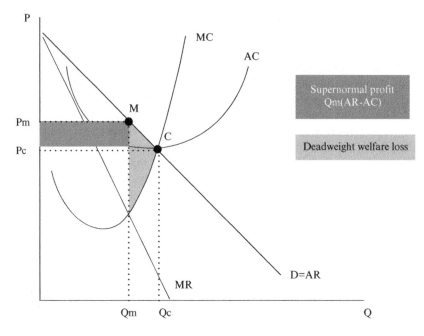

Notes:
P= Price per unit supplied
Q= Quantity supplied
MC= Marginal Costs
AC= Average Costs
MR= Marginal Revenue
AR= Average Revenue
D= Demand
M= Monopoly equilibrium
C= Competitive equilibrium
Pm= Price in Monopoly equilibrium
Pc= Price in Competitive equilibrium
Qm= Quantity supplied in Monopoly equilibrium
Qc= Quantity supplied in Competitive equilibrium

The difference between the Competitive equilibrium and the Monopoly equilibrium is that the quantity supplied is reduced and the price per unit is increased. Creating a welfare loss to the consumers and a supernormal profit to the producers, as the figure illustrates.

Figure 5.1   Illustration of the monopoly profit and welfare loss to society

of cartels are, however, not enough to explain the actual existence and 'success' of cartelization. The success of a cartel depends on four factors connected with the behavior of the cartel (Crèmer and Isfahani, 1991). A cartel must:

1. Determine a price for the group as a whole;
2. Determine a production level for the group as a whole;
3. Allocate output among members; and
4. Detect and punish cheaters.

The first two points have to do with the cartel's relations to the market, while the last two points are concerned with internal bargaining problems.

The model presented above suggests how a monopolist should set the price in the market in order to maximize profit – in theory. In practice, this is not so easy. In most actual cases there are some imperfections – there are some other producers outside of the cartel, the products are not fully homogenous, the consumers have some possibility of substitution, or there are some weaknesses in the barriers to entry into the market (cf. definition of monopoly above). Thus, the theoretical optimal price might not be achievable, as it might attract new producers, or discourage demand. In the case of Standard Oil, the continuous discoveries of new oil fields in the US posed a challenge for the price regardless of the initial market control exerted by the company. In OPEC's case, the increase in non-OPEC producers during the 1970s and 1980s had the same effect. With a cartel the problem of disagreement over the optimal price can emerge and likewise a lack of adherence to the agreed price can cause problems. The total production of the members of the cartel is meant to be fixed according to a level of production that will realize maximum profit. However, this level can also become a matter of dispute among the members.

Bargaining over the quota is of special importance as the actors bargain at two levels: first, over what the level of total quotas is to be; second, over what the quota for each individual members is to be. Then, there is the problem of compliance. If one assumes that the level of total quotas is set to achieve a certain price in the market, this level of total quotas is not negotiable – given the price target and assumed demand. Whether the agreed production level realizes the price target is another matter. The members might disagree about whether the assumptions are correct, and they might disagree on the price target. It follows that the quota-setting bargaining is mostly distributive bargaining – it allocates individual quotas within the limit of the total quotas, which are set exogenously. While the criterion for setting the total level of quotas is rather rigid, the criterion for individual allocation is virtually nonexistent. Obviously, historical production level is important, but production capacity (and spare capacity) might prove to be the most important factor. Also, income requirement, poverty, war costs, and reconstruction programs have been directly or indirectly put forward as arguments for increased quotas. Among the OPEC members, some 40 different criteria have been introduced at one point or another.

Furthermore, setting the quotas is an example of an iterated game. Thus, agreeing to one quota level at one moment is not formally binding for more than a period of months. However, agreeing to a 'low' quota level at one point in time might make it harder for a member of a cartel to argue for higher quotas at a later point.

Once the quotas are set, the game changes to one of collective action. If the total quota level is correctly set and thus achieves the decided price level in the market, the members of the cartel find themselves in a traditional prisoner's dilemma situation. This could be analyzed on the basis of a high oil price being a collective good for the oil producers (Malnes, 1983).

Applied to oil-producer relations, the point of departure for the collective good is that all actors have an interest in limiting production to ensure a high oil price. At the same time, it is in the actors' interest to sustain their own production volume. In such a case, the actors can gain by cooperating (reducing production), but individually they can gain more by not cooperating while the others do. The oil price can thus be regarded as a collective good. A collective good is, in this context, understood in accordance with Olson's definition:

> If person X_i in a group $X_1 \ldots X_i \ldots X_n$ consumes it, it cannot feasibly be withheld from others in the group. In other words, those who do not purchase or pay for any of the public or collective good cannot be excluded or kept from sharing the consumption of the goods, as they can where non-collective goods are concerned. (Olson, 1965)

Olson then distinguishes between exclusive and inclusive goods (Olson, 1965). Exclusive goods are goods whereby one actor's consumption reduces other actors' consumption equally. Inclusive public goods are similar to pure public goods, as defined by Samuelson: "each individual's consumption of such a good leads to no subtraction from any other individual's consumption of that good, so $X_{n+j} = X^i_{n+j}$ simultaneously for each and every individual and each collective consumption good" (Samuelson, 1954). Obviously, the price of oil can induce rivalry among the producers, and thus fail to satisfy the definition of inclusiveness. The oil price will consequently be regarded as an exclusive collective good for the oil producers.

One key problem for any cartel is the potential overambitious goal to set both price and production levels at the same time, unless it controls all, or almost all, the production. A cartel that does not control all production will work only if it sets a price and defends it by increasing production if the price is above the target or reducing production if the price is below the target. This will discourage other producers from entering the market, as the price will not rise substantially above the target price, and it will secure income as production is curtailed to keep the price at the target level.

The internal allocation of production and the subsequent adherence to a set production level create additional problems for the cartel's members. As pointed out by Willett (1979), "while all of the oil exporting countries have a mutual economic interest in restricting supply and keeping oil prices well above competitive levels, they have substantial differences of interest concerning just how high prices should be and how great the supply restrictions of each individual producer should be." Let us now turn to the history of oil producers' attempt to control the oil market.

Two historical cases illustrate how *companies*, at particular times, have achieved almost total control over the oil market. The first is the dominant position of Standard Oil in the US from 1870 to 1880, the second is the collusion between the International Oil Companies (IOC), known as the Seven Sisters, before and after the Second World War. The latter case was, to some extent, backed by the interests of the home countries of the companies.

There are also cases where *governments of states* have tried to control the oil market, through producer cooperation. The historic case of the Texas Railroad Commission is briefly described in this chapter. The primary case is the Organization of the Petroleum Exporting Countries (OPEC). The entire next chapter is devoted to this organization, since it is the pre-eminent instance of political actors' ability (and disability) to govern the oil market.

5.2 THE US OIL INDUSTRY AND STANDARD OIL

The history of the modern oil industry began in the 1850s. Over the next decades oil drilling commenced in places like Baku, Sumatra, Burma, Persia and in the United States. The most famous was the drilling conducted by Edwin L. Drake in Titusville in the western part of Pennsylvania – later named the Oil Region. Extreme price volatility characterized the first phase of US oil history.

Several factors contributed to an instability in production and subsequently in prices. These included a lack of geological knowledge which led to sudden new discoveries of large reservoirs, short leasing terms which put pressure on rapid development and production of the individual fields. Nevertheless, the legal provision of the 'rule of capture' meant that the individual lease owner could drain a common reservoir regardless of the extension of the reservoir under other leases (cf. Section 1.3.1). Owners of adjacent wells thus engaged in heated competition to produce as much as possible as fast as possible: "Production in western Pennsylvania rose rapidly – from about 450,000 barrels in 1860 to 3 million barrels in 1862

... Prices, which had been $10 a barrel in January 1862, fell to 50 cents by June and, by the end of 1861, were down to 10 cents" (Yergin, 1991, p. 30).

While low prices increased the demand, many producers went bust and by 1863 the market was experiencing a shortage of supply and the price increased to $7.25 a barrel by 1863 (Yergin, 1991, p. 30). A similar pattern of boom and bust appeared after the Civil War. Given the rule of capture there were no possibility to control or govern the overcapacity in exploration and production. However, the next stages of the production chain – transportation and refining – were obviously not affected by the implications of the rule of capture. In fact, activities such as the provision of barrels, the construction of refineries and, in particular, the construction of oil pipelines or transportation by trains, were more suitable for gaining market control.

These were the targets for John D. Rockefeller. He formed the Standard Oil Company, and began buying up refineries, either by friendly take-overs or by dropping prices to outcompete other refineries. From 1870 to 1880, Standard Oil's share of refinery capacity rose from 10 to 90 percent. The company also controlled pipelines and transportation. In the 1880s, Standard Oil also took control of the marketing of oil products, achieving almost the same market share as it had with refining (Yergin, 1991, pp. 35–55).

The market power exercised by Standard Oil cannot be explained without an understanding of the vertical dimension of the market structure. The characteristics of the various stages of the oil product chain determined the strategy of the company: "Standard had stayed out of one of the critical parts of the business – the production of oil. It was too risky, too volatile, too speculative . . . Better to let the producers carry that risk and stick to what could be rationally organized and managed – refining, transportation and marketing" (Yergin, 1991, p. 51). In the 1890s, having secured control of the downstream sector, Standard Oil also got involved in oil production.

The market power of Standard Oil also relied on the internal structure of the company. It was organized as a so-called 'trust,' whereby nine trustees controlled a large number of different companies across several states. Although the stocks were owned directly by the shareholders, the trustees didn't have to be shareholders themselves. Rockefeller tested unexplored territory in the judicial aspects of his business, and refined the legal concept of the trust as public and political attention increased with the increased market dominance of the company. There were some attempts by producers to challenge Rockefeller and Standard Oil – for instance by constructing a competing pipeline in Pennsylvania. As the oil industry spread to new oil provinces in Ohio, Oklahoma and California, the dominance of Standard Oil was somewhat reduced. The company never had absolute control of the industry. Nevertheless, Rockefeller's market power was significant, and provided the shareholders with a massive dividend. As the consumer markets for various oil products developed, so too did public scrutiny of the oil industry in general and Standard Oil in particular.

As Daniel Yergin (1991, p. 43) concludes: "There remained only one way to hold this giant in check, and that was through the political system and the courts." In 1890, the US Congress passed the Sherman Antitrust Act, as a "comprehensive charter of economic liberty aimed at preserving free and unfettered competition as the rule of trade." This was the first federal antitrust law. The Act declared:

> Every contract, combination in the form of trust or otherwise, or conspiracy, in restraint of trade or commerce among the several States, or with foreign nations, is declared to be illegal ... Every person who shall monopolize, or attempt to monopolize, or combine or conspire with any other person or persons, to monopolize any part of the trade or commerce among the several States, or with foreign nations, shall be deemed guilty of a felony.[4]

Several words in the legislation, like 'combination', 'trust' and 'restraint of trade', lacked a specific definition. The courts spent years determining the boundaries of the Act. The ideas of public regulation of competition within industries were novel and it took time achieve efficiency in such legal regulation.[5] In 1906, the US Justice Department brought charges against Standard Oil for restraint of trade. In 1909, the Federal Circuit Court of the Eastern District of Missouri found Standard Oil guilty of violating the Sherman Antitrust Act. The company appealed to the US Supreme Court, which upheld the ruling on May 15, 1911, and ordered Standard Oil to dissolve into 34 independent companies. Some of these merged with other companies and became well-known companies, such as Exxon (Standard Oil of New Jersey), Mobil (Standard Oil of New York), Amoco (Standard Oil of Indiana), ARCO (Standard Atlantic), Marathon Oil (The Ohio Oil Company), Chevron (Standard Oil of California). The Supreme Court ruling became a landmark in the economic history of the United States and formed a new doctrine in antitrust policy, known as the 'rule of reason'. This states that a trade practice violates the Sherman Act only if the practice is an unreasonable restraint of trade, based on economic factors.

Figure 5.2 illustrates the price effect of the dominant position of Standard Oil. Other factors also influenced price and production, but without doubt, Standard Oil's monopoly created a stable low price, which then laid the foundation for expanding markets for oil products.

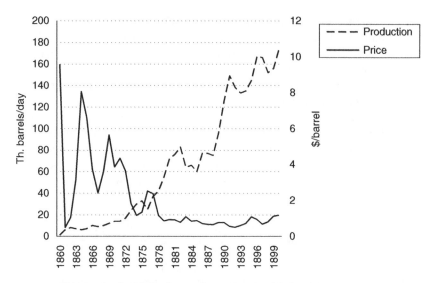

Source: EIA. Production: https://www.eia.gov/dnav/pet/hist/LeafHandler.ashx?n=PET&
s=MCRFPUS2&f=A; Price: https://www.eia.gov/dnav/pet/hist/LeafHandler.ashx?n=PET
&s=F000000__3&f=A (both accessed July 3, 2018).

*Figure 5.2   US crude production and price 1860–1900 (th.barrels/day,
            $/barrel)*

The legal actions against Standard Oil removed the unreasonable concentration of market power in the US oil industry, and thus also the inef-
ficiencies related to the lack of competition (cf section 5.1.3). However, the
Supreme Court decision did not remove the vagaries of the market. New,
large discoveries across the US created repeated booms and busts. With
the antitrust legislation in place, it became the responsibility of state and
federal government to regulate production. An important case that was to
become an example for later producer cooperation was the Texas Railroad
Commission (TRC).

5.3   THE TEXAS RAILROAD COMMISSION

In 1891, the Texas legislature had set up a commission to regulate the
railroads in Texas. The body, known as the Texas Railroad Commission
(TRC), was given jurisdiction over the operation of railroads, terminals,
wharves, and express companies. It could set rates, issue rules on how to
classify freight, require adequate railroad reports, and prohibit and punish

discrimination and extortion by corporations. In 1917, the scope of the commission was extended to regulating oil pipelines, two years later to gas production and in 1920 to gas delivery systems. The TRC was to become the key instrument for regulating the US oil industry from the 1930s and implicitly the main institutions setting the world oil price up until the 1960s.

The discovery of the Spindletop oil field in Texas in 1901 was important both in terms of the development of better drilling technology and because it coincided with the transition of oil consumption from illumination to transportation (Vasiliou, 2009, pp. 469–70). The ensuing oil boom marked the entry of Texas into the family of US oil states, which it was later to dominate. The field was outside the control of Standard Oil and thus contributed to the fall of the Rockefeller oil empire. On the other hand, it also heralded new challenges for price stability in the US oil industry.

In 1900, Texas oil production was about 2.3 thousand barrels per day. In 1902, Spindletop alone produced more than 47.7 thousand barrels per day. The massive increase in supply drove the oil price down to 3 cents per barrel. Then followed a 30-year period of oil discoveries in Texas, which made the state the dominant oil-producing state in the country. In the 1930s, the East Texas oil boom created a huge oversupply in the market, and another price crash followed. The price dropped from about one dollar to 10 cents per barrel (Downey, 2009, p. 8). The oil producers were unable, by themselves, to resolve their collective action problem of reducing overproduction. In Texas, the Railroad Commission tried to set up local proration agreements with the producers. The problem was that the un-prorated fields continued to overproduce. At the state level, the problem was that the regulation of production in one state could be countered by increased production in another, as the legislation differed across the oil states.

In August 1931, East Texas produced more than one million barrels per day, while the TRC regulation set a limit of 220,000 barrels per day. At this point, the governors of both Oklahoma and Texas used military forces to curb oil production, leading to an almost complete shut-down in East Texas and increased prices. New regulations gave the TRC more muscle, but its legitimacy among the producers remained weak. Cheating on assigned quotas was a widespread problem. In 1933, prices fell back to about 10 cents per barrel, and in May of that year were as low as four cents per barrel (Yergin, 1991, p. 254). On the federal level, a new presidential administration took office in 1933, led by Franklin D. Roosevelt. The Secretary of the Interior became Harold L. Ickes. The new administration rapidly signaled a willingness to intervene. With prices as low as four cents per barrel, even the private oil companies welcomed federal intervention.

Ickes took full control over the regulation of the oil industry. He "dispatched Federal investigators into the East Texas field to examine refinery records, test oil gauges, inspect tanks, even to dig up pipelines to measure the accuracy of sworn records. Subsequently, Federal certificates of clearance were required to move any oil out of East Texas" (Yergin, 1991, p. 255). The federal government took an unprecedented role in regulating the oil business. In September 1933, Ickes sent telegrams to the governors of the oil states giving them individual production quotas (Yergin, 1991, p. 256). A new form of cooperation between the federal and state level emerged, and was accepted by the private companies, in dire need of stable prices. The Texas Railroad Commission became a major inspiration for the members of OPEC 40 years later (cf. Chapter 6).

5.4 THE SEVEN SISTERS

In 1900, the production of crude oil in the US was 174,000 barrels per day, which represented 42 percent of world production, Russia was the leading oil producer. By 1925, US production had increased to 1.7 million barrels per day which represented 70 percent of world production. In Baku, oil drilling had started as early as 1848, but it was not until the 1870s that oil production took off. In 1885, oil was discovered in Sumatra, and in 1908, discoveries were made in Persia, leading to the establishment of the Anglo-Persian Oil Company – later to become British Petroleum.

Although the US dominated the oil industry, it was becoming a global business. Standard Oil was active in several oil provinces outside the US. The geology of some of the new oil provinces seemed to be as good, or even better, than in the US. In 1874, the oil fields discovered in Baku were released from their status as a state monopoly, and production was expanded under the leadership of Robert and Ludwig Nobel. During the 1880s, the Rothschild family also entered into the Baku oil industry, and was behind the construction of a railway from Baku to the Black Sea, which made Baku's oil competitive with US oil in the emerging European market (Howarth, 1997, pp. 30–31).

On the Island of Sumatra in Indonesia, a Dutch plantation manager struck oil in 1885 and founded the Royal Dutch Company, increasing production in Indonesia, but lacking efficient access to consumer markets. In 1907, the company joined with the Shell Transport and Trading Company, a British oil transport company in the hands of the Samuel family. The Royal Dutch Shell group is another illustration of the tendency to vertical integration in the oil business. Royal Dutch Shell also created a strong challenger to Standard Oil, outside the US.

The activity of these emerging oil companies were mostly the result of the commercial aims of European or US capitalists. The fourth oil province that was opened up during the first decade of the 20th century was, however, more tightly connected to political aims of one country – or rather one man. In 1901, William K. D'Arcy acquired exclusive exploration rights from the Shah of the Qajar dynasty in Persia. In 1908, oil was discovered, and the following year the Anglo-Persian Oil Company was established. In 1913, oil production commenced. At this point, the UK's First Lord of the Admiralty, Winston Churchill, made the bold move of switching the fuel of the Royal Navy from coal to oil. Certain that war with Germany was imminent, he desperately needed to secure oil supplies. His eyes fell on The Anglo-Persian Oil Company. In 1914, the British government bought a controlling share of the company, in exchange for the guarantee of secure supplies to the British navy.

By the outbreak of the First World War, the scene was set for a global oil industry, dominated by large corporations, vertically integrated along the product chain from exploration and production to marketing and sales. The relationship between these major oil companies and the host governments in the oil-producing states was discussed in Chapter 2. As the case of Standard Oil showed, the US government did not permit the market concentration and cooperation among US oil companies that followed from the Standard Oil trust. In most of the new international oil provinces, governments were weak, or nonexistent. Thus, there were no antitrust laws. Today, corporations find their behavior in foreign countries increasingly subject to the competition laws of their home countries. This was not the case in the first half of the 20th century. To some extent, the political interests of the Great Powers coincided with the interests of the companies.

In the inter- and post-war period, the companies performed a vital task for their home countries by providing secure access to affordable oil supplies. The fact that the companies performed this task through secret collusion and cooperation did not disturb the home governments, since the negative effects of this international cooperation did not affect the home market or raise prices to unreasonable levels. In fact, although the commercial consumption of oil rose at an unprecedented rate after the Second World War, the price was low and fell slowly during the 1950s and 1960s. The main reason was that new discoveries and falling production costs more than kept pace with rapidly increasing demand.

Just before the First World War, the Anglo-Persian Oil Company acquired 50 percent of the Turkish Petroleum Company, which had been established in 1912, in order to gain an oil concession for Mesopotamia, which was then part of the Ottoman Empire. The other partners were Royal Dutch Shell and Deutsche Bank, both of whom had a 22.5 percent share, and the Armenian entrepreneur, Calouste Gulbenkian, who acquired a 5 percent share. The concession was promised but never fulfilled. After the First World War, the Ottoman Empire was falling apart, and France and the UK took control of large parts of its former possessions. Mesopotamia became a British mandate under the League of Nations. In connection with the San Remo agreement, an Anglo-French oil agreement was negotiated,[6] with the consequence that the German share of the Turkish Petroleum Company was transferred to France, resulting in the establishment of the Compagnie Française des Pétroles (CFP) – later to become Total.

Until the First World War, the US government did not involve itself with Standard Oil's operations outside of the US. However, the war created concerns that US oil reserves might become scarce, and they became uneasy over the fact that US companies abroad faced barriers to entry by the European colonial powers (Maugeri, 2006, pp. 28–29). With the Middle East as the most promising area for new oil discoveries, the US government and companies started a fight for influence in the formerly Turkish-dominated area by invoking 'the open door policy.' It argued (i) that the nationals of all nations be subject, in all mandated territories, to equal treatment in law, (ii) that no economic concessions in any mandated region be so large as to be exclusive, and (iii) that no monopolistic concession relating to any commodity be granted.

The US government asserted that, as the war had been won by the Allied powers fighting together, any benefit – whether in oil interests or otherwise – should be made available to the citizens and companies of all the victorious countries. The US claimed that the San Remo agreement discriminated against the rights of US citizens and that no rights in Iraq were vested in the Turkish Petroleum Company. The UK government argued that British nationals had 'acquired rights' and that these rights should be respected. Although the United States had been an ally, this could not override British acquired rights. The term 'acquired rights' referred to the rights held by the Turkish Petroleum Company and the rights promised to that company by the Ottoman Grand Vizier, as evidenced by his letter of June 28, 1914, to the British and German Ambassadors (FTC, 1952, pp. 51–52).

After year long negotiations the United States, the United Kingdom and France reached a compromise in 1928. As shown in Table 5.1, the US companies got about a fourth of the Turkish Petroleum Company concession. The agreement also included a so-called self-denying clause, stating that all parties should work jointly – and only jointly – in the region (Yergin, 1991, p. 204). The region included the Arabic peninsula (except Kuwait), Iraq, and Turkey. This was the so-called Red Line Agreement (see Figure 5.3). In the areas inside the red line, the companies would pursue joint concessions.

By 1928, more than 50 percent of oil production outside the United

Table 5.1   The division of the Turkish Petroleum Company in 1928

Owner	Subsidiary	Share
Anglo-Persian Oil Co., in which the British government held 51%	D'Arcy Exploration Co. Ltd.	23.75
Royal Dutch/Shell (Royal Dutch: 60%; Shell: 40%)	Anglo-Saxon Petroleum Co. Ltd.	23.75
Compagnie Francaise des Pètroles (cfp), in which the French government held 35%		23.75
Standard Oil Co., New Jersey: 25%; Standard Oil Co. of New York: 25%; Gulf Oil Corp.: 16.66%; Atlantic Refining Co.: 16.66%; Pan American Petroleum and Transport Co. (subsidiary of Standard Oil of Indiana): 16.66%	Near Eastern Development Corp.	23.75
C.S. Gulbenkian	Participation and Investments Co.	5

Source: Anderson (1981, p.19).

States was controlled by the Standard Oil Company of New Jersey (later Exxon/Esso), Shell, and the Anglo-Persian Oil Company (later BP). In September of that year, the leaders of these companies met at Achnacarry Castle in Scotland and worked out a market-sharing deal, known as the Achnacarry Agreement or As-Is Agreement. This was an agreement to keep the existing percentage market shares of sales in various markets. Another important point in the agreement was the 'Gulf plus pricing system,' according to which crude was to be priced as if produced in the Mexican Gulf regardless of its actual origin. Later the companies also agreed to control production.

The various agreements covered operations in all countries except the United States and the Soviet Union. By the end of the 1920s, the companies had set up agreements governing their interrelations in the whole vertical production chain. The scarcity that had made the US companies so eager to move into the Middle East production area soon turned into a giant surplus, as new discoveries were made both inside and outside the Red Line area. Thus, the downward pressure on prices increased.

After the Second World War, the international oil market was dominated by seven companies, known as the Seven Sisters.[7] The Seven Sisters

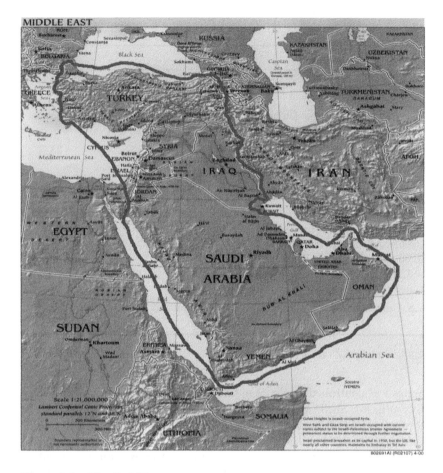

Figure 5.3   The Red Line

accounted for virtually all the oil produced outside the United States and
under the control of the Soviet Union. They were integrated in the sense
that they controlled the entire vertical production chain from exploration
to sales of refined products. As of 1953, these companies controlled 95.8
percent of the reserves, 90.2 percent of production, 75.6 percent of the
refining capacity, and 74.3 percent of the product sales.[8] This created a
very stable market structure.

> Only a few firms were capable of the risky search for oil in remote often harsh
> places. In each consuming country, refining and marketing was a small industry,
> protected by distance and government, making entry difficult and unprofitable.

Production was too risky without an assured outlet, known as "finding a home for the crude." Refining was too risky without an assured supply of crude. Hence in each country the few sellers were confronted by few buyers, and neither side wished to be at the mercy of the other. The obvious solution was vertical integration. (Adelman, 1995, p. 44)

Table 5.2   Ownership shares in Middle East production distributed to companies (%)

Company	Iran	Iraq	Saudi Arabia	Kuwait
Exxon	7	11.875	30	
Texaco	7		30	
SoCal	7		30	
Mobil	7	11.875	10	
Gulf	7			50
BP	40	23.75		50
Shell	14	23.75		
CFP	6	23.75		
Iricon	5			
Gulbenkian		5		

Source: Church (1974).

The Sisters also organized their operations in the Middle East through a consortium in which all the companies were engaged in at least two countries. In this way, the Sisters stood stronger against possible regulation by the producing countries, as none of them were totally dependent on the will of any one government (cf. Table 5.2). Middle East oil became increasingly important to the companies as it gradually replaced oil from US domestic sources, which became split up into several owner interests after American anti-monopoly legislation had been enforced against Standard Oil earlier in the century. Later the anti-trust laws made extensive cooperation between the Sisters impossible in the United States (Odell, 1986, p. 16).

As oil consumption increased, the economic gains from maintaining control over the international oil market increased. After the war, the need for governmental involvement was perceived as less immediate. Together with the overall establishment of a somewhat liberal international trade regime, this prompted the most important political actors (the UK and US governments) to withdraw from direct involvement in the international oil market, leaving a large space for the international oil companies. In a period marked by an abundance of oil available at low prices, political interference in the market disappeared during the 1950s and 1960s: "Parent governments could almost forget about the oil industry which, with a few isolated exceptions, was obviously being successfully controlled by the majors [read: the seven sisters and CFP]" (Turner, 1983, p. 23).

Thanks to a combination of rapidly increasing oil consumption and low production costs in the Middle East, the international companies reaped a considerable profit. This profit naturally proved attractive to private companies other than the 'Sisters', as well as to national oil-importing companies. There were two strategies open to these companies if they wished to gain entry to the market – they could develop a new area for oil production outside the area controlled by the Sisters, or they could attempt to break the dominance of the 'majors' in the Middle East.

The French company CFP employed the former strategy, opening production in Algeria in 1959, while the Italian national company ENI (Ente Nazionale Idrocarburi) chose to enter into a joint venture agreement with NIOC (the National Iranian Oil Company) in 1957, providing it with access to Iranian offshore territory. A number of similar agreements between exporting countries and small companies followed (Schneider, 1983, pp. 79–81). This created steadily increasing competition in the market, which in turn put pressure on prices. Among the main newcomers were companies such as Getty Oil, Phillips, and Occidental. The last played a crucial role – in 1970 it became the first company to yield to Libya's pressure to raise prices and increase tax rates to producer countries (Terzian, 1985, p. 120). This forced Shell's independent partners in the Oasis Group to follow suit, and only a month and a half later Shell itself gave in to Libya's demands.

5.5   THE MARKET POWER OF POLITICS

The developments in the international oil market during the 1960s illustrate the general point that, as markets expand, competitive pressure increases. It is easier to be a monopolist in a small market than in a large one. The integrated structure created barriers to entry at the company level, but when the market grew, these barriers became impossible to maintain. This set the stage for the next revolution in the oil market – the take-over by the oil-producing countries, the topic of the next chapter.

Regarding the political reactions to cooperation among companies, the comparison of the two cases is striking. In the US case of Standard Oil, the government's reaction was to abolish the corporation. In the case of the Seven Sisters, the home governments of the companies facilitated and encouraged the cooperation. It is a well-known insight in political science that national and international political systems have fundamentally different structural features. A defining feature of a national political system is the "institutions and processes that make and implement authoritative decisions for a society" (Lenz and Holman, 2013, p. 2). The international political system is regarded by many as anarchic, which is to say that its principal defining characteristic is the absence of overarching government (Bull, 1977; Buzan, 1991).

Thus, the power of any government is profoundly different in the national system, compared to the international system. The ability of any individual state to control companies' activities in other countries or across state borders is far more limited than inside the jurisdiction of the state. Today, the US and EU competition authorities can prosecute unlawful cooperation by foreign firms, but only based on the effects this collusion has on the US or EU market. Furthermore, the interests of the states might be very different regarding companies' cooperation internationally and domestically. The Seven Sisters ensured secure supplies of oil at relatively low prices. In the 1950s and 1960s, this fueled the economic growth of both the US and Europe and the profit of the companies. Thus, there was a compatibility between the interests of the home governments and the international oil companies.

NOTES

1. The exception to this is if the monopolist can sell at different prices to different customers, so-called price discrimination. Crude oil has different qualities, and thus there are some price variations across these qualities, but, in general, oil is a homogenous product, and thus price discrimination is hard to achieve.
2. Marginal revenue is the additional revenue to the monopolist by increasing sales by one unit. In other words it is the revenue generated from the last unit sold.
3. Economic efficiency is a "general term for making the maximum use of available resources" (Black and Nigar Hashimzade, 2017, p. 157).
4. Act of July 2, 1890 (Sherman Anti-Trust Act), July 2, 1890; Enrolled Acts and Resolutions of Congress, 1789–1992; General Records of the United States Government; Record Group 11; National Archives. https://www.ourdocuments.gov/doc.php?flash=fal se&doc=51&page=transcript (accessed July 3, 2018).
5. In 1914, Congress passed two additional antitrust laws: the Federal Trade Commission Act, which created the FTC, and the Clayton Act. With some revisions, these are the three core federal antitrust laws in the United States still in effect today.
6. The San Remo agreement was primarily between France and the United Kingdom and concerned the mandates in the Middle East. France was awarded the mandate for Syria and Lebanon, and the United Kingdom received the mandate for Palestine and Mesopotamia (later Iraq).
7. The designation "the Seven Sisters" was first used by the Italian oil man Enrico Mattei, and later used as the title of Anthony Sampson's book about the seven largest oil companies (Sampson, 1975, p. 11). This group included Exxon, Mobil, Standard Oil of California, Texaco, Gulf (all American), BP (British Petroleum) (51% of the shares were formerly held by the British government), Royal Dutch/Shell (60% Dutch and 40% British). CFP (Compagnie Francaise des Pètroles) is sometimes included in this group, despite representing a minimal share of world production (approx. 1.2% in 1950) (Schneider, 1983, p. 39).
8. The figures refer to markets outside the United States and the Second World, and include CFP.

6. OPEC

6.1 HOW TO STUDY OPEC

A search on OPEC in Google Scholar brings about 180,000 hits, 3,850 since 2017 alone! Energy-related journals in economics and political science publish a constant stream of analysis of OPEC from almost any possible angle. In newspapers covering international politics, markets or businesses, hardly a day goes by without an article related to OPEC. The nearly sixty-year-old Organization of the Petroleum Exporting Countries has been in the limelight of politics and economics since the early 1970s at least. Putting together a single book chapter on OPEC is bound to do the organization an injustice. My only excuse is that I have devoted an entire book to the question of oil-producer cooperation and OPEC before (Claes, 2001). This chapter is a combination of historical narrative and a discussion of the reasons behind OPEC's attempt and its ability to govern the international oil market. The concluding section addresses one of the most common mistakes in scholarly studies of OPEC (and even more so in public and political debates) – to start out with the presumption that OPEC is a cartel. I fully agree with Ramady and Mahdi (2015, p. 216) that while OPEC "may have some *cartel-like features*, it was not a cartel … [The notion] 'OPEC is a cartel' has evolved into a self-sustaining 'rational myth', with a life of its own." In fact, the question of whether OPEC is a cartel or not is a very interesting question to ask. In my mind, it is far more interesting to "explore the extent that collective action has been a necessary condition for the producers to exercise influence over the international oil market and thereby increase their economics gains" (Claes, 2001, p. 239). This could be followed by the counterfactual question of what the oil producers' behavior and the oil price would have been in the absence of OPEC. Counterfactual questions like this cannot be answered analytically, but explaining what actually happened can sometimes require a discussion of what future the actors tried to avoid. Economic models of cartel behavior or by statistical studies of marginal changes in price and production are of the highest value for our understanding of the oil market and the role of OPEC. However, they need to be supplemented by 'analytical narratives' which are able to capture the role of individual and collective decision-makers within their institutional framework, in order to fully understand the remarkable history of OPEC and the oil market.

6.2 THE PRICE SHOCKS OF THE 1970s

On September 14, 1960, OPEC was established in Baghdad, with the principal aim of "coordination and unification of the petroleum policies of member countries and the determination of the best means for safeguarding their interests, individually and collectively" (Article 2 of the Statutes (OPEC, 1990, p. 32)). The founding members were Iran, Iraq, Kuwait, Saudi Arabia, and Venezuela. During the 1960s, OPEC served as a focal point for the members' self-assertiveness as oil-producing countries (cf. Chapter 2). It did not attempt to regulate the market.

6.2.1 The Tehran and Tripoli Agreements, 1971

As discussed at the end of the previous chapter, the unity and control over the oil market by the Seven Sisters were breaking up in the late 1960s, as new independent oil companies started to engage themselves in oil production in the Middle East. At the same time, OPEC had established a stronger solidarity among the oil producers during the 1960s. It became obvious that the IOC and OPEC would have to negotiate price policy, taxation, royalties, and so on. After some internal differences, the companies united in a common front and sought to negotiate with OPEC as a whole. They conducted two sets of negotiations, one with the Gulf exporters and one with the Mediterranean exporters. On February 14, 1971, the so-called Tehran agreement between the international oil companies and the OPEC members exporting through the Persian Gulf was signed. On April 2, 1971, a similar agreement for the OPEC members exporting through the Mediterranean was signed, called the Tripoli agreement.

The Tehran–Tripoli agreements of 1971 implied a 21 percent price increase for Saudi Arabian crude (from $1.80 to $2.18) and an increase in revenue of 38.9 percent. What was more important, however, was that the producer countries gained some control over the price-setting. The distribution of market power in the international oil market had changed: "Before Tripoli and Tehran, the OPEC nations had exerted defensive market power. Their excise taxes had put a floor of tax-plus-cost under the price. But raising taxes in concert, to raise the worldwide price floor, was indeed new" (Adelman, 1995, p. 80). The agreement was a result of a combination of lack of unity among the companies and a new unity among the OPEC members (cf. the end of Section 5.4). One could argue that both factors were necessary, but neither of them alone was sufficient to explain the events of 1971. A unified OPEC strategy would not have succeeded unless the companies' unity had begun to crack. The lack of unity among the companies would have meant nothing unless the OPEC members had gained some ability to act in concord. It is reasonable to argue that with competition for production concessions among the companies, the producer countries would have been able to increase taxes individually, as, in fact, was the case in both Libya and Venezuela.

6.2.2   The Oil Weapon: The 1973 Embargo

The idea of using the control of oil resources as a political weapon was an old idea. As early as 1948, oil exports were stopped in connection with the conflict between Israel and the Arab countries. The same happened in the Suez crisis in 1956 and the Arab-Israeli war in 1967 (Schneider, 1983, p. 212). Foremost among advocates of this policy were Iraq, Algeria, and Libya. The only country in opposition was an important one – Saudi Arabia. In 1973, the political use of oil reach its peak. On October 17, a Conference of Arab Oil Ministers was convened in Kuwait, with the aim of discussing the use of oil as a political weapon in the ongoing Arab–Israeli war.[1] The conference announced the intention to reduce production by 5 percent per month until Israel retreated from the occupied territories and the rights of the Palestinians were restored (Blair, 1976, p. 264). On October 20, they agreed to stop oil supplies to the United States and the Netherlands altogether due to their outspoken support of Israel. Saudi Arabia's Sheik Yamani later called the embargo a legitimate political action: "We watched America and learned how they use one's economic power to meet political objectives. We studied this carefully" (Robinson, 1988, p. 95). The embargo and the production limitations, itself, removed very little oil from the market, and were short-lived (Blair, 1976, pp. 266–268). No shortage of oil emerged, but expectations that the future might lead to a supply shortage drove up prices: "Nobody knew how long the cutback would last or how much worse it would get" (Adelman, 1995, p. 110). Kissinger (1982, p. 873) finds the embargo "a symbolic gesture of limited practical importance . . . The true impact of the embargo was psychological." The uncertainties about the future supply of oil created a highly favorable environment for price increases. On October 6, the OPEC countries effected a first price increase without the involvement of the companies (Terzian, 1985, p. 170), and thus buried the Tehran and Tripoli agreements, and in effect put the price setting in the hands of the oil-producing countries alone and left the companies as pure price-takers. With the market power now in the hands of the governments of the producer countries, followed the challenge of *how* to manage their new-gained power. The decision to increase oil prices after the oil embargo was not an OPEC decision, but made by a group among the members. "OPEC, therefore, found itself, largely by accident, with a price of $11 instead of $5" (Skeet, 1988, p. 150). With the price increases, the change from posted price to official selling price, and the nationalization of production, the focus turned to the internal OPEC bargaining. "No longer could OPEC governments fix a price floor by fixing per barrel taxes and letting the companies compete freely above the floor. They now had to fix prices in concert and to trust each other not to undermine those prices by trying too hard for additional sales. It was an endless exhausting struggle" (Adelman, 1995, p. 143). One could say that with market power comes great responsibility and the endless challenges of collective action (cf. Section 5.1.4).

6.2.3 The Two-tier Price Structure

Although oil consumption is generally regarded as inelastic, meaning that consumption is slow to react to price changes, the market experienced a slowdown in demand after the price increases of 1973–1974. The OPEC countries had to absorb it all, and their production fell by 3.5 million barrels per day (mbd) from 1974 to 1975. The industrialized economies experienced an economic recession partly fueled by the increase in oil prices. This recession also created high rates of inflation, thus reducing the value of the price increase, causing some OPEC members to call for further price increases. In this situation, there was more oil available than the market demanded. Saudi Arabia, which had reluctantly agreed to the 1973 embargo, was strongly opposed to further price increases. Theodore H. Moran (1981, p. 255) claims that the Saudi Arabians were ready to "accept whatever price the conditions of surplus would produce." He refers to journals claiming that Yamani, as early as in May 1974, proposed to cut the posted price of Arabian Light to $9 per barrel, and invited Iran to cooperate on this.[2] The Saudi Arabian position brought about severe internal tension (Moran, 1981, p. 257).

When the OPEC members met in May 1976, the organization's Economic Commission had estimated that to compensate for inflation the price would have to be raised by another 20 percent. Eight countries favored such a price increase: Iraq, Libya, Nigeria, Iran, Gabon, Qatar, Indonesia, and Ecuador. Three countries proposed a 10 percent increase: Algeria, Kuwait, and Venezuela. Only one country opposed any price increase at all: Saudi Arabia. The decision was postponed until the meeting in Doha in December 1976. At the Doha meeting Saudi Arabia proposed a 5 percent increase, supported by the United Arab Emirates. The members did not agree, and the other countries increased their oil price by 15 percent, while Saudi Arabia and the United Arab Emirates increased theirs by 5 percent. A two-tier price structure was thus established. After the meeting Saudi Arabian Oil Minister Sheik Ahmed Zaki Yamani threatened to initiate a price war: "We will remove the production ceiling of 8.5 million barrels a day. We will damp the market – it means the whole structure of price will collapse all over the world" (Terzian, 1985, p. 244). Saudi Arabian production did actually increase from 8.5 mbd in 1976 to 9.2 mbd in 1977. By 1977 Iran, too, advocated a price freeze. When these two countries, which together accounted for a full 48 percent of OPEC's total production, opposed price increases, there was little the other countries could do. However, unexpected events were to play havoc with the oil market again.

6.2.4   The Second Oil-price Shock, 1979–1980

The Iranian revolution
On October 13, 1978, 37,000 Iranian oil workers went on strike. It took only five days to bring the Iranian oil production to a complete standstill (Terzian, 1985, p. 257). The production was restarted, but in January 1979 Iranian oil production was 445,000 barrels per day, down from more than 6 million mbd in September 1978.

At the same time, Saudi Arabia and some other OPEC countries increased their sales of oil, filling the gap left by the Iranian shortfall. Therefore, there was no actual physical shortage of crude oil during the rest of 1978. However, the market actors perceived a shortage and the prices began to climb. The OPEC countries increased their official prices following the increase in the spot prices, although not to the same level.

As the events evolved in the first months of 1979, OPEC, on February 21, 1979, summoned an extraordinary meeting of the Conference on March 26.[3] A week later, on February 28, the Secretariat issued another statement: "Conference decisions in setting crude oil prices do not prevent Member Countries from making an upward adjustment in light of their prevailing circumstances . . . In the present circumstances, the actions of Member Countries in exercising their sovereign rights can not be construed as prejudicing the solidarity and unity of OPEC" (OPEC, 1990, p. 163). At the meeting on March 26, the marker crude price was raised from $13.335 per barrel to $14.546 per barrel from April 1. At this time the spot price was above $20 per barrel. But the Conference confirmed the above statement regarding upward price adjustments: "Besides this adjustment [the changed marker crude], it is left for each Member Country to add to its price market premia which it deems justifiable in the light of its own circumstances" (OPEC, 1990, p. 164). The Conference also made an appeal to the consuming countries to restrain the international oil companies: "the Conference calls upon all consuming countries to take such measures as to prevent oil companies from charging them prices beyond the price decided upon by the OPEC Conference" (OPEC, 1990, p. 164).

This demonstrates that the organization did not have any intention to curb the upward pressure on the oil price itself. While the OPEC members were free to add to the agreed prices as they saw fit, the organization called upon the consumers and companies to hold back the price escalation. A working cartel has to be able to counter a price increase with increased production, as well as to cut production when the price falls. An effective cartel organization would also have been able to prevent the crisis, as it could have prohibited sales at prices higher than what would clear the market. As it turned out, only Saudi Arabia stood firm on official prices and traded mostly in the contract market, while other members exploited the high prices in the spot market.

In May 1979, Iran was again selling oil on the international market. The fall out of Iranian production had lasted only four months. OPEC met again in June 1979. Although Saudi Arabia had changed its position and was willing to agree to a price adjustment ($18 per barrel), the other countries wanted far more. The compromise was to adjust the marker crude price to US$ 18 per barrel, but to also allow members to add to the price of their crude a maximum premium of two dollar per barrel over their normal differential. However, the Conference also set a maximum price that could be charged at $ 23.50 per barrel (OPEC, 1990, p. 165). Skeet (1988, p. 160) concludes that:

> [I]n terms of price management these two meetings of OPEC were an admission that they neither had, nor wished to have, any control. *Carte blanche* was given, or taken, to obtain the highest possible price. The inclusion of a ceiling price in the June communiqué was a weak effort to restrain the worst excesses of price greed, but it had no practical effect.

Terzian (1985, p. 269) reads the same events as follows: "This 'ceiling price' was quite a development . . . in this month of June 1979, OPEC was not only not shoring up prices, it was actually holding them down by imposing a 'ceiling.'" It is, however, hard to find any evidence that the ceiling price had any effect whatsoever on OPEC members' behavior. Skeet's interpretation seems more adequate.

The Iran–Iraq War

In January 1980, Saudi Arabia increased its oil price by $2 per barrel to align its price with those of the other OPEC members. This failed, as the other members immediately increased their prices by the same $2 per barrel (Terzian, 1985, p. 275). The same happened in May, bringing the official Saudi Arabian price up to $30 per barrel. In the second half of 1980, the increase in spot prices came to a halt. So did the increases in the official prices of the OPEC countries. The OPEC ministers met in Vienna in the middle of September. With OPEC's twentieth anniversary coming up, it seemed a good time to standardize prices. Saudi Arabia once more increased its price by $2 per barrel, and this time the others remained unchanged. A summit of heads of state was scheduled for November 4 in Baghdad, with the prospect of a renewal of the organization. It was never to take place, since, on September 22, 1980, the Iran–Iraq War broke out.

The outbreak of this war did not affect the oil market in the same way as did the revolution in Iran. At the time the war broke out, there was a supply surplus in the market of about 2 mbd. The outbreak of war led to a reduction in both countries' production of some 4 mbd, leaving only 2 mbd of actual shortage. This was easily replaced by the other members. The exceptionally high oil price accelerated the drop in consumption. This brought OPEC production down. On December 15, 1980, the OPEC Conference met in Bali, with representatives of the two warring countries attending. A substantial surplus had emerged in the market, even with Iran and Iraq at war. At the same time, several OPEC countries used the political situation to increase their selling prices. This caused Saudi Arabia to use its idle production capacity as a threat, in order to achieve its long-sought goal of a unified price structure. In the words of Yamani himself, the price increases were a mistake:

> We believe that we made a mistake in 1979/1980 by raising our prices without paying attention to the real supply-demand situation. There was only a false demand, because the oil companies and governments panicked and bought oil to build up stocks at a very high price. We in OPEC took this false demand for real. And we made a mistake: we raised our prices further.[4]

6.2.5   A Unified Price Structure

Saudi Arabia, at the time producing above 10 mbd, refused to lower its production unless the other countries lowered their prices. Saudi Arabia was creating a surplus situation in order to force the other countries to lower their prices. This conflict continued at OPEC's next meeting in Geneva in May 1981. The press release issued after the meeting read as follows: "The Conference . . . decided to maintain the deemed marker crude price at a ceiling of US$ 36 per barrel with a maximum OPEC price of US$ 41 per barrel until the end of the year. The majority of Member Countries decided to cut production by a minimum of 10 percent, effective 1st June, 1981" (OPEC, 1990, p. 194). Saudi Arabia refused, and Iran and Iraq were excluded from the production cuts as they needed money for their warfare. Although Nigeria, Venezuela, Kuwait, and Qatar cut their production by more than 10 percent, the market was still in a surplus situation. Saudi Arabia continued to produce about 10 mbd, making buyers switch from the more expensive sellers to Saudi Arabia, which, as in past years, kept its prices well below the others. The official selling price of Nigerian oil was at this time $40 per barrel, and the Saudi Arabian price was $32 per barrel. The other OPEC members experienced an imposed cut in production, as there were simply no buyers for their crude oil. Terzian (1985, p. 288) puts these forced cuts in production at 30 percent for Algeria, 40 percent for Kuwait, and 50 percent for Nigeria (all 1981 figures).

In August, it became known that Nigeria was giving the buyers a $3 discount, and thereby de facto reducing its selling price. The oil ministers were summoned to a consultative meeting in Geneva, August 19 to 21, with the intention to convert the meeting into a full conference if they reached an agreement. A unified price was the obvious goal of the meeting. A compromise of $35 per barrel was put on the table, and eleven countries agreed. Iran refused and demanded $36 per barrel, while Saudi Arabia insisted on $34 per barrel. The meeting ended without any decision. However, the problems got worse. With reduced demand for OPEC oil, and the indecisiveness of the OPEC meeting, the companies foreseeing lower prices started to reduce their stocks of oil. By the same logic when prices increased, there was no reason to keep large stocks in a surplus market with falling prices. The destocking increased the downward pressure on the OPEC official prices. By October, even the high-price countries agreed that it was necessary to have a united OPEC. An extraordinary meeting of the Conference, held on October 29, 1981, decided as follows: "The Conference . . . recognizing the necessity to adopt a unified pricing system for OPEC crude . . . has resolved to set the official price of the marker crude at US$ 34 per barrel" (OPEC, 1990, p. 199). At last, the Saudi Arabian fight for a unified price structure had succeeded. However, the reason for the other countries' abidance was not any kind of organizational discipline or the negotiating skills of the Saudis. It was the market forces of reduced demand for OPEC oil, which left the countries with no other options.

There was therefore no 'role of OPEC' in market governance until 1981, in the sense that the member states' price and production behavior in the market was a result of institutional factors or collective action. The increase in the oil price in the first half of the 1970s was created by individual countries' utilizing the opportunities the market created. The market conditions were such that the actions performed by the members of OPEC would most likely have been the same without the presence of the organization.

When the market forces started to press the price down, the OPEC countries, having experienced this second oil shock, had to cut back production to sustain prices. This created the need for cooperation regarding the second and third aspects of cartel theory outlined in section 5.1.4 – the determination of a production level for the group and the allocation of output among the members of OPEC. So far, the OPEC countries had experienced high prices and high production at the same time, now OPEC had to live up to the hard part: either cut prices to sustain production, or cut production to sustain prices. They tried the latter first.

6.3 THE PRODUCTION POLICY OF THE 1980S AND 1990s

6.3.1 The Quota Decisions of 1982–1984

The OPEC decision of October 1981 was not sufficient to keep prices at $34 per barrel. Since the Iranian revolution the spot prices has been above the official selling prices of OPEC, at the end of 1981, the spot prices were below the official selling prices. The market forces now put a downward pressure on prices. Instead of surcharges, discounts became the order of the day. At the Arab Energy Conference in Doha on March 6, 1982, Yamani said:

> Destocking has reached unprecedented levels: my experts estimate it at 4 million barrels a day . . . We have to take an initiative. There can be no question of altering the price structure it took us so much trouble to set up again: on the other hand, my country is prepared to make an effort in terms of production. (quoted in Terzian, 1985, p. 296).

Two weeks later an extraordinary OPEC conference was held in Vienna, where the price of the marker crude at $34 per barrel was confirmed, but it was "decided that, as of April 1, 1982, the total OPEC production will have a ceiling of 18 mbd. This ceiling will be reviewed at the next Meeting of the Conference in the light of market developments" (OPEC, 1990, p. 202). Production quotas were allocated among the members, except Saudi Arabia. The Kingdom was to act as a swing producer, regulating production to create market equilibrium. The initial quotas of March 1982 were not based on any criteria at all. "The system was first established as a result of negotiations made more or less on the spur of the moment and influenced, to a great extent, by Member Country production levels which prevailed at the time" (Al-Chalabi, 1989, pp. 25–26). In fact, not even the present production at the time is recognizable in the quota allocation (Claes, 2001, pp. 183–184).

The Saudi Arabian role as swing producer allowed OPEC to maintain some control of the price level, but from 1983 to 1984 OPEC's dominance and control over price-setting crumbled. This was due to two important developments. In the first place, the growth in demand for oil came to a halt, due partly to higher prices, partly to a general reduction in economic growth that occurred prior to OPEC's price increases, and partly to new energy sources such as natural gas and nuclear energy. Second, competition between oil producers increased, in the same way as it had twenty years earlier between the companies. The new profitability of oil production made fields in non-OPEC countries profitable, and new producers took a larger share of the market. Both factors were caused by the market behavior of the OPEC countries during the 1970s. By the time of the OPEC Conference in December 1982, the market did not have room for 18.5 mbd of OPEC crude. Several other producing countries had increased their production in the times of high prices, and there was nothing stopping these non-OPEC countries from producing at full capacity. Although the total production was set at 18.5 mbd, adding the individual quota claims at the December 1982 meeting would give a figure of about 23.5 mbd. Iran claimed a quota of 3.2 mbd and called for a cut in Saudi Arabian production to below 5 mbd. Iran also argued that the following criteria should guide the establishment of national production quotas: (i) historical output levels, (ii) size of oil reserves, (iii) size of population, and (iv) extent of current economic and social needs. Venezuela argued for a national quota of no less than 2.1 mbd . . . Libya no less than 1.3. Iraq argued for a quota increase equal to whatever Iran obtained or the historical level of 10 percent of OPEC production, which meant 2.3 mbd (Evans, 1990, p. 607; Terzian, 1985, p. 310). The December meeting ended with a decision that "OPEC production for the year 1983 should not exceed 18.5 million b/d. However, an agreement of establishing national quotas for the distribution of that total amount would require further consultations among the respective Governments . . . every effort should be made by each Member Country to preserve the price structure and to stabilize the market conditions" (OPEC, 1990, p. 206). Again, there was no actual institutional pressure on the individual member countries to abide by the 18.5 mbd production ceiling. Furthermore, the previously agreed price level of $34 per barrel was sustained. In a declining market, this price level could not last. The price on the spot market fell, while at the same time OPEC members began to relate their sale contracts to the spot price, undermining their own organization. There was no reason for Yamani or the Saudi Arabians to bear the political costs of pressing for a price reduction, as they were convinced that the market, or, more correctly, the non-OPEC producers, would do it for them in the following months, if not weeks. On February 18, the British National Oil Corporation (BNOC) reduced its price from $33.5 to $30.5 per barrel. Nigeria had to follow suit and cut its price to $30; "they also made clear that they would match cent for cent any UK price cut below $30" (Skeet, 1988, p. 191). Yamani wanted a $4 cut in the marker crude price from $34 to $30. Now, with the Nigerian oil at $30, the marker would have to go below that level due to the different quality of the oil. "This was the situation when OPEC began a series of consultative meetings in Riyadh, Geneva, Paris, and, finally, London. The London meeting lasted twelve days, with only the last hours on March 14 transformed into an official Extraordinary Conference, OPEC's 67th" (Skeet, 1988, p. 191). The Conference resolved to:

> [S]et the official price of the Marker crude . . . at US $29 per barrel . . . To establish a ceiling for the total OPEC production of 17.5 million barrels per day, within which individual Member Country quotas were allocated . . . The Member Countries shall avoid giving discounts in any form whatsoever and refrain from dumping petroleum products into the world oil market at prices which will jeopardize the crude oil pricing structure. (OPEC, 1990, p. 208)

Most OPEC members cheated either on the price floor or on the production quota. This led to new pressure on the agreed price level. Especially, the Saudi Arabian build-up of a floating stock of oil tankers created downward pressure on prices.[5] OPEC had set up a Market Monitoring Committee in order to impose some discipline on the member countries. It was immediately attacked by the Saudi Arabians, who did not tolerate any interference in their sovereign oil policy. The extraordinary conference from October 29 to 31, 1984, upheld the price floor of $29 per barrel, but cut the total production quota by another 1.5 mbd to 16 mbd.

6.3.2 Changing Market Strategy, 1985

OPEC's policy was dependent on Saudi Arabia cutting back production to sustain prices. However, the market price did not react to the Saudi production cuts. In June 1981, Saudi Arabia produced above 10 mbd, in June 1985 the production was 2.5 mbd. None of the other OPEC members were anywhere near this dramatic reduction in production. In addition, some members also undercut the agreed price level, by selling oil with a discount. For Saudi Arabia, this policy was impossible to maintain. In the summer of 1985 there were definite signs that the Saudi Arabians would no longer accept production beyond the quotas by other OPEC countries, as long as they themselves produced only half their quota.[6] In October, Saudi Arabia shifted policy and increased production by introducing the so-called netback pricing system. In essence, ensuring crude oil buyers a profit when selling the refined oil products. This led to considerable over-supply in the market and heavy pressure on spot prices, a circumstance several countries tried to compensate for by increasing production. In this atmosphere, OPEC gathered for its meeting in Geneva on December 9, a meeting that was to change the oil market yet again.

At this meeting, the OPEC members had no choice, but to follow the Saudi policy. OPEC changed its market strategy from the defense of a high oil price to the defense of the OPEC countries' market shares. "Having considered the past and likely future developments in the world oil market and the persistently declining trend of OPEC production, the Conference decided to secure and defend for OPEC a fair share in the world oil market consistent with the necessary income for Member Countries' development."[7] The Saudi threat had failed. The price fall was dramatic. The oil market entered a price war between all oil producers. Saudi Arabia now turned their attention to producers outside of the organization. In a press conference held after the December 1985 meeting the Saudi Arabian oil minister, Ahmad Zaki Yamani made a clear warning to the non-OPEC producers, when answering a question about the likelihood of a price war: "It all depends on what the non-OPEC producers will do."[8] At first they did nothing. By May 1986, the spot for Brent crude oil was below $10 per barrel. At this point, some of the non-OPEC producers started to change their strategy, at least in words, if not in actual production cuts (Claes, 2001, pp. 281–295; Lie and Claes, 2018). At the December 1986 meeting of the OPEC Conference, a new accord was agreed upon for the first half of 1987. Now the price issue was resolved by the introduction of the OPEC basket. As the basket included several different OPEC oil qualities, the reference price was that of a composite of OPEC oil, rather than the single marker crude which had been used as a reference in the 1970s. Furthermore, the price differentials were fixed, and a system for revision of price policy and monitoring was established.

6.3.3 The Iraq–Kuwait War, 1990–1991

In July 1990, the Iraqi leader Saddam Hussein accused Kuwait of 'stealing' oil from Iraq and demanded repayment, declaring that "Iraqis will never forget the maxim that cutting necks is better than cutting the means of living."[9] The Iraqi foreign minister wrote a letter to the Secretary-General of the Arab League, stating that he regarded the stealing as "a direct military attack on Iraq" and declaring the Iraqi "right to return all the money that was stolen from our oil fields."[10] After the 87th OPEC Conference in July 1990, Iraq and Kuwait met for negotiations, which immediately broke down. A few days later, on August 2, Iraq invaded Kuwait and subsequently declared a "comprehensive, eternal and inseparable merger" between the two countries.[11] The UN Security Council declared a full boycott of Iraq and the new regime in Kuwait. This immediately brought to a halt all oil flows from the two countries. The oil price skyrocketed from $18 per barrel to almost $30 per barrel in a couple of days. On August 29, OPEC issued a press release stating that the organization would "consequently increase production, in accordance with need in order to maintain . . . market stability and regular supply of oil to consumers" (OPEC, 1990, p. 310). This implied an abandoning of the quota system until further notice. Other producers, particularly Saudi Arabia, quickly filled the gap. There was no shortage of oil. After a few weeks, total OPEC production was almost back at the prewar level.

The disappearance of oil from Kuwait and Iraq eased the pressure on the OPEC quota system, especially the Saudi restraints. The continuous UN blockade of Iraq enabled the other OPEC countries to continue a high production policy without disrupting the oil price. Saudi Arabia almost completely covered the loss of Iraqi oil, as Saudi production in the period 1991–1994 increased by almost 2.8 mbd, and the Iraqi reduction in the same period was just above 2.8 mbd (Claes, 2001, pp. 191–192).

The Iraq–Kuwait War gave the other OPEC producers room for increased production without risking a fall in oil prices, as the Iraqi production remained under 1 mbd until 1997. At the meeting of the Ministerial Monitoring Committee in February 1992, the quota allocations were reestablished, with Kuwait being allowed to produce as much as possible. Iraq was not allocated a quota but was included at its current production level. In January 1993, new quotas were set, including one for Kuwait. The UN sanctions against Iraq continued to block regular Iraqi oil exports. The Security Council of the UN was in effect a part of the OPEC production sharing efforts, and a very abiding one as well, as the UN curbed an increase in Iraqi exports that would otherwise have taken place. In the spring of 1996, the UN and Iraqi authorities worked out an oil-for-food deal. Iraq was to be allowed to sell oil in order to pay for food and medicine under an UN-monitored distribution system. As the implementation of the deal seemed imminent, OPEC included Iraqi oil production of 1.2 mbd in the quota agreement of June 1996. This created an increase in the total quota, as no other country cut back.

6.3.4 Muddling through the 1990s

During the 1990s OPEC also experienced two cases of members leaving the organization. In November 1992, the OPEC conference accepted the Ecuadorian suspension of membership effectively from January 1993.

In July 1996, the OPEC Conference accepted Gabon's termination of its membership effectively from January 1995. Amuzegar (1999, p. 56) describes the Ecuadorian dilemma as follows: "Facing an increasing need for foreign exchange and having a small crude output, Ecuador regularly exceeded its OPEC quotas, fell behind in its membership fees and finally left the organization as of January 1993." What would be the reason for any country to leave OPEC? Given the prominent role of the production limitations in the internal OPEC bargains, it can be assumed that countries leaving the organization believe they will be able to increase production further outside OPEC than inside. Comparing the Ecuadorian production increase outside OPEC with the development of OPEC production in the same period, such a strategy seems to have been unsuccessful in that case. While the Ecuadorian production increased with 16.7 percent from 1992 to 1998, the OPEC countries increased their production with 17.9 percent in the same period. In the case of Gabon, which announced its intention to terminate its membership in 1994, a similar pattern can be observed. From 1994 to 1998, Gabon's oil production increased with 6 percent, while the OPEC production in the same period increased with 13 percent. These two countries were large overproducers inside OPEC; measured in percentage of overproduction above allotted quotas, their small market shares made their lack of compliance a minor problem.

A more dramatic effect on the oil price followed the economic downturn in Asia in the autumn of 1997. The fall in demand following this recession implied a weaker, not stronger, market for OPEC crude. The sensible response would have been to cut production in order to balance the market at a lower level of demand. However, in November 1997, the OPEC countries increased the quotas. The Brent oil price fell from $19.88 per barrel in October 1997 to $13.11 per barrel in March 1998. When OPEC reduced the production ceiling again in March 1998, the new agreed production was not based on the quotas but on reduction from actual production the month before. Robert Mabro argued that "OPEC [had] abandoned its production quota policy." Since the price policy was abandoned back in 1986, there was not much left of the market-governing role of OPEC; and thus he concluded that: "OPEC today has neither a price nor a quota policy" (Mabro, 1998, p. 10).

In March 1999, OPEC agreed on significant cuts in production.[12] The meeting was over in ten minutes. The agreement had been negotiated before the meeting. Ministers from Algeria, Iran, Saudi Arabia, Venezuela, and non-OPEC country Mexico met two weeks before the OPEC conference and agreed on a 2 mbd production cut for OPEC and cooperating non-OPEC countries. The OPEC Conference was simply a confirmation of this agreement. This procedure would be repeated sixteen years later. At the end of the decade OPEC also improved the price strategy, introducing a price band and establishing a firm mechanism for market interventions. The renewed efforts in oil-producer cooperation, now including the non-OPEC producers Mexico, Russia, and Norway, paid off. By the summer of 2000, the oil price reached $30 per barrel. It had gone from $10 to $30 in eighteen months. From OPEC's perspective, the world economic outlook at the end of the 1990s seemed good. The Asian economies were recovering, and the already unprecedented sustainability of the US growth seemed to go on. The fact that several non-OPEC producers were included in the negotiations also reduced the probability that they would capture potential increased demand. It seemed OPEC was finally coming around to tackling the long-term challenges, as outlined by former Saudi Arabian oil minister Ahmad Zaki Yamani in September 1999:

> Regarding the longer term, OPEC needs to develop a strategy that keeps oil prices constant in real terms at a level low enough to deter non-OPEC producers from adding to their reserves and keep worldwide oil demand growing at a healthy rate. What this level should be, of course, is open to vigorous debate, but whatever it is it should ensure that the demand for OPEC oil rises steadily to absorb its huge excess capacity – both at present and in the future.[13]

6.4   THE MARKET PRICE DRIVE OF THE 2000s AND 2010s

6.4.1   The Market Driven Price Increase, 2003–2013

From 1986 to 2000 the average oil price was about $18 per barrel. Except for the period around the Iraq–Kuwait war, the price was hardly above $20 per barrel. The price increases of the 1970s were triggered by deliberate political use of oil such as the embargo of 1973, or by political events which directly reduced the supply of oil in the marketplace – such as the Iranian revolution and the Iran–Iraq war. From 2003 to 2004, Chinese oil consumption increased by almost one million barrels per day, representing an annual increase of 16.5 percent. Oil producers, traders, analysts and the media, started to speculate about whether this surge in Chinese demand was going to continue. A forgotten ghost of the 1970s reappeared – scarcity (cf. Section 2.2). The market actors continued to raise the price from 2003 to 2008, without any help from OPEC. OPEC reacted with consecutive increases in the overall production quota, and then in effect abandoned the quotas and opened up for production at full capacity. The oil price continued to increase, from $30 per barrel in December 2003, to a high of $143.68 on July 11, 2008. Then the financial crisis brought the price down to $40 per barrel in December 2008. It then climbed up again to over $100 per barrel by 2011, and was stable at that level until the summer of 2014. This period can adequately be explained as primarily the result of cyclical factors and short-term pressure on installed production capacity, blended with the psychology of market actors' behavior, in a situation of unexpected increased demand from China, and to an extent India, followed by a highly unexpected drop in demand with the financial crisis. Nevertheless, the market took over the driving seat from OPEC regarding price development. The economic downturn following the global financial crisis also turned the situation in the oil market around in just a few months. In fact, total oil consumption fell both in 2008 and 2009, in 2009 by as much as 1.7 percent (4.8 percent in OECD countries).[14] Neither the price increase from 2003 to 2008, the price fall following the financial crisis, nor the subsequent price recovery, can adequately be seen as the result of OPEC decisions. Indeed, although market actors expected OPEC to resume its role as market governor, the price collapse which followed in 2014 cannot only be laid at OPEC's door either.

6.4.2 The OPEC Non-decision of November 2014

Increased non-OPEC production has been a challenge to the organization since the early 1980s. Around 2010 a new unexpected group of challengers appeared, as the technological revolution in shale oil production in the US turned oil deposits in rock formations from a geological resource into commercial reserves (cf. Section 2.3). The shale oil revolution in the US was the major factor behind the price fall of 2014. Increased US production combined with flat or slightly falling consumption created a sharp fall in US oil imports. The market was oversupplied. It did take some time for the market to react. This is probably because the market actors had got used to a continuous increase in demand, in particular from China, and in the same period the sanctions against Iran cut Iranian exports. This contributed to a delay in the price effect of the increased US production. But in the summer of 2014 the downturn in the oil price began. Slowly at first, but then it was pushed off the cliff by a non-decision from OPEC. By November 2014 the market surplus was acknowledged by all market actors. The upcoming OPEC meeting on November 27 was intensely anticipated. To many, the obvious answer was for OPEC to cut its production in order to balance supply with demand, and thus sustain the price level. However, the outcome of the meeting was that no action was to be taken by OPEC. The organization's collective quota of 30 million barrels a day was maintained. No signals were given to indicate that OPEC would defend the price.[15] Two weeks later the Saudi Arabian oil minister, Ali al-Naimi, countered claims of a link between the kingdom's oil policy and wider political motives, saying it was difficult for the Gulf nation and other members of OPEC to reduce output and sacrifice market share in the current environment.[16] In effect, the OPEC meeting, by not acting on the oversupply in the market, initiated a price war against US tight oil producers. The situation was very similar to the early 1980s, and the lessons from then were prominent in the minds of the Saudi Arabian leadership:

> The experience of the first half of the 1980s was still in our minds. At the time, we cut our production several times. Some OPEC countries followed our lead, and the aim was to reach a specific price that we thought was achievable. It didn't work. In the end, we lost our customers and the price. The Kingdom's production dwindled from over 10 MMBD in 1980 to less than 3 MMBD in 1985. The price fell from over $40 per barrel to less than $10. *We are not willing to make the same mistake again.*[17]

A key implication of the shale oil revolution for OPEC and the producer governance of the oil market was the possibility that US shale producers might take over the role of swing-producers from Saudi Arabia. "The future role of shale oil in shaping oil price stability is one of the biggest open questions for the near future . . . Shale oil may prove to be a much more flexible . . . form of oil production . . . to provide the oil industry with natural self-adjusting features" (McNally, 2017, pp. 232–234).

Claes, Goldthau, and Livingston (2016, p. 191) find it is a myth that US shale producers acted as an effective swing producer balancing the global oil market. They obviously introduced new competition into the market. They also have some relevant features such as low upfront capital costs, short time spans from drilling to production and the ability to turn production 'on and off' relatively quickly in line with price movements. On the other hand, they lack the essential instrument behind Saudi Arabian market power; the Kingdom's spare production capacity. Furthermore, the individual shale producer will be moving in and out of the market as a competitive price-taker, responding to price movements with the simple decision to produce or not. Saudi Arabia is capable of centralized strategic thinking in the exercise of its market power (Claes et al., 2016).

6.4.3   The Phoenix 'Cartel,' 2016

The reluctance by Saudi Arabia to embark on new production regulation kept prices relatively low throughout 2015 and 2016. In January 2016, the average price was just above $30 per barrel. During 2016, oil producer diplomacy started with the aim of re-establishing producer cooperation in order to shore up prices through collective production cuts. In April 2016, 18 producer countries met in Doha, hoping to close a joint deal to freeze production. The meeting failed. Saudi Arabia backed out at the last minute. "The ongoing geopolitical tension with Iran is clearly a key consideration in Saudi Arabia's oil policy, preventing it from joining in even a vague agreement to freeze oil production at already inflated levels, and knowing that an oil price drop is likely as a result"[18] Other commentators dismissed the notion that the Saudi position was dependent on Iranian participation.[19] Bilateral discussion between Saudi Arabia and Russia had been going on for some months. The failure of the meeting in Doha was interpreted as the end of OPEC/non-OPEC cooperation. Russian cooperation with OPEC, and with Saudi Arabia in particular, seemed to be the key to effective producer governance. Nevertheless, on November 30, 2016, the OPEC conference decided to cut production and implement a production adjustment of about 1.2 million barrels a day (mbd). On December 10, OPEC met with 11 non-OPEC producers (Azerbaijan, Bahrain, Brunei, Equatorial Guinea, Kazakhstan, Malaysia, Mexico, Oman, Russia, the Republic of Sudan, and the Republic of South Sudan). These countries committed themselves to cut production by 558,000 bd. Two years after the OPEC non-decision, a new producer agreement was signed. This time with 24 participating countries, and two of the three largest oil producers in the world, Russia and Saudi Arabia, in the drivers' seat. The agreement has been prolonged through consecutive 'Declarations of Cooperation' during 2017, the latest in November 2017, which prolonged the production agreement for the whole of 2018.[20]

6.5 A CARTEL OR A SUCCESS?

As pointed out in the previous chapter (section 5.1.4), the success of a cartel depends on the ability to:

1. Determine a price for the group as a whole.
2. Determine a production level for the group as a whole.
3. Allocate output among members.
4. Detect and punish cheaters (Crèmer and Isfahani, 1991, p. 30).

The first two points depend on the cartel's market behavior. The last two points depend on internal collective action to enforce, in particular, production quotas.

6.5.1 Market Behavior

The first challenge for a cartel is the relationship between the optimal price and optimal production. Unless the cartel controls almost 100 percent of the market, attempts to fix both the selling price and production level are futile. OPEC's share of the world oil market reached a peak in 1973 at just above 50 percent, representing, in nominal terms, 30 million barrel per day (mbd), and its nadir occurred in 1985 at less than 30 percent (16 mbd). Since the early 1990s, OPEC's market share has been stable at around 40 percent. In the same period, total world production has increased from 65 mbd to 92 mbd, leaving OPEC with a production above 39 mbd in 2017. This suggests that OPEC's ability to perform the role of a cartel is limited by the behavior of oil producers outside the cartel. As the historical exposition above clearly shows, these constraints have been more prominent at certain junctures in the history of OPEC, in particular in 1986 (Basosi, Garavini, and Trentin, 2018), and 2014. The general prescription for OPEC to behave like a cartel would be to "set a fixed price, based on perceived demand conditions and the assumed production outside the cartel, and then increase production if the price rises above the agreed level, and decrease production if the price falls below the same level" (Claes, 2001, p. 247). When the production quotas were introduced in 1982, OPEC unfortunately tried to fix both price and production at the same time. The result was that neither price nor production was under control. The fixed price was undermined in the tight market of the 1980s, as OPEC members discounted and sold at prices below the official OPEC price. At the same time, the production level was unattainable, placing unbearable burdens on Saudi Arabia as the swing producer of the organization. Since 1986, OPEC has modified the price setting to a 'target price' that only indicates a policy aim, and does not constitute a binding or regulative figure in OPEC's deliberations. The swing-producer has also been very reluctant to take on the burden of defending the price by itself. Figure 6.1 compares the behavior of Saudi Arabia in the two periods, 1981 to 1985 and 2014 to 2017. The latter clearly demonstrates the change from a benevolent hegemon assuming the burden of trying to provide the collective good of a high oil price, to a coercive hegemon, insisting on the contributions of other producers in order to achieve a price increase. As mentioned above, in the early 1980s, Saudi Arabia cut production which fell from over 10 mbd to a low of 2.5 mbd in the summer of 1985. After the oil price fall in November 2014, Saudi Arabia actually increased production, behaving competitively against other producers, trying to compensate for the income effect of the price fall with increased production volumes. These observations are related to the extraordinary situations of dramatic price falls. Claes (2001, pp. 249–250) tries to track cartel-like behavior among the OPEC members in 'normal' situations between 1973 and 1995, excluding volatile periods related to price shocks or revolutions and wars. Cartel-like behavior would imply a strong positive correlation between changes in price and changes

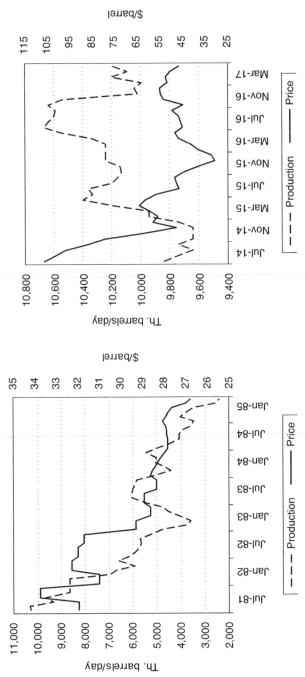

Source: BP (2017).

Figure 6.1 Saudi Arabian production, and market price, 1981–1985 and 2014–2017

in production. According to the criteria for a successful cartel, any price movement – positive or negative, large or small – should be accompanied by similar changes in production.

No such correlation is identified for any member for the period as a whole, although there are some brief periods of positive correlations. More striking is the fact that, for several members, there was a strong, negative, and significant correlation between price and production (Gabon, Iran, Kuwait, Libya, Nigeria, Qatar, and Venezuela). This suggests that the relationship between production and price is the *opposite* of the cartel-theory assumption. The individual producer tries to compensate for falling prices with increased production, and reduces production when prices increase above the target. The former correlation is easy to understand as an attempt to preserve income by compensating for a falling price with increased volumes. The latter correlation has been formalized in the economic model called the "backward-bending supply curve model" (Crèmer and Isfahani, 1991, p.45). In general, the point is that the producer does not try to maximize income, but seeks a more or less specified target for its revenue; the strategy can be called an "income target" strategy. The model is based on the Hotelling theorem (Hotelling, 1931); see Section 2.1. Behavior in accordance with a target revenue model would contradict cartel-like behavior. A simple method of identifying any strategic market behavior by OPEC is to observe production reactions to price changes.

As Table 6.1 indicates, OPEC's production reactions to price changes are almost equally distributed between reaction according to the target revenue assumption (46.3 percent) and production change in accordance with cartel theory (53.7 percent). None of the strategies is sustained over time. The longest period is nine months. One reason for the lack of cartel behavior might be that the understanding of demand and non-OPEC supply was inaccurate. "To calculate actual elasticities of demand and of non-cartel supply is worth doing, but the results seem too weak and inaccurate for direct application. The cartel will never hear the clang of a market bell: you have raised prices too high, start a retreat!"(Adelman,

Table 6.1   *Production under various price changes and models, 1982–1999, number of months*

	Decreasing Prices	Increasing Prices	Months
Cartel Behavior	Decreased production	Increased production	109 (53.7 %)
Revenue Target Behavior	Increased production	Decreased production	94 (46.3 %)

Note: Only the direction of price and production change is measured.

1982, p. 54). Another, more obvious reason for the lack of cartel behavior is the failure of the member states of OPEC to comply with their assigned production quotas.

6.5.2 Quota Compliance

The production quotas have been a prominent part of OPEC's deliberations since their introduction in 1982. With the quota system, OPEC proved its ability to formally allocate the agreed production volume. However, the question that immediately emerges is to what extent the quotas have limited production and raised prices. There has been an enormous interest among economists on the possible cartel behavior of OPEC, starting with Griffin (1982). The models applied have been increasingly sophisticated. Nevertheless, the literature as a whole remains inconclusive as to whether OPEC is a cartel or not (Kisswani, 2016, p. 172). There is no conclusive evidence of cartel behavior in the economic sense of either strict price control or production behavior that could imply a working cartel. Colgan (2014, p. 606), finds that, calculated in months, between 1982 and 2009 the production of the OPEC countries exceeded the quotas 96 percent of the time. He also correlates production and quotas and finds that "at most 1.8 percent of the variation in the month-to-month changes in [the members] oil production can be explained by changes in their OPEC quotas" (Colgan, 2014, p. 607). Claes (2001, p. 258), shows that OPEC members' production was consistently above quotas every month between April 1982 and April 2000, with a very few exceptions. However, *changes* in production and quotas are strongly correlated. This, however, can imply causality either way. The quotas can constrain production, even though it still is above quotas. But it could also be the other way around – that the quotas are adjusted to changes in production. The fact that OPEC made 38 adjustments in the quotas between 1982 and 2003 could indicate the latter (OPEC, 2003).

One can surely understand the reflections of a former Secretary-General of OPEC. "OPEC is not the cartel that some of our friends outside like to portray us as; if we acted as a true cartel, prices wouldn't be where they are right now!"[21] The problem is that the focus tends to be on a narrow and strict definition of a cartel, here identified by the four criteria in the introduction to this section. The same authors state: "Cartel is by far the most widely used term to describe OPEC . . . However, there is general agreement that the textbook definition of a cartel does not apply to pre-1982 OPEC, and specialists have spent much time identifying the internal features that make OPEC successful despite this fact" (Crèmer and Isfahani, 1991, p. 31). The question is whether

OPEC can be seen as a success even without acting as a cartel? This exposes the discussion to the fundamental challenge of social science in general; counterfactual claims. Basically, counterfactual claims suggest that if *A* had not occurred, *C* would not have occurred (Lewis, 1973). In this case, we cannot know with certainty how the OPEC members would have behaved if they had not cooperated within the framework of OPEC. It is equally hard to determine with certainty what the oil price would have been without the existence of OPEC. In the spring of 1986, when OPEC abandoned the strategy of defending the price level and began pursuing a strategy to protect its market share, the price fell to about $10 per barrel. The same level was reached during the price fall of 1998–1999. Since the price only stayed at that level for short periods of time, the actual effect on investments and replacement of reserves was not empirically tested. Adelman (1986) estimates the competitive price of oil – that is, the price without producer cooperation in any form – to be $8 in the short run and $5 in the longer run. He claimed that these prices would maintain investments in new reserves and capacity.

The conclusion regarding the relationship between cooperation and the price is thus a mixed one. OPEC has not behaved as a cartel, but the oil price has certainly been above what would have been obtained in a competitive international oil market. In a recent study, Aquilera and Radetzki (2016, p. 25) describe OPEC as "a less than entirely coherent producer group able to extract prices somewhat above the competitive level for limited periods." They are less interested in the concept of a 'cartel'. "Whether this description warrants the label 'cartel' is a semantic and, for our purposes, not very important question" (Aquilera and Radetzki, 2016, p. 25).

The picture becomes even more uncertain if we address how OPEC has achieved its influence on the market and the price. Has it been instigated by deliberative cooperative efforts, or has it been the result of uncoordinated but similar and simultaneous behavior of individual rational actors based on favorable market conditions? A solid test of the importance of cooperative behavior is only possible when the individual and the collective rationally diverge. This was not the case during the 1970s. One does not need to cooperate with others in order to raise prices when the producer can sustain or increase its individual production level. This became apparent during the Iranian revolution of 1978–1979 and with the outbreak of the Iran–Iraq War of 1980–1981. In these situations the restrictions agreed at the OPEC Conference were abandoned in favor of a free-for-all price increase. The fact that the price could not be raised without negative consequences for OPEC's market outlets became evident at the beginning of the 1980s. When the market-sharing mechanism – the quotas – was introduced, the costs of cooperation followed suit as the free-rider incentive appeared. So, we are back at the fundamental collective action problem described in Section 5.1.4. It follows that cartels are least effective when they are most needed. Internal cohesion is the key issue.

> Under competition, market-sharing is automatic. Each operator produces all it can, up to the point where the cost of additional output would exceed the price. But a cartel exists for only one reason: to keep the price above the marginal cost. Thereby, the cartel shuts off the automatic market-sharing mechanism. A joint decision by the members must replace it. But market sharing is a zero-sum game: any member's gain is another member's loss. (Adelman, 1995, p. 6)

However, applying economic models of cartels in order to understand OPEC brings us only so far. It is easy to subscribe to the conclusion by Fattouh and Sen (2016, p. 91) when they emphasize the importance of "relying on dynamic models that allow for changes in OPEC's conduct depending on market conditions, the interactions with other players, and the nature of the shock hitting the oil market."

NOTES

1. The participating countries were equal to the members of OAPEC. The conference met in OAPEC headquarter, but was "formally constituted on an ad hoc basis outside of the institutional framework of OAPEC" (Evans, 1990, p. 440). OAPEC is the Organization of Arabian Petroleum Exporting Countries. It was formed in 1968 by Kuwait, Libya, and Saudi Arabia. Algeria, Bahrain, Egypt, Iraq, Qatar, Syria, and the United Arab Emirates have subsequently joined the organization (Jenkins, 1986, p. 429).
2. Middle East Economic Survey May 31, 1974 and *Oil and Gas Journal*, June 17, 1974, p. 38; cited in Moran (1981, p. 254, note 33).
3. The meeting was intended as a consultative meeting of the oil ministers of OPEC member countries, but was converted into a full conference "in view of the current situation and due to the important developments that have been taking place in the oil industry" (OPEC, 1990, pp. 162–163).
4. Middle East Economic Survey July 18, 1983.
5. In August 1983, Saudi Arabia set up a trading company in Switzerland called Norbec. This company hired oil tankers, filled them up with oil, and sent them to different locations outside the Persian Gulf. This was explained as a precaution if the Strait of Hormuz should be blocked in the ongoing war between Iran and Iraq. However, approximately 60 million barrels stocked at sea led market actors, not surprisingly, to perceive a supply surplus in the market (Terzian, 1985, pp. 323–324).
6. This is expressed particularly clearly in two interviews with Yamani in the Jeddah newspaper Asharq al Awsat, quoted in Middle East Economic Survey, June 3, 1985, and *Petroleum Intelligence Weekly*, June 17, 1985.
7. Press release from the 76th OPEC Conference, quoted in *OPEC Bulletin*, December/ January 1986. The resolution promptly triggered a price drop for crude of $3 in three days (*International Herald Tribune*, December 11, 1985). "The market has gone mad," an oil broker told Aftenposten (Oslo). "No serious oil expert dares to predict what the oil price will be tomorrow, next week, or in 1986" (*Aftenposten*, December 12, 1985).

8. Middle East Economic Survey, December 16, 1985.
9. Platt's Week, July 23, 1990.
10. Platt's Week, July 23, 1990.
11. *International Herald Tribune*, August 10, 1990.
12. Press release from the 107th OPEC Conference, Vienna, March 23, 1999.
13. Speech by Sheik Ahmed Zaki Yamani, at the Centre for Global Energy Studies and Oil and Gas Journal Joint Conference: Oil Price Challenges into the Next Century in Houston, Texas, September 9–10, 1999.
14. BP statistical review of world energy, 2010.
15. Press release: http://www.opec.org/opec_web/en/press_room/2938.htm (accessed June 21, 2018).
16. http://www.ft.com/cms/s/0/b6e5ac64-86a4-11e4-8a51-00144feabdc0.html#ixzz3MHRitw fq (accessed June 21, 2018).
17. Speech by Saudi Arabian Oil Minister, Ali al-Naimi, in Riyadh, April 7, 2015, https://uk.news.yahoo.com/full-text-saudi-oil-ministers-speech-riyadh-084034690--business.html (accessed December 26, 2017). My italics.
18. Jason Bordoff, Director of the Center on Global Energy Policy at Columbia University. Quoted in *The Washington Post*, April 17, 2016. https://www.washingtonpost.com/news/energy-environment/wp/2016/04/17/whats-so-important-about-the-oil-meeting-in-doha/?utm_term=.b4bd3c2b5cdb (accessed December 26, 2017).
19. *Financial Times*, April 19, 2016.
20. Equatorial Guinea is not part of the prolonged agreements.
21. OPEC's Secretary-General, Rilwanu Lukman, interviewed in *Petroleum Economist*, March 1999, p. 8.

PART III

Political conflict

7. Oil and the US hegemony

7.1 THE US HEGEMONY

The third part of this book turns the table, from looking at how politics influence oil, to how oil influence politics. Politics is everywhere. In the two chapters following this one, the scope is limited to political conflicts, like interstate and civil war, and terrorism, with a geographical focus on the most oil-rich region in the world, the areas surrounding the Persian Gulf. This is also one of the most conflict-ridden areas in the world since the Second World War. The obvious question relevant for this book is to explore the role of oil in these conflicts. Chapter 8 discusses the role of oil in *inter*state conflicts in this region, while the role of oil in *intra*state conflicts is discussed in Chapter 9. The final chapter of the book, Chapter 10, relates to the role of oil in combating climate change. In the present chapter, the topic is the role of oil in international geopolitics, from the perspective of the United States, the world's hegemonic power, a power strongly connected to oil.

7.1.1 The Concept of Energy Security

Energy security is an underlying concept for understanding the petro-political behavior of oil-consuming countries. A well-established definition of energy security reads as follows: "adequate, reliable supplies of energy at reasonable prices in ways that do not jeopardize major national values and objectives" (Yergin, 1988, p. 111). This is a rather narrow and practical definition. Over the last decade, the academic interest in energy security has exploded, in particular in Europe, related to disruptions in supply of natural gas from Russia in 2006 and 2009. Szulecki (2018, pp. 7–12) identifies three categories of approaches to defining energy security: inductive, abductive, and deductive. Important observations are related to the need for security in the vertical value chain and in the energy system as such. More nuanced question are raised like security for whom, for which values and from what threats (Szulecki, 2018, p. 11; see also Cherp and Jewell, 2014).

Within the field of International Relations, the Copenhagen School emphasizes the way an issue becomes a security issue, through a process of securitization. Securitization is defined as a successful speech act "through which an intersubjective understanding is constructed within a political community to treat something as an existential threat to a valued referent object, and to enable a call for urgent and exceptional measures to deal with the threat" (Buzan & Wæver, 2003, p. 491). As Holger Stritzel (2007, p. 360) points out, this has immediate and significant implication for policy:

> The articulation of 'security' entails the claim that something is held to pose threat to a valued referent object that is so existential that it is legitimate to move the issue beyond the established games of 'normal' politics to deal with it by exceptional, i.e. security, methods. This puts an actor in a very strong position to deal with an issue as he/she thinks is appropriate.

The point following the Copenhagen School is that in itself by defining reliable and affordable energy supplies as a security issue, certain policy implications follow: in particular what kind of means that are available and appropriate.

When the oil producers organized themselves in the early 1970s and took control over the upstream segment of their oil industry through nationalization, it was perceived as a fundamental threat to the Western way of life. Reducing the dependency on foreign oil was given top priority: "Aside from our military defense, there is no project of more central importance to our national security and indeed our independence as a sovereign nation" (Kissinger, 1982, p. xx). This statement and many subsequent statements by representatives of the US government and US analysts are prime examples of securitization speech acts. Kissinger's reference to 'our independence as a sovereign nation' defines the threat as an utmost severe and dramatic threat. Although this perspective is most prominent in newspaper and general political journals, also some academic studies in the energy field have expressed a similar securitization perspective (Barnes & Jaffe, 2006; Kalicki & Goldwyn, 2013).

7.1.2 Hegemonic Governance

In the literature on global governance, two perspectives stand out. First, a realist-based perspective finding the international system to be anarchic and thus that governance in world politics primarily depends on the will and behavior of the most powerful states. Kenneth Waltz proclaimed that "Self-help is necessarily the principle of action in an anarchic order" (Waltz, 1979, p. 111), thus disregarding the role of international institutions. More explicitly related to the economic order is the claim by Charles Kindleberger that "for the world economy to be stabilized, there has to be a stabilizer, one stabilizer" (Kindleberger, 1973, p. 305). Second, a

liberal-institutional perspective claiming that even in the anarchic international system cooperation takes place as actors' policies are coordinated,
usually with the help of international institutions. Robert Keohane claim
that anarchy does not preclude cooperation defined as "a process through
which policies actually followed by governments come to be regarded by
their partners as facilitating realization of their own objectives, as the
result of policy coordination" (Keohane, 1984, p. 63).

The first perspective does not disregard the presence of international
institutions, but their existence and perseverance is dependent on the will
of the powerful states. The liberal perspective suggest that international
institutions to some extent have an independent effect on the behavior of
states, even on the dominant actors. The liberal perspective was outlined
and formed the basis for the discussions in Chapter 4. The theoretical
discussion among realists has been focused on the implication for state
behavior from the anarchic feature of the international system. By taking
a realist starting point, this chapter turns from studying the role of politics
in the oil states and in the governance of the oil market, to emphasizing
the role of oil in national and international politics. This also implies that
we part with the references to the economic models that has served as a
background for the discussion of politics of oil states and effective governance of the oil market in chapter 5 and 6. Economic models of the market
behavior of states have been developed from the assumptions underlying
the behavior of economic entities (i.e. firms). However, the rationale
of states is different from the rationale of firms. States have a more
complex set of interests, and tend to place primacy on security interests.
Furthermore, states are more complex organizations that contain more
potential for internal conflicts over aims and means. Finally, states have to
pay attention to aspects at the societal level in a way that firms seldom have
to do – if for no other reason than the fact that political leaders of democratic states usually seek re-election, and leaders of non-democratic states
seek to avoid revolution. It is the strong opinion of this author that only
through a combination of political and economic analysis can one gain an
understanding of the intrinsic world of international oil, as "the economics of oil influence the politics of oil, and vice versa" (Amen, 1996, p. 360).
Furthermore, the international oil market is not isolated from the rest of
the international economy, nor from international relations in general. The
changes in the oil market can be a result of not only an individual actor's
non-oil interests and behavior but also the actor's position in international
political structures.

Ideally, we should cover the role of oil security from the perspective
of all oil-consuming countries in the world. This would require a book
by itself. Instead, the focus in this chapter will be on the dominant world

power since the Second World War – the United States. The question based on the outlined concept of energy security is to what extent, and how, the United States has governed the global oil market, to ensure *availability, affordability, accessibility and acceptability* in oil supplies (Cherp and Jewell, 2014).

7.1.3 The Strategic Role of Oil in the US Hegemony

We tend to think of the US as a hegemonic power, implying that it can control the conditions in almost any corner of the world. Also the international oil market has been approached from such a starting point. The international oil market is, of course, not isolated from the rest of the international economy or international politics. To capture this aspect of the international oil market, Simon Bromley, in his study of US oil policy, develops what he calls a conjunctural approach, combining realism with orthodox economics. "By . . . placing the developments of US oil policy in the context of its wider management of the world economy and nation-state system, [the approach] demonstrates the central role which oil played in the organization of US hegemony" (Bromley, 1991, p. 242). His conclusion is that the explanation of oil-market development is connected with the overall development of the international post-war economic system:

The economic crisis can be more readily understood as the results of general contradictions within the maturation of postwar capitalism, evidenced also in an overall shift of US hegemony to an increasingly unilateral and predatory form; and second, the response of the United States to these wider challenges played a significant role in the origins of the oil price increases. (Bromley, 1991, pp. 242–243)

This indicates an interrelationship between the position of the US in international relations at large, and the role of oil in enhancing US political power:

Understanding how oil fueled the "American century" is fundamental to understanding the sources, dynamics, and consequences of U.S. global dominance. Essential to both military power and the functioning of modern society, oil fueled American power and prosperity during the twentieth century. . . . Control of oil boosted U.S. military and economic might and enabled the United States and its allies to win both world wars and the Cold War. (Painter, 2012, p. 24)

The oil crisis of the 1970s changed this picture, and represented a severe challenges to the US control of international oil, both economically and politically. It coincided with the Watergate crisis and the Vietnam War. The price increases weakened the oil dependent US economy relatively to emerging economic powers like Japan, while the Iranian revolution made US control of oil flows from the Middle East more challenging, to put it mildly. The US invasion of Iraq in 2003 highlights how US Middle East policy has become more complex and unpredictable. The anticipation that the invasion would increase Iraqi oil production was not realized. On the other hand, the oil shale technological revolution starting in 2008 has increased US oil production dramatically and reduced import dependency. The intertwined relationship between the economics and geopolitics of oil seems to continue. This chapter only allows for a discussion of a few key historical events. I start out with the fundamental bilateral relationship that has been the cornerstone of US international oil politics since the Second World War.

7.2   THE US–SAUDI ARABIAN 'SPECIAL RELATIONSHIP'

"Few relationships are as vital, under as much pressure, and as poorly understood as that between the United States and the Kingdom of Saudi Arabia" (Bronson, 2006, pp. 2–3). It is also of vital importance for Saudi Arabia – the hegemonic power among the oil producers. "The dimensions of potential incompatibility relate to the very core of Saudi foreign policy. The informal alliance with the United States both strengthens and weakens the Saudi position on most key issues" (Niblock, 2006, p. 143).

In May 1933, Standard Oil of California was granted a sixty-year concession for oil exploration and production in eastern Saudi Arabia (cf. Section 2.5.2). In July 1941, President Franklin D. Roosevelt, after considering a request from the US companies operating in Saudi Arabia that the US government give financial aid to ibn-Saud, instructed one of his aides: "will you tell the British . . . I hope they can take care of the King of Saudi Arabia. This is a little far afield for us" (Yergin, 1991, p. 394). The US policy changed during the war, partly due to the perception of an increased need for imported oil, and partly due to the perception of the lack of Britain's capacity to secure Western geopolitical interests in the region. In 1943 the US companies operating in Saudi Arabia persuaded the US government to extend 'lend lease' aid to Saudi Arabia. This laid the foundation for the political ties between Saudi Arabia and the United States. Roosevelt and the Saudi Arabian King ibn-Saud, met in early 1945, and a US security guarantee to Saudi Arabia was established in 1947. In October 1950, President Harry S. Truman wrote to the King: "I wish to renew to your majesty the assurances which have been made to you several times in the past that the United States is interested in the preservation of the independence and territorial integrity of Saudi Arabia. No threat to your Kingdom could occur which would not be a matter of immediate concern to the United States."[1] The US–Saudi relationship developed both at the political level, through the military guarantee and weapons deliveries, and at the economic level, through the US company Aramco. Ibn-Saud's political position inside Saudi Arabia was strongly enhanced by the state revenues generated from the oil industry. The oil income not only made the economic modernization of Saudi Arabia possible, it also secured the rule of the royal family – the House of Saud.

Governments did not engage themselves too much in the governance of the oil market during the 1950s and 1960s: "For decades, the international petroleum system was managed by private oil companies which explored, developed, produced, transported, refined and marketed crude oil and petroleum products. Governments in both producing and consuming countries demonstrated varying degrees of involvement in that system, but the predominant pattern was laissez faire" (FEA, 1975, p. v). The notable exceptions to this was the role of the US in preserving the Western influence and control in the Middle East. Both in a short- and long-term perspective, the Middle East countries are paramount for the determination of oil prices. The fact that two-thirds of the world's proven oil reserves are located in the Middle East indicates the long-term role of this region. More than a third of the word's oil supply comes from the Middle East. Any conflict that could potentially disrupt any aspect of this supply will immediately affect the price of daily traded oil. This makes the region important for all oil-consuming countries; regardless of to what extent they receive oil directly from the region. Even today, when US tight oil production has made the US less dependent on long-haul oil supplies from the Middle East, the price of gasoline in the US is no less vulnerable to a disruption in Middle East supplies.

The overarching US political hegemony and the Seven Sisters control of the oil market, co-existed to their mutual benefit until the early 1970s. "Immediately after World War II, the United States was hegemonic in the world economy: it had strong control over raw materials, including Middle Eastern oil resources; it was the major source of capital and by far the most important market in the world" (Keohane & Underdal, 2011, p. 51). "Between 1945 and 1970, the United States played a central role in building and maintaining a stable international monetary system, a regime of liberal trade, and dominance in world oil markets leading to stable prices and open access to supplies" (Keohane and Underdal, 2011, p. 53). The events in the oil market in the 1970s "reflected a new *inability* of the United States to control events" (Keohane and Underdal, 2011, p. 54, my italics).

In the oil market, a key instrument for the US government was the relationship with the country that after the Second World War emerged as the major oil exporter in the world – Saudi Arabia. In 1950, the Saudi Arabian oil production was one tenth of the US production. In 1974, the Saudi Arabian production level was more than 80 percent of US production. In the early 1950s, the US turned from net exports to net imports. As consumption continued to increase and production leveled off in the late 1960s, the import gap widened. The possibility of depletion of domestic oil resources had for decades been a repeated issue in US energy administrations. During the Cold War, the issues also had an imminent security dimension. Thus, the need for oil-rich political allies in the Middle East was one of the exceptions to the political 'laissez faire' in the era of the Seven Sisters' rule of the oil market.

While the international oil companies naturally emphasized the economic relations, the US government primarily focused on the political relationship. This is illustrated by the following passage of a letter from the US Ambassador to Saudi Arabia to the State Department in 1959:

> Assistant Secretary Irwin, who appeared exceptionally well briefed, made as his central theme the point that United States Government decisions to train the Saudi military forces and to provide them with arms was basically a political one. Therefore, no matter what our military problems with the Saudis are they should be accepted up to the limit of our national interests . . . He said one of the worries of Defence was that the Saudis might accuse us of failing to carry out our commitments . . . I replied I thought Faisal was coming around more to understanding the value of the United States friendship. (US Department of State, 1993, p. 743)

In 1970, President Richard M. Nixon stated what became known as the Nixon doctrine:

> Neither the defense nor the development of other nations can be exclusively or primarily an American undertaking. The nations of each part of the world should assume the primary responsibility for their own well-being; and they themselves should determine the terms of that well-being. We shall be faithful to our treaty commitments, but we shall reduce our involvement and our presence in other nations' affairs. (Palmer, 1992, p. 87)

Before the ink dried on the Nixon doctrine, the US was dragged into a diplomatic quagmire involving foreign countries, US oil companies, and not least an international organization called OPEC.

The government of the United States played an important role in the events surrounding the Tehran and Tripoli agreements of 1971 (cf. Section 6.2.1). Based on the experience in Libya, where the new president, Muammar al-Qadhafi was able to play the companies out against each other, the international oil companies realized they needed to negotiate jointly with the oil-producing states. Such openly coherent market behavior could violate the US antitrust legislation. In January 1971, before the Tehran and Tripoli negotiations began, the oil companies approached the US government and got a so-called business review that, given the information available, the Justice Department would not take criminal action against the companies if they pursued a united negotiation strategy with the oil-producing governments (Church, 1974, p. part 6: 224). With this clearance, the companies signed the Libyan Producers Agreement, a safety-net agreement that ensured other companies would provide a company with oil if it was forced by a government to reduce its production (Church, 1974, pp. 224–230).

OPEC, at its 21st Conference in December 1970, agreed on a resolution adopting a 55 percent minimum tax rate on oil companies' income, and a uniform general increase in prices. The resolution demanded negotiations with the companies within thirty-one days. On January 16, 1971, the companies were ready to negotiate on all issues, but only jointly, one team from the companies and one from OPEC. The following day Undersecretary of State John N. Irwin met with the Shah of Iran. Based on this conversation, Irwin suggested that the State Department urge the companies "to agree to negotiate in Tehran with the Gulf producer" (Church, 1974, p. part 5: 167). The US government had in effect hanged its position in the coming negotiations between the international oil companies and the oil-producing states.

The importance of this change in US government policy has been debated. Morris Adelman claims that: "had the US government not destroyed the new-found solidarity of the companies . . . the Persian Gulf producers might have been frustrated . . . The historian can only record that the US government helped the cartel in its hour of greatest need" (Adelman, 1995, p. 80) A key actor in these negotiations was the companies' adviser John J. McCloy. Although he was not "too much impressed . . . by the attitude of the US government," he argues that the US policy "wasn't decisive . . . I wasn't disturbed so much by what the Government's position was. I rather took for granted that Mr. MacArthur would side with the Shah" (Church, 1974, pp. part 5: 266–267). Also Stephen Krasner discusses how the US policy can be explained. He partly attributes it to ignorance, but he also emphasizes the conflicting interests of the US government:

The fact is that American policy did satisfy the objective of keeping the Shah and Faisal happy, even if it did not keep prices down. American policy-makers acted to preserve the stability of noncommunist regimes even though this strategy meant accepting higher prices and opposing the preferences of the oil companies. It was only after 1973 that prices themselves became a matter of concern. (Krasner, 1978, p. 265)

7.3   THE OIL WEAPON

During the Arab–Israeli war of 1967, several Arab countries advocated the use of oil-export restraints as a political weapon against Western countries that supported Israel. This strategy failed due to several factors: the main Israeli ally, the United States, imported only 5 percent of its total consumption from the Arab producers; the exports from non-Arab countries, like Iran and Venezuela, increased as the Arab producers cut back. Furthermore, the embargo was not a total volume restraint, and the IOCs were therefore able to swap shipments among different destinations. The main consequence of the 1967 embargo was a loss of revenue for the Arab producers.

In the early 1970s there was a desire among radical Arab powers to once again use oil as a weapon against Israel, as the United States had experienced an increased dependence on imported oil from OPEC. Foremost among the advocates of this policy were Iraq, Algeria, and Libya. The only country in clear opposition to this strategy was Saudi Arabia. This opposition can be explained by several factors. Schneider (1983, p. 213) maintains that Saudi Arabia's security interests were particularly important. The Saudi authorities perceived two separate threats to the safety of their state: (i) Israel's existing and potential expansion; and (ii) Arab radicalism. These were understood as being closely intertwined, as increased Israeli expansion would strengthen Arab radicalism. US support for Israel and its lack of support for conservative forces in the Arab world had, in the eyes of King Faisal, the same effect. Even though an Arab oil boycott could have solved this question, Saudi Arabia did not wish to confront the United States, which they considered to be the only possible guarantor of Saudi Arabia's security. "As late as October 1972, King Faisal said in an interview, 'It is useless to talk about the use of oil as an instrument of pressure against the U.S. – it is dangerous even to think of that'."[2] Furthermore, the stake for the international oil companies (IOCs) was as high as one could only imagine. At a meeting between Faisal and the Aramco partners in May 1973, Faisal, according to a transcribed confidential notes, said the following: "Time is running out with respect to US interests in the Middle East, as well as Saudi position in the Arab world. Saudi Arabia is in the danger of being isolated among its Arab friends because of the failure of the US Government to give Saudi Arabia positive support . . . you will lose everything" (J. Robinson, 1988, p. 89). To the companies, 'everything' meant the oil concessions; to the US government, it meant a vital political ally in a region of the utmost economic and strategic importance. When it turned out that the United States rejected Saudi Arabia's wish for a more 'balanced policy' (J. Robinson, 1988, p. 73), and Egyptian President Anwar Sadat pressured to obtain the support of Saudi Arabia in the ongoing conflict with Israel,[3] Faisal changed his mind. On August 30, 1973, Faisal declared: "We do not wish to place any restrictions on our oil exports to the United States, but America's complete support for Zionism against the Arabs makes it extremely difficult for us to continue to supply the US petroleum needs and to even maintain our friendship with the United States."[4]

The 1973 embargo imposed a severe test on the relationship (cf. Section 6.2.2). The Saudi regime did not seek the embargo, but felt pressured by other Arab countries. In fact, the US government and the Saudi Arabian leadership misread each other's situations in connection with the Yom Kippur/October War and the following oil embargo:

> Washington continued to view the Saudis as Arab moderators who could influence large sections of the Arab world through oil largess. By adopting such a stance, Washington misread Saudi (and Arab) public opinion, and more importantly, the ability of the al-Saud to disregard the strong currents flowing around them. The Saudis committed the same mistake vis-à-vis Washington. Most Americans supported Israel, and would not let it be defeated or destroyed by its Arab enemies; this attitude, in turn, entered into American policy considerations. (Wilson & Graham, 1994, p. 100)

On October 17, 1973, a conference of Arab Oil Ministers followed a Saudi Arabian proposal and decided to cut oil production by 5 percent and to cut it by a further 5 percent each month until "Israeli forces have completely withdrawn from all Arab territories occupied in June 1967 and the legitimate rights of the Palestinian people are restored" (Evans, 1990, p. 440). Three days later, they agreed to stop all oil supplies to the United States. This, obviously, represented a major blow to the US-Saudi relations. The Arab–Israeli war was over in 18 days, and the embargo of the US was rather ineffective (cf. section 6.2.2). Also on the diplomatic level, the conflict level was reduced when: "at a further meeting held on December 24 and 25 the Conference modified its policies after hearing a report by the Saudi Arabian and Algerian Oil Ministers on their recent visits to various Western countries, which had led them to conclude that a more positive attitude should be adopted towards 'friendly' countries" (Evans, 1990, p. 442). However, the events had dramatic effects on the oil price in the spot market. The OPEC members then used the opportunity to raise their official selling prices. At a meeting between the Gulf oil ministers in Tehran in December 1973, Yamani strongly opposed large price increases, arguing that they might drive the industrialized countries' economies into recession. On the other hand, the Shah of Iran pressed for maximum exploitation of the market situation, and a price increase as large as possible. To preserve OPEC unity, Yamani agreed to raise the price.[5] However, he made it clear that this was not the preferred policy of Saudi Arabia, as later confirmed by King Faisal.

Having joined the embargo, Faisal gained prestige among other Arab countries and relieved some of the internal pressure on the regime. However, the oil embargo did not change the US-friendly policy pursued by Faisal and Crown Prince Fahd. Already in June 1974, Fahd made an official visit to Washington, resulting in a comprehensive agreement on economic, technical, and military cooperation. "Riyadh expressed its readiness to help maintain a regular supply of oil to the market and to curb the rise in oil prices" (Abir, 1993, p. 67).

> The agreement was described by Secretary of State Kissinger as "a milestone in U.S. relations with Saudi Arabia and Arab countries in general." It involved massive American assistance to the kingdom in planning and implementing its economic and military development and in return called for Saudi cooperation in meeting the energy needs of the United States and its Western allies. (Golub, 1985, p. 22)

In July 1974, Saudi Arabia announced an oil auction of 1.5 mbd, without any minimum price, confident that no one would pay over $11.651 per barrel.[6] As demand had slackened, an auction would most likely put the official OPEC prices under pressure. After intense pressure from other OPEC countries, the plan was canceled. However, the stage was set for tense OPEC bargaining over the price issue, which prevailed for the rest of the 1970s (cf. Section 6.2). In the following years the most prominent opponent of the Saudi Arabians was the Shah of Iran. After the oil auction was called off, "the Shah led the counterattack against Saudi Arabia, insisting that the cartel's principle be that producer revenue should not be allowed to decline (i.e. prices or taxes should rise if volumes dropped)" (Moran, 1981, pp. 255–256). This confrontation between Saudi Arabia and Iran was the beginning of a lengthy conflict between these two major OPEC producers on the price issue. The Saudi Arabians were not able to influence the Shah's oil policy: "Yamani later insisted that if the United States wanted the kingdom to use its production capacity on behalf of moderation . . . the US government would have to play a more active role in relieving pressure from Iran" (Moran, 1981, pp. 255–256).

7.4 US AND THE MIDDLE EAST – TANGLED UP IN CONFLICTS

The US policy in the aftermath of the 1973 oil crisis seems to be somewhat incoherent. Apart from the aim of creating cooperation and solidarity among the consumer countries (cf. Section 4.2.2), the US Secretary of State, Henry Kissinger, in his memoirs emphasized the aim of separating the moderates from the radicals within OPEC (Kissinger, 1999, p. 677). Military aid to Saudi Arabia and Iran was a key element in this strategy, which also served the purpose of deterring Soviet expansion. The problem was, of course, that these two major oil producers were not on the best political terms, to say it mildly. Thus, the Saudis did not want to moderate the oil price themselves, without contributions from Iran. According to Francisco Parra, the US government did not put any pressure on the Shah to change his hawkish oil price policy: "The policy of arming Iran and allowing the Shah to purchase practically whatever arms he wanted remained in effect after the January 1974 OPEC price increases" (Parra, 2004, p. 205). The combination of Watergate and the Vietnam War reduced the capacity of the US government, in particular for overseas engagements. As the security of oil supplies from the Middle East was becoming a prominent concern, the need to bolster strong regional allies was important (Sick, 1985, p. 14). In fact, these security concerns might have been regarded as more important than the oil price.[7] In 1977, President Jimmy Carter finally got the Shah to join Saudi Arabia in moderating the OPEC oil price strategy.

A number of political issues are related to the embargo in the autumn of 1973 – internally among the OPEC members, in the relationship between oil producers and consumers in general and for the foreign policies of the US and European countries. The aim of reducing the dependency on foreign oil became a matter of highest political urgency, as indicated by the quote from Henry Kissinger on page 163. In the context of this chapter, the reactions in consumer countries are most relevant. In many consumer countries, the price increases were seen as a symptom of resource scarcity, not of market intervention by the oil producers. It fitted well with a recent influential publication from the Club of Rome called *Limits to Growth* published in 1972. "Its arguments were a potent element in the fear and pessimism about impending shortages and resource constraints that became so pervasive in the 1970s, shaping policies and responses of both oil-importing and oil-exporting countries" (Yergin, 1991, p. 569). Robert Pindyck (1978, p. 36) refers to a CIA report claiming that "a crisis is likely to occur in the early 1980s as world energy demand exceeds supply, resulting in shortages of energy, rapidly rising prices, and economic contraction in all of the industrialized countries . . . This view has had an important role in forming the rationale for the Carter administration's energy program." There was no shortage; the price increase was a result of OPEC exercising market power, not a lack of available resources. As Pindyck (1978, p. 51) concludes: "The kind of worldwide energy crisis of concern to the CIA and the Carter administration is unlikely to occur." Nevertheless, the oil price was to increase once again. In the autumn of 1978 opposition to the Shah of Iran intensified, including strikes in the Iranian oil industry, which almost brought production to a halt in January 1979 (cf. Section 6.2.4). Despite the fact that the other OPEC countries easily compensated for the disappearance of Iranian oil, demand increased as the buyers clamoured to secure their access to crude oil in case of a future supply shortage. From December 1978 to October 1979, the spot price increased from $13.80 per barrel to $38.35.

The Carter administration's unfortunate handling of the Iranian crisis and the hostage affairs weakened its credibility in the eyes of the Saudi Arabian regime, which could vividly imagine itself in a position similar to that of the Shah. The Reagan administration relied more one-sidedly on market forces, and was willing to follow the market even in times of crisis: "In the event of an emergency, preparedness plans call for relying primarily on market forces to allocate energy supplies."[8] However, the military commitment to Saudi Arabia was maintained. The Soviet intervention in Afghanistan in 1979 solidified the US–Saudi alliance. Now they had a common cause countering Soviet expansion and communist uprising in the Middle East and elsewhere. The Iran–Iraq war presented another threat to Saudi Arabia as there was a "widespread perception that if Iraq were to suffer defeat, the Kingdom would be the next domino to fall, with a tide of Iranian Shiite expansionism covering the region" (Niblock, 2006, p. 145). The formation of the Gulf Cooperation Council (GCC) in 1981 was an attempt to counter such a development. Furthermore, the United States partly intervened in the tanker war during the Iran–Iraq conflict by reflagging Kuwaiti and Saudi Arabian oil tankers and providing protection for these ships in the Gulf area (cf. Section 8.3).

A major conflict affecting the US–Saudi Arabian relationship was the Iraqi attack on Kuwait in August 1990 (cf. Section 8.4). The attack immediately triggered the US–Saudi alliance. Symbolically the first military operation of the US was named 'Desert Shield'. The aim was to protect Saudi Arabia. The operation gave Saudi Arabia weapons deliveries and military support on a tremendous scale during 1990–1991, but the subsequent operation 'Desert Storm', in which the US-led 'Coalition of the willing' attacked the Iraqi forces in Kuwait, also created some lasting negative effects on the US–Saudi Arabian relationship as US military personnel became present in the Kingdom. This provoked Islamic fundamentalists in both Iran and Saudi Arabia. Bomb attacks against US facilities and personnel in Saudi Arabia attest to the level of tension created. It worsened the dilemma of the royal family, between the need for US support against external security threats and the possibility that this support itself increases internal security threats, most vividly demonstrated by the emergence of Usama bin Laden and Al-Qaeda: "Radical Islamists movements which had been funded by Saudi money, and shaped by Whahabi precepts, were now directing their critique at the Saudi regime" (Niblock, 2006, p. 153).

In 2001, the 9/11 terrorist attack changed the US–Saudi alliance overnight. Most of the hijackers were Saudi Arabian citizens. In the eyes of US leadership, the Saudi royal family seemed unable to control its own Islamists, let alone the global threat they constituted. They also feared popular reaction towards Saudis in the US. About six hundred Saudis left the US in the weeks following 9/11. Saudi Arabia neither participated nor publicly supported the next two major US military operations in Afghanistan and Iraq. In 2003, all US troops were withdrawn from Saudi Arabia. On both sides the alliance became contested and debated. The Saudi regime had to tread extremely carefully in order to preserve the security guarantee from the US and not provoke more internal radical Islamists, with the potential of undermining the regime itself. In the US, the alliance became subject to open public debate, and criticism. "Even with these heavy pressures on the relationship, however, oil continued to provide a massive incentive for the United States and Saudi Arabia to cooperate" (Colgan, 2013, p. 241). The statement made by Gregory Gause III in the aftermath of 9/11 also calls for reflection on the US–Saudi Arabian alliance. "We [the US] should think of Saudi Arabia not as a friend, or as an enemy, but as a strategic partner on a number of very important issues for our interests: most importantly, on oil issues and the stability of the Persian/Arabian Gulf area."[9]

7.5 THE IRAQ WAR

The outbreak of some wars is more easily explained than others. The US invasion of Iraq in 2003 can be compared with the outbreak of the First World War, as particularly hard to explain (Cramer & Thrall, 2012, p. 3). Robert Jervis (2012, p. 28), quotes Richard Haass, Director of the Policy Planning Staff in the Bush administration, and thus as close to the decisions as any, stating, "I will go to my grave not fully understanding why." The history behind the invasion, and the deplorable developments in Iraq since, is well-known, and outside the scope of this book. However, among the most popular explanations for the invasion, were various US motives related to the Iraqi oil resources. Thus, the Iraqi War is an excellent case for reflections related to the relationship between US foreign policy and oil. It is very easy to make causation from the correlation between two facts: Iraq has large oil resources and the US did invade the country in March 2003. Here I will propose a different twist, and ask: if oil was the motive, to what extent could occupying Iraq be an adequate instrument? (Claes, 2005).

The most immediate argument suggests that the United States was concerned about its own dwindling oil reserves, and thus occupied Iraq in order to add the Iraqi oil reserves to US controlled oil reserves. A moderate version of this argument is that the US is concerned with the general supply of oil, and thus wanted to ensure that Iraqi oil would continue to flow to the market, preferably in increased quantities. The war did coincide with the so-called peak oil debate (cf. Section 2.2.3). This idea of an emerging depletion of global oil resources has later been dismissed. But this does not exclude the possibility that such an argument could have been part of the US administration's decision in 2003. The energy policy of the Bush administration reveals a strong belief in the threat of shortage. Even though the oil was available in ample quantities globally, the United States could suffer a shortage, as was the case in 1973, when the US was the main target of the embargo. The reference to the 1970s was made very clear in the introduction to the 2001 report of the National Energy Policy Development Group which warned, "America in the year 2001 faces the most serious energy shortage since the oil embargoes of the 1970s."[10] Nevertheless, even then, any sober analysis would have told the US administration that there were plenty of oil reserves available and that the change of control over the Iraqi reserves would not play an important market role. "In the run-up to our current misadventures in Iraq, Deputy Secretary of Defense Paul Wolfowitz famously demonstrated his ignorance of the region and lack of understanding of oil economics when he predicted that the Iraqi oil industry would finance Iraq's reconstruction and pay for the costs of the war."[11] Separating the oil security of the United States from the rest of the world is a perspective uninformed of the structural changes that have taken place in the international oil market over the last three decades. The dominance of the vertical integrated oil companies is long gone (cf. Section 5.4), and the close contractual relations between buyers and sellers has been replaced by an international around the clock oil trading market, where single cargos of oil might be sold dozens of times before finally arriving at the refinery. Under these market conditions the producers have ceded control of the final destination of the cargos sold. The prominent perspective of energy independence in the political debate related to the Iraq war missed the fact that the oil market had turned it into a matter of energy interdependence, not independence (Verrastro et al., 2004, p. 2). However, supply stability should not be confused with price stability. One could very well have a situation with ample supplies, but where the price fluctuated widely, and became a heavy economic burden for the oil consumers. Then the question becomes whether or not it is possible for the United States to use political means to control oil prices.

During the late 1980s and early 1990s, one of the most prominent features of oil trading was the increased activity in the paper market or semi-paper market. The forward market is actually a market for spot transactions in which oil is traded for delivery at a future time. So the forward market is a semi-paper market, as it is actual physical crude that is traded. A more genuine paper market is the so-called futures market. Futures contracts are at the outset designed for financial purposes. In contrast to a physical market, in a futures market "the trader will buy or sell not because she/he has a physical need for the item but entirely on the basis of expectations about subsequent price movements" (Mabro, 2005, p. 11). The futures market reduces not only the buyers' costs of ensuring access to the commodity, but also the producers' access to market outlets. Fixing the price of oil through political decisions by the oil producers is no longer an option. The only way to have effect on the market price is to influence the oil traders' perception of under- or over-supply (Claes, 2010). As argued above, oil from the Middle East is important in the global oil market, as about a third of the world's oil supply comes from the area and the fact that two-thirds of the world's proven oil reserves are located in the region. Nine percent of the global reserves are located in Iraq. But it is a prodigious leap from acknowledging that Iraq has the geological potential to become a major producer to claiming that the one who controls Iraqi oil also controls the world oil price.

Although beyond the scope of this book, the potential economic gains to the US from the Iraqi war have to be compared to the costs. In this respect it is sufficient to direct the reader to the detailed discussion in the book with the telling title, *The Three Trillion Dollar War – the True Costs of the Iraq Conflict* (Stiglitz & Bilmes, 2008). The oil price effect, if any, is obviously far from compensating the costs of the Iraqi war. In line with the focus of this book, the conclusion of oil as a motive for the Iraqi war is that neither the security of supply nor the price of oil can be effectively controlled by occupying Iraq: "Trying to shape world oil prices on the basis of a war in Iraq is sort of like trying to sculpt an iceberg with the Titanic" (Cordesman, 2002, p. 17).

7.6   THE SHALE OIL REVOLUTION

Technological change can have immediate implications for the economics
and politics of energy. There have been several technological improvements
in the oil industry. As late as 1972 offshore oil accounted for only 5 percent
of global production. Today this figure is about 30 percent. In the 1990s
the drilling technology was revolutionized, making it possible to extend
oil wells horizontally, with a range today of up to 10–15 kilometers. This
has dramatically increased the recovery rate and reduced the number
of wells necessary to drill into the individual reservoir. Since 2008, the
introduction of horizontal drilling in the exploration of oil and gas in rock
formations has contributed, together with more efficient fracking, to the
so-called shale gas and tight oil revolution (Aquilera & Radetzki, 2016,
pp. 81–83).[12] The presence of such resources has been known for decades,
but the technological change over the last two decades has made them
commercially viable in large scales. IEA finds the total amount of remaining technically recoverable tight oil in the world to be 436 billion barrels,
constituting 7 percent of overall technically recoverable oil resources (IEA,
2017, p. 175). As discussed in Section 2.2.1, there are important differences
between technically recoverable resources, and so-called proven reserves
that are possible and profitable to extract immediately. In 1996 US proven
reserves was estimated to 29.8 billion barrels, a figure which by 2006 had
dropped slightly to 29.4 billion barrels. In 2016, the US proven reserves
was estimated to 48 billion barrels: an increase of more than 60 percent.[13]
US tight oil production increased from about 500,000 barrels per day in
2008 to reach almost 5 million barrels per day in 2015. The US Energy
Information Administration (EIA) estimates that US tight oil production
would reach 7 million barrels per day by 2040.[14] The increase in production
follows from rapidly falling production costs, as is usual with new technology. "Efficiency gains in the shale sector have been large and accelerating
and are now hovering at around 25 percent a year . . . In the oil sector, most
drilling now brings adequate return on investment at prices below $50 per
barrel, and within a few years, that level could be under $40 per barrel"
(Morse, 2014, pp. 3, 6).

With a trend of sustained level of consumption and downward domestic
production, a future of increased oil imports seemed to be the destiny of
the world's most powerful nation – a situation deemed unacceptable by the
last eight presidents. The import share had been increasing since the days
of President Nixon. The future as an import-dependent oil-consuming
country was certain. This is just one example of the conventional wisdom:
"Oil import levels will range between 65 and 75 percent of total demand by
2025. The natural gas situation is almost the same" (Verrastro et al., 2004,

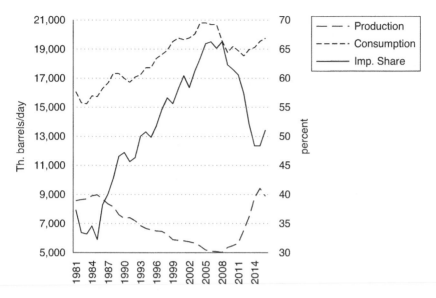

Source: BP (2017).

Figure 7.1 *US production consumption (th. barrels per day), and import share (percent) of crude oil and petroleum products, 1981–2016*

p. 3). The shale gas and tight oil revolution changed all of this (Figure 7.1). In September 2017, the oil import level was 49.5 percent. At the same time, the US became a net exporter of natural gas for the first time since 1958.

The importance of reducing US oil import dependency is portrayed as a matter of setting the country free. As an illustration, the Citigroup report on the effect of tight oil is called: *Energy 2020: Independence Day* (Morse et al., 2013). Newspapers made comments like this: "The shale energy revolution is likely to shift the tectonic plates of global power in ways that are largely beneficial to the West and reinforce U.S. power and influence during the first half of this century."[15] Daniel Yergin connected the dots by pointing to how the first oil shock of 1973 created incentives to develop oil fields outside of the Middle East, in particular in the North Sea and Alaska. The current tight oil revolution follows the same logic. Since it involves the development of domestic US resources, the economic benefits are even higher, as the tight oil industry creates jobs, investment and increases household income in the US.[16] With a reduced share of oil import, US energy security increases. Amid this euphoric mood of energy independence, it seems appropriate to mention that the US still imports about half of its oil consumption, most of it from the Western hemisphere.

(see Figure 7.2). Saudi Arabia has had downstream activities in the US for many decades, including a joint venture refining company between a US subsidiary of Shell and a subsidiary of Saudi Aramco. Although this joint venture was split up in 2017, Saudi Aramco seems to extend its downstream activities in the US. Among the minor exporters, we find Iraq, Kuwait and Algeria with a combined export to the US of 816,000 barrels per day in 2016. None of these are particularly antagonistic toward the US. One interesting challenge for an adequate US foreign oil policy is the discrepancy between public perception and reality regarding the source of oil imports. Figure 7.2 shows the actual distribution of imports and the distribution of imports in the eyes of the US public. The difference between the two figures is striking.

7.7 US, CHINA AND THE PERSIAN GULF

By securing oil supplies domestically, or at least on the home continent, the US gains freedom of action that could be used to pursue more adventurous projects in the Middle East. After the experience in Iraq and Afghanistan, this seems less likely, at least for the foreseeable future. However, the US might turn its attention elsewhere:

> The move towards US energy independence will give the country additional freedom to focus attention, and its diplomatic, military and other resources, on the Asia-Pacific region. This leaves China in the awkward position of needing to work with the US to ensure stability in the Middle East, but in so doing enabling the US to become more active in Asia. (Robinson & Qinhua, 2013, pp. 4–5)

Oil producers outside of North America will be able to redirect their oil exports to other markets, particularly the still-growing Asian market. In particular, the oil trade relationship between the Middle East producers and China seems destined to grow stronger. This creates a trilateral strategic interplay between the US, Chinese and Middle Eastern oil producers, particularly Saudi Arabia. Until recently, many believed this relationship would be characterized by increased rivalry over diminishing resources: "As global demand for energy, particularly from China, continues to increase exponentially, the stage is set for intense competition over the remaining oil and gas in the Middle East" (Dorraj & English, 2012, p. 174). With the US approaching self-sufficiency, the fundamental premises for the strategic interaction among these actors have changed. The US might want to reduce its engagement in the Middle East. The increased domestic oil production makes it possible. The question is whether it will be a geopolitically prudent strategy. China wants to increase its control over

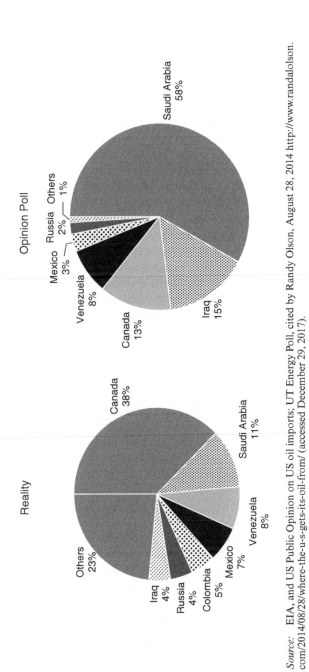

Source: EIA, and US Public Opinion on US oil imports; UT Energy Poll, cited by Randy Olson, August 28, 2014 http://www.randalolson. com/2014/08/28/where-the-u-s-gets-its-oil-from/ (accessed December 29, 2017).

Figure 7.2   US oil imports 2016 by country

oil supply sources. The most important ones are the producers around the Persian Gulf, in particular Saudi Arabia. All three actors – the US, China and Saudi Arabia – have a dilemma, strongly influenced by the actions of the others.

The US has so far provided important collective goods for all actors in the oil market – for instance by ensuring freedom of navigation through the Hormuz strait, and other chokepoints in oil trade, and securing the political stability of Saudi Arabia, the dominant exporter and swing producer. If the US wants to save money and let others contribute more to the provision of these collective goods, the uncertainty regarding the security of global supplies might increase. Neither the European allies nor China has anything approaching the naval and military capacity of the US.

China has the opposite dilemma. Should it invest what is necessary to take over the US role as guardian of the straits, and secure Saudi Arabia? Such a strategy could easily be perceived as a challenge by the US, and would in any case be costly. A more subtle strategy is not to challenge the US, but remain 'number two' and let 'number one' provide the collective goods. We have a kind of 'Chicken-game' between the US and China. If the US decides to leave the Middle East it will be easier and more necessary for China to move in. Should the US remain in the Middle East, there is no reason for China to move in and create a potential confrontation with the US.

Saudi Arabia faces the dilemma of choosing an ally between the US and China. The US has proved its ability to secure the Kingdom, but might become less willing to do so in future. China might be willing, but is so far unable. The Saudi strategic dilemma is two-folded: First, does Saudi Arabia risk having an ally that is willing but unable to protect the Kingdom from military threats? Second, does Saudi Arabia risk having a security guarantee from an ally that is not dependent on Saudi Arabia for its energy security? Saudi Arabia might prefer not to have to choose between China and the US.

The United States and China have a strong common interest in a stable and low oil price. In order to achieve this in the present global oil market, output from key oil-producing areas has to be perceived as reliable. In most oil provinces outside the Middle East this presumes continuous investment in new production capacity. The presence of available low-cost resources is not a problem in the Middle East, however. Although the accessibility of the oil is not an issue, political conflicts and regime instability are regarded as far more prominent in this region compared to other oil provinces. From a more academic point of view the puzzle is rather why the oil flow from the Middle East has been so reliable given the amount of political conflicts that have occurred in this region. The Middle East is by far the oil province with the lowest production costs, and it has the greatest ability to serve as the marginal supplier, but it also comes with a high level of political instability. Convincing the oil traders that Middle East supplies are reliable demands the use of political means. Although the military presence and support of regime stability in the region can be costly for the US, it can be a small price to pay for the stable and reliable flow of low cost oil and thus a reasonably low price per barrel both in the global market and in the US.

7.8 OIL – A BLIND SPOT IN THE US HEGEMONY

An energy independent US might increase multilateralism in the field of energy, or create a more isolationistic US energy strategy, relying on its own resources and becoming less politically engaged in international energy affairs and markets. President Donald Trump has taken several initiatives indicating the latter option. Nevertheless, US interests in the oil market have become more mixed. The dilemma arising is due to the fact that although the cost of producing tight oil in the US is declining rapidly, the level is way above the average production costs in the Middle East. This is no problem as long as the world market price is far above the cost level of the US tight oil producers. However, this was not the case after the price fall of November 2014.

As indicated above, even without US imports from the region, the Middle East countries are paramount for the determination of the market price of crude oil. Although it will matter for the US trade balance if the oil is produced in the US or abroad, US car drivers will be equally affected should the price go up. In this respect, increased US oil production will benefit all oil consumers by putting a downward pressure on the world market price of oil.

This chapter started with establishing a connection between the international oil market and US hegemonic power in international relations. The relationship between oil and US political power is obvious. Stokes and Raphael (2010, p. 38) make this connection explicit: "US hegemony within the postwar order era has been reliant to no small extent upon Washington's ability to exert control over oil reserves in the global South as well as the conditions under which those reserves are released onto international markets." However, the direction and strength of the influence between the two phenomena is more complicated to untangle, as this chapter has tried to demonstrate. In particular, Washington's ability to exert control over oil reserves in the global South has been questioned and at least modified. No one should be surprised that a country that consumes a quarter of the world's oil finds the region holding two-thirds of the world's oil reserves to be of the highest political importance. This has been confused with the idea that the US defines the geopolitics of the Middle East. The structural conditions in the oil market, and the costs connected with the use of military force, suggest that any direct influence on the world oil market price is hard to achieve, even for the world's hegemonic power – the United States. If US hegemonic power is so strong and dominant, should not the politics of the Middle East and the international oil market have been working according to the interests of the United States?

> If the United States were able to wish into existence a world that would favor its terms of trade and superpower status, all NOCs would be privatized, foreign investors would be treated the same as local companies and OPEC would be disbanded, allowing free trade and competitive markets to deliver the energy that is needed worldwide at prices determined solely by the market.[17]

This is not what we have observed.

Furthermore, the dependency on imported oil at occasionally high prices has imposed costs on the US economy. Estimates suggests that the total cost to the US economy from 1970 to 1999 amounts to more than $10 trillion (2017 dollars) (Duffield, 2008, p. 61). These are the direct economic costs of importing oil. Duffield extends his study to include the costs of both economic and political policy responses aimed at moderating negative effects and reducing the risks of foreign oil dependency. This adds an *annual* burden of between $30 and $50 billion (Duffield, 2008, p. 206). It is hard to imagine that the hegemonic power in the world would incur economic costs of this magnitude if it had full political control over the behavior of key actors in the international oil market.

The conclusion is rather that, since the beginning of the 1970s, the United States is a *policy-taker* in the international oil market, not a *policy-maker*. The US has primarily struggled to compensate for its lack of influence in this market, using whatever power it found available: diplomatic skills, economic rewards or military force. The use of these instruments has been a sign of weakness, not strength. We should not confuse the fact that the US influences actors in the oil market and the Middle East, which it clearly does, with the illusion that the US deliberately designs and controls the Middle East and the international oil market, which it does not.

NOTES

1. FRUS, 1950, vol. 5, pp. 1190–1191, cited in (Yergin, 1991, pp. 427–428).
2. Quoted from the Egyptian magazine al-Musawwar in *Middle East Economic Survey*, and subsequently in Golub (1985, p. 9).

3. On August 23, Sadat visited Faisal in Riyadh, and probably informed him of his plans for war with Israel (J. Robinson, 1988, pp. 85–86; Schneider, 1983, p. 219).
4. Speech on American television, printed in *Petroleum Intelligence Weekly*, September 10, 1973, and referred to in (Schneider, 1983, p. 220).
5. The marker crude posting was raised to $11.651 for Saudi crude 34° Ras Tanura f.o.b.
6. There are different opinions about who initiated the auction plan. Moran (1981, p. 255) claims that it was US Treasury Secretary William Simon who "got the leadership of Saudi Arabia to announce publicly an auction"; Robinson (1988, p. 137) argues that it was Yamani's idea.
7. Parra provides a detailed argument for this. He refers to public statements by the then Treasury Secretary, William Simon like "we had to make sure our allies were in strong positions," concluding that Kissinger was the best friend that the OPEC [price] hawks ever had and his decision not to press seriously for lower prices was a monumental error (Parra, 2004, pp. 204–205).
8. Summary of National Energy Policy Plan, US Department of Energy, Energy Insider, Washington, DC, August 3, 1981, p. 3, cited in (Lieber, 1992, p. 157).
9. "The future of U.S.–Saudi Relations," testimony before Subcommittee on Middle East and South Asia, House Committee on International Relations, May 22, 2002.
10. "National Energy Policy," Report of the National Energy Policy Development Group, May 2001 (US Government Printing Office).
11. Chas. W. Freeman, Jr., President, Middle East Policy Council, in Verrastro, Placke, and Hegburg (2004, p. 1).
12. Tight oil is oil that has not yet migrated to a conventional trap, but instead remains in the porosity of the source rock unit in which it was generated. Shale oil is also used to describe this type of oil.
13. All figures from *BP Statistical Review of World Energy*, June 2017.
14. "Future U.S. tight oil and shale gas production depends on resources, technology, markets," *Today in Energy*, August 22 2016. Energy Information Agency https://www.eia.gov/todayinenergy/detail.php?id=27612 (accessed December 29, 2017).
15. Alan Riley: "The Shale Revolution's Shifting Geopolitics," *The New York Times*, December 25, 2012.
16. Daniel Yergin: "Why OPEC No Longer Calls the Shots," *The Wall Street Journal*, October 14, 2013.
17. 'The Changing Role of National Oil Companies in International Energy Markets' Baker Institute Policy Report no. 35, April 2007, p. 17. Oddly enough, (Stokes & Raphael, 2010, p. 45) include the same quote, only a few pages after their claim regarding US hegemony.

8. Oil and regional security

8.1 NATIONAL SECURITY

The previous chapter ended with the conclusion that the world's hegemonic power – the United States – cannot fully control the Middle East. This generates the question of whether anyone else can. The Middle East is a hotspot for both interstate and intrastate conflicts. I will deal with them in turn, focusing the role of oil in Middle East interstate conflicts here and the role of oil in intrastate conflicts in the next chapter. There are a number of conflict dimensions present in the Middle East: ethnicity, religion, overlapping territorial claims, waterways, great power influence (both during colonial times and the Cold War), and, of course, resources. Today the Middle East holds 48 percent of the world's proven oil reserves, down from 58 percent 20 years ago. The Middle East also represents 34.5 percent of world oil production, and 46 percent of inter-regionally traded oil (BP, 2017). In addition, the average production costs in the Middle East are probably one-tenth of the average costs elsewhere. It is obvious that the oil resources of the Middle East have political importance. The aim of this chapter is to relate these oil resources to the political conflicts between states inside the region. I start out with the theoretical model of how oil can cause leaders of oil-rich states to follow an aggressive foreign policy developed by Jeff Colgan (2013b) in Section 8.2. Then I explore two empirical cases: the Iran–Iraq war (1980–1988), and the Iraqi invasion of Kuwait (1990) (Sections 8.3 and 8.4). There are reasons to consider the interstate relations between the countries surrounding the Persian Gulf more narrowly. In their overarching study of the regional level in international relations, Buzan and Wæver (2003) categorize the Persian Gulf as a sub-region of the Middle East. Gregory Gause III (2010) has developed this perspective in more empirical detail, which will be the discussed in Section 8.5. Finally, I discuss the paradox of oil cooperation in such a conflict-ridden region (Section 8.6). First, a discussion of the concept of national security is necessary.

In the previous chapter we discussed the concept of 'energy security' which was defined as "adequate, reliable supplies of energy at reasonable prices in ways that do not jeopardize major national values and objectives" (Yergin, 1988, p. 111). This concept is not directly related to the general concept of 'national security', which is the starting point of this chapter, although some conceptual connections are relevant (Szulecki, 2018). National security has to do with the absence of threats toward core values. For the individual, the absence of threats to life and the means of subsistence are fundamental (cf. Section 1.2). National security would then relate to the preservation of the collective of citizens within the state's borders. The prime caretaker of the security of the citizens is the government. "No purpose of government is more central than the protection of its citizens' physical security. Philosophically, many thinkers have held that this, in fact, is the ultimate reason why humankind forms governments" (Smoke, 1975, p. 247). In states governed by law, institutions are established to protect the citizens, the judicial system and the police. These institutions have the authority to legitimately authorize and use force against those constituting a threat to the life of others. Between states such authoritative institutions do not exist. Thus, the international system is regarded as anarchic. It follows that states have to protect themselves against external threats. This international system is a self-help system, and thus creates a security dilemma as the defensive measures of one state can be interpreted as offensive measures by another, and vice versa. Such dynamics can be especially prevalent in regional settings such as the Middle East.

According to Buzan (1991, p. 8), the concept of security has been dominated by the concept of power in the literature on international relations. "[R]educed to little more than a synonym for power," he claims, "security had little independent relevance in wider systemic terms." Buzan quotes several definitions that highlight, in his view, important aspects of national security, such as "the centrality of values, the timing and intensity of threats and the political nature of security as an objective of states" (Buzan, 1991, p. 18). He goes on to divide the security concept into five categories related to the sectors affecting national security. Three of these are particularly relevant for this chapter:

- *Military security* concerns the two-level interplay of the armed offensive and defensive capabilities of states, and states' perceptions of each other's intentions.
- *Political security* concerns the organizational stability of states, systems of government and the ideologies that give them legitimacy.
- *Economic security* concerns access to the resources, finance and markets necessary to sustain acceptable levels of welfare and state power (Buzan, 1991, p. 19).

These relate to the physical protection of the citizens of the state, the protection of the state institutions and the protection of the economic welfare of the citizens. Self-preservation is the fundamental goal of the state. In certain circumstances the state might have to resort to the use of power. In order to do so the state must have the capabilities to exercise power. These capabilities can be physical (such as oil reserves in the ground), organizational, financial, technological, or purely political (including the deployment of military forces). Usually, military force, or coercive force, is regarded as an ultimate capability. "Survival is the primary goal of all states, and in the worst situations, force is ultimately necessary to guarantee survival. Thus military force is always a central component of national power" (Keohane and Nye, 1977, p. 27). In addition to such fundamental resources, states need the skill and will to use their power resources effectively (Baldwin, 1979, p. 163). The resources themselves are of no use unless the state is able and willing to use them. Another problem is the context of power resources: "the capabilities (or potential power) of an actor must be set in the context of a 'policy-contingency-framework' specifying who is trying (or might try) to get whom to do what" (Baldwin, 1979, p. 164). Particular types of capabilities might not be effective in certain situations or in the context of specific issues. Baldwin argues that political power resources are relatively non-fungible, compared to, for instance, money.

These concepts and arguments are particularly relevant as we approach the intertwined relationship between oil and security in the Middle East. Can the possession of oil resources increase the oil state's security, or does it make it susceptible to more threats? Can military capabilities be used to gain access to oil resources, or does the use of force destroy or reduce the access to oil resources? I think the answer to these questions is yes – both, that is, the relationship between oil and security depends on the contextual factors surrounding the specific situation of the individual actor or group of actors. The Middle East is a region where countries play out an intrinsic set of strategies to achieve both security, power and oil wealth, at the same time.

8.2   OIL AND INTERSTATE CONFLICT

Oil resources can be related to international conflicts in a number of ways. Colgan (2013a, p. 152) identifies eight different causal mechanisms, many of which are discussed elsewhere in this book as part of other topics than oil and interstate conflict. A too narrow focus on energy security would miss oil-related factors that are unrelated to the energy consumers' search for security of supplies, but still important for political conflicts. For instance the Iraqi claim that Kuwait tapped a border crossing oil field was probably one of several motives for the attack in 1990. But this has nothing to do with consumers access to reliable and affordable oil. A too broad approach would risk including international conflicts where energy is not the cause, motive or target of the parties in conflict, but, nevertheless, important for the conflict itself. For instance, in no other conflict has oil played a more crucial role than the Second World War. We would, nevertheless, find it inappropriate to call the Second World War an oil war, or suggest that oil was the primary cause of the war. Although oil was a crucial motive behind particular battles and a vital factor in determining the outcome of other important battles during the Second World War. Thus, I'm cherry-picking two mechanisms from Colgan's list: oil resources as a possible target or motive for interstate conflict, and oil resources as a factor creating a more aggressive foreign policy. The two cases described in sections 8.3 and 8.4 are related to each of these mechanisms.

In his book *Petro-Aggression – When Oil Causes War*, Jeff Colgan (2013b) outlines a theory which relates oil resources to international conflicts. His starting point is in line with the discussions in Chapters 3 and 9 of this book, as he identifies an apparent paradox in the resource curse literature. "[O]il generates stability in one sense (i.e., persistent autocratic regimes) while simultaneously generating instability in another sense (i.e., frequent violent rebellions) . . . Thus even in the face of frequent domestic conflicts . . . petrostate leaders tend to have greater domestic political autonomy" (Colgan, 2013b, p. 29). Colgan then establishes a crucial interaction between oil income and revolutionary government in fomenting an aggressive foreign policy (Colgan, 2013b, pp. 32–37). Based on empirical data from the Correlates of War dataset (see, for instance Gleditsch, Salehyan, and Schultz, 2008; Weeks, 2012), he finds that petrostates with a revolutionary government are strongly overrepresented as aggressors in so-called 'militarized interstate disputes' (MID).[1] In essence, the "interaction of oil and revolution often leads to a state with unrestrained, warlike government capable of harnessing a significant portion of the state's resources toward international conflict" (Colgan, 2013b, p. 88). Colgan's study supports the argument that oil, combined with revolutionary government, fuels aggressive foreign policies in petro-states.

Another aspect following from the starting point of this chapter is the degree to which oil resources represent a target, or motive, of interstate conflicts. "Oil is a highly valuable, and lootable commodity, meaning it can be exploited relatively easily and profitably by a new owner. The presence or perception of oil reserves therefore creates a significant incentive for conquest of the associated territory" (Colgan, 2013a, p. 154). Colgan finds the Iraqi invasion of Kuwait in 1990 to be a prime example of this kind of 'resource war', or 'oil war' to be more precise. This argument depends on his claim that "the opportunity to seize control of Kuwait's oilfields and extend Iraq's influence over the Organization of the Petroleum Exporting Countries (OPEC) was a powerful incentive for an invasion" (Colgan, 2013a, p. 154).

One of the most profiled advocates of oil as an explanatory factor behind international conflicts – from the Arctic, through to the Caspian Sea and Africa, and the Persian Gulf – is Michael T. Klare: "The struggle over oil and natural gas is driven by two fundamental considerations: a widely shared belief that energy constitutes a vital commodity whose acquisition is a matter of national security, and a geographic disconnect between the major sources of hydrocarbons and the major consuming nations" (Klare, 2017, p. 23). When it comes to the US invasion of Iraq in 2003, discussed in the previous chapter, Klare is crystal clear: "Certainly anyone who was paying close attention to the administration's planning for the invasion would have seen ample evidence of Washington's interest in securing control over Iraq's prolific oil reservoirs" (see also Klare, 2004, pp. 98–101; Klare, 2012a, p. 129). Emily Meierding (2016, p. 259) is somewhat critical of the evidence for the decisive role of oil behind interstate wars. "Most people assume that competition over control of oil resources is a significant cause of interstate conflict. However, there is little empirical evidence to support this claim." Although she agrees that oil is an "extremely valuable natural resource" she asserts that "proponents of what I label the oil war hypothesis err by overlooking the extensive obstacles to seizing, producing, and marketing foreign oil resources" (Meierding, 2016, p. 260). Meierding provides empirical observations on both the Iran–Iraq war and Iraq–Kuwait war dismissing oil as the prime motive behind the conflicts. As the following exposition shows, several oil-related physical features were affected by the two wars, such as oil fields, terminals, other facilities, and tanker vessels. The political relations among oil producers in general, and the Persian Gulf producers in particular, were also affected. Nevertheless, I follow Meierding's skepticism against claiming that it was all about oil.

8.3   THE IRAN–IRAQ WAR, 1980–1988

Iran and Iraq have been involved in most military conflicts between oil-producing countries. With one exception – a border dispute between Saudi Arabia and Qatar in 1992, which killed two border-guards – Iran or Iraq has been involved in all disputes between OPEC members since the Second World War. Iran and Iraq have never been on the same side as any other OPEC member during the same period, except for the Kuwait–Iraq War of 1961 where Iran supported Kuwait (Claes, 2001, p. 101). Most prominent among these conflicts is the war between the two countries from 1980 to 1988.

The factors behind the Iran–Iraq War were many. Traditional conflicts between Sunni and Shiite Muslims, historical conflicts concerning disputed land and river areas, and expansionist objectives by former leaders have created clashes between the two countries for centuries. Thus, Iraq's declaration of war on Iran on September 22, 1980, was in line with a traditional conflict pattern in the region. Meierding (2016, p. 282) very clearly dismisses the importance of oil as a motive for Iraq's action, asserting that "seizing foreign petroleum resources was not one of Saddam's initial aims in the conflict. Instead, his goal was to retake only 335 square kilometers of territory along the central portion of Iran and Iraq's boundary, and to regain full control over the Shatt al-'Arab waterway."

Iraqi troops soon made substantial advances into Iran, but then Iraq stopped and offered to negotiate. The Iranians refused, gaining time to mobilize. At the end of 1981, the Iraqi advances came to a complete halt. In the spring of 1982, the Iranian counterattacks had substantial success, and the temptation to continue into Iraq became irresistible for Tehran. Although the Iranian forces gained some Iraqi territory, the war soon ran into a stalemate; neither of the parties was able to advance forcefully over a longer period. Iran conducted several offensives against Iraq between 1984 and 1987, but none of such a magnitude to decisively end the war. In February 1984, as Iran started the first of these so-called final offensives, the war turned to the Persian Gulf waters, and the tanker war commenced. Iraq attacked ships going into Iranian ports, probably with the aim of provoking an Iranian blockade of the Strait of Hormuz, which in turn would prompt the Western countries to take more severe action against Iran. Iran did not fall for the trap, but launched attacks on tankers serving Kuwaiti and Saudi Arabian ports in order to deter these countries from supporting Iraq. By 1985, the intensity and brutality of the land war had increased again. The use of chemical weapons contributed to a substantial increase in civilian deaths; estimates range between 450,000 and 730,000 on the Iranian side, and 150,000 and 340,000 on the Iraqi side (Cordesman and Wagner, 1990, p. 3). Combining the direct and indirect costs of the warfare, estimates have been put at $627 billion for Iran and $561 billion for Iraq.[2] Most important for the oil market was the war in the Persian Gulf initiated in 1984. Three hundred ships were hit from 1984 to 1988. Furthermore, Iraq tried to destroy Iranian oil-loading facilities, particularly on Kharg Island. Although Iraq received laser-guided bombs and navigation equipment from France, the number and small size of loading points at the Kharg installations made the bombing ineffective. Iranian oil production varied during this period but, on average, a substantial level was sustained.

The West did not pay much attention to the conflict until 1984. Not even the Iranian advances into Iraq caused much concern. One reason was that, until June 1982, there was virtually no activity at sea. The first sea war efforts were also characterized as small, single attacks and not part of a broader strategy of a naval war battle. The oil production of the two belligerent countries was already low, so this did not change the flow of oil from the Persian Gulf. While Iran in 1984 started using the "human wave" tactic, Iraq escalated the war into the Gulf waters. This obviously brought the warfare closer to the other Gulf countries' territories, and they were soon directly affected. On May 14, two Kuwaiti tankers were attacked, followed by an attack on a Saudi Arabian tanker on May 17. This development also brought the United States into the conflict, as Washington decided to supply Saudi Arabia with 400 Stinger anti-aircraft missiles (Kechichian, 1990, p. 100). Saudi Arabia was set to defend the Gulf waters. On June 5, 1984, a Royal Saudi Air Force jet shot down an Iranian F-4 Phantom fighter-bomber. The kingdom tried not to let this incident broaden the war.[3] However, after this point the other Gulf countries' ability to mediate or end the conflict by other diplomatic means was severely weakened (Kechichian, 1990, p. 1). The next major shift in the war came when Iraq intensified its attacks on Kharg Island and the Iranian shuttle traffic to the more distant islands of Sirri and Larak, and the Iranians intensified their attacks on sea traffic to pro-Iraqi countries like Kuwait and Saudi Arabia. Since Iran's air force was insignificant, its light naval forces conducted hit-and-run attacks on tankers, a kind of naval guerrilla warfare. Thus, the ability to actually sink supertankers was limited until Iran was supplied with heavier rockets, particularly by China. By 1986, the Iranian attacks on ships in the Gulf increased, and the attacks became more severe. In January 1987, Kuwait sought US naval protection of its tankers by suggesting that the ships be "re-flagged" to fly the "Stars and Stripes." Kuwait also leased three Soviet tankers, which the Soviet Union agreed to escort. By June, the first ships with US flags and protected by the US Navy entered the Gulf. This led to an increased internationalization of the conflict. Both superpowers were now directly involved in the Gulf War. In spring of 1987, Iranian forces attacked two Soviet tankers. In May, Iraq attacked the US frigate *Stark*, killing thirty-seven mariners. This caused a political crisis in the United States, and Western public attention to the war increased dramatically. When Iran laid out mines that reached Kuwaiti ports, minesweepers were sent to the area, and a joint operation with Saudi Arabia, using Saudi Arabian AWACS (airborne warning and control system) surveillance planes, was established. On July 20, 1987, the UN Security Council passed UN Resolution 598, calling for an immediate cease-fire.

Saudi Arabia strengthened its position in the Gulf both as a result of the US presence and through its own military build-up. In particular, the Royal Saudi Air Force became the strongest air power in the region during this period. Saudi Arabia's increased self-confidence also meant that it became more willing to challenge Iran. After the eighth summit of the Gulf Cooperation Council (GCC) in 1987, the Saudi Arabian foreign minister, Prince Saudi-al-Faysal, stated that "the aim of the GCC countries [was] to end the war and put an end to Iranian attacks against the GCC states" (Kechichian, 1990, p.106). While Kuwait and Saudi Arabia wanted to take a tougher position against Iran, the United Arab Emirates and Oman sought continuous dialogue with Tehran (Kechichian, 1990, p. 106). Also the gunning down of 400 Iranian pilgrims in Mecca on July 31, 1987, must be understood as a result of a more potent and confident Saudi Arabian regime. The war thus influenced the overall power relations between the three major powers in the region.

The next question is what effects the war had on the economic oil-related relations between the affected countries. The price effect was short-term, and the lasting importance for the market was the disappearance of the two countries' production capacities. This made the hegemonic role of Saudi Arabia even more prominent, as these two countries, given their installed production capacity prior to the outbreak of the Iranian revolution, were the possible challengers to the Saudi Arabian position. The Iranian oil production had been about 6 million barrels per day (mbd) in September 1978, while Iraq produced about 3.5 mbd in the first half of 1980. With the outbreak of the war, the Iranian production fell from 1.3 mbd in August to 350,000 barrels in October. Iraqi production fell from 3.4 mbd to 500,000 barrels over the same period.

The war did have some direct consequences for cooperation inside OPEC. On November 4, 1980 a summit of heads of state was scheduled in Baghdad to celebrate the twentieth anniversary of the organization in its founding city. The meeting never took place. However, on December 15, 1980, the OPEC Conference met at Bali, with representatives of two belligerent parties. The head of the Iranian delegation, Oil Minister Javad Tondguyan, was in fact a war prisoner captured by Iraqi troops at the beginning of the month. Terzian (1985, pp. 286–287) describes how OPEC handled this first meeting after the war broke out:

> The Iranian delegation entered solemnly, bearing a portrait of their captured minister . . . installed the photo of Tondguyan on the chair reserved for the head of delegation and took their places behind it. Suharto, the President of Indonesia, arrived next and, after his inaugural speech, launched an appeal for a cessation of hostilities between Iraq and Iran . . . the Iraqi and Iranian delegations were given the floor. They exchanged endless accusations, each

country blaming the other for the war. Finally, when the diatribes were over, the ten other OPEC members adopted a resolution backing the call for peace issued by Indonesia. Once all these matters had been settled, the delegates moved on to the other items on the agenda, and it was business as usual.

The official OPEC reaction was expressed in very diplomatic terms:

> The Conference endorsed the sincere and honest appeal made by His Excellence the President of the Republic of Indonesia in his inauguration speech to the two Member Countries – Iran and Iraq – who are presently in dispute, to quickly seek the best possible solution to their conflict leading to a peaceful settlement of their differences. (OPEC, 1990, p. 192)

Due to the war, Iran became a pure price-taker, maximizing its oil exports. Iranian oil production rose throughout 1982, from 1.1 mbd in March to 2.8 mbd in December. On April 10, 1982, Syria cut off the Iraqi pipeline to the Mediterranean, cutting 400,000 bd of Iraqi export capacity. Iraqi production fell from 1.3 mbd in the first quarter to about 850,000 bd in the second half of 1982. The OPEC production quotas allocated to the two countries in April 1982 were 1.2 mbd each. At the 65th OPEC Conference in July 1982, Iran "demanded a quota of 2.5 mbd and that its increase should be taken from the Saudi share" (Skeet, 1988, p. 188). The boldness of this demand was fueled by the success on the battlefield. In 1982 Iran had stopped the Iraqi advances and was ready for its counterattack, and only weeks after the meeting, Iran invaded Iraq. The resolution of the 65th Conference simply states that "the Conference . . . decided to suspend the deliberations of the Conference until further notice" (OPEC, 1990, p. 204). Iran did not at all abide by its quota in the following months. On the battlefield the Iranian offensive was soon stopped, and the war became a war of attrition. Saudi Arabia and the other GCC countries became more relaxed, no longer fearing rapid Iranian expansion. They accordingly began to take a tougher stand against Iran, a stand that extended to the OPEC negotiations. A statement from the GCC oil ministers' meeting in Salala on October 14, illustrates this. "The other producers should know that the GCC Ministers expect them to shoulder their responsibilities and if they continue their misguided actions they will not be protected by the member countries from the GCC from the consequences of these actions"(Skeet, 1988, p. 189). In his opening address at the following OPEC meeting, the chairman of the Nigerian delegation, Alhaji Yahaya Dikko, with a clear reference to the above statement, said that "threats are never a basis for cooperation"(Evans, 1990, p. 607).

As discussed in Chapter 6, OPEC in this period tried to cut production in order to support the market price. Saudi Arabia was not allocated a quota but was officially given the role of "swing producer to supply the balancing quantities to meet market requirements" (OPEC, 1990, p. 208). Obviously, the following downswing of Saudi Arabia would have been harder had both Iran and Iraq had their exporting capacity intact. Given these facts, one should expect there to have been a turbulent situation when the war ended in 1988. However, by that time, the price had crashed (in 1986), and the market to some extent had taken into account the production capacity of the warring parties. As the war damage to oil installations was reduced through the US presence in the Gulf and the military build-up of the GCC countries, the production of Iran and Iraq picked up gradually, giving room for a smoother market adaptation.

The OPEC negotiations were only modestly influenced by the war. Aside from the incident involving the captured minister, and some exchange of accusations, the negotiations were business as usual. However, the power basis for the different countries' positions in OPEC and in the oil market in general, was dramatically changed by the war. Both Iran's and Iraq's oil production dropped significantly at the beginning of the war, from above 3 mbd to under 1 mbd each. Iran was able to regain a production level of about 2 mbd, while the Iraqi production remained at about 1 mbd until 1985, and then started to climb slowly. This severely reduced these two countries' positions in the OPEC bargaining and in the market compared with those of other countries like Saudi Arabia and the other Gulf states.

8.4 THE IRAQ–KUWAIT WAR, 1990

At the Arab Cooperation Council meeting in February 1990, Saddam Hussein asked King Hussein of Jordan and President Mubarak of Egypt to tell the Gulf States to forgive their loans to Iraq. Saddam perceived the loans as payment for Iraq defending the Gulf States against Iran. "Let the Gulf regimes know that if they do not give this money to me, I will know how to get it," he said.[4] At the Arab summit meeting in May 1990, Saddam argued that the continued violation of OPEC quotas by some Arab countries was equivalent to a declaration of war against Iraq. In a radio speech in July, his argument was even stronger:

> War is fought with soldiers and much harm is done by explosions, killing, and coup attempts – but it is also done by economic means. Therefore, we would ask our brothers who do not mean to wage war on Iraq: this is in fact a kind of war against Iraq . . . we have reached a point where we can no longer withstand pressure.[5]

In mid-July, the build-up of military forces and a diplomatic offensive began. On July 16, the Iraqi foreign minister, Tariq Aziz, delivered a

memorandum to the Secretary-General of the Arab League, presenting
the Iraqi indictment. Among other accusations, Kuwait and the United
Arab Emirates were accused of having created a glut in the oil market,
bringing prices down with devastating economic impact on the Middle
East and Iraq. Furthermore, Kuwait was claimed to have robbed Iraq by
setting up oil installations in the southern section of the Iraqi Rumaila oil
field (Freedman and Karsh, 1993, pp. 47–48). The following day, Saddam
increased the tension by an address to the nation. He accused Kuwait
and the United Arab Emirates of conspiring with world imperialism and
Zionism to "cut off the livelihood of the Arab nation," and threatened
that "if words fail to afford us protection, then we will have no choice but
to resort to effective action to put things right and ensure the restitution
of our rights."[6] Kuwait responded by "refuting the Iraqi accusations and
expressing strong indignation at Iraq's behavior" (Freedman and Karsh,
1993, p. 49). The Arab League tried to mediate and chose Husni Mubarak
as mediator. He went to Baghdad on July 24. Saddam Hussein assured
Mubarak that the military forces along the border were meant for intimidation, but asked Mubarak not to let the Kuwaitis know. "Brother Husni, do
not let the Kuwaitis rest easy before the meeting" (Freedman and Karsh,
1993, p. 50). When Mubarak arrived in Kuwait, Iraq announced that the
Kuwait issue had not been discussed in Baghdad. Mubarak was annoyed
and told the Kuwaitis that Saddam did not intend to invade. "When asked
what Saddam wanted the Egyptian leader replied: 'It seems he needs some
money'" (Freedman and Karsh, 1993, p. 50). On July 31, representatives
from Iraq and Kuwait met in Jeddah for negotiations after Iraq had placed
100,000 men along the Kuwaiti border. The talks ended the next day. The
parties disagreed on the reason for the breakdown of the talks. The Iraqi
version is that they asked for $10 billion in compensation for the Rumaila
oil field, but the Kuwaitis humiliated them by offering only $9 billion.
The Kuwaiti version is that Iraq was not content with $10 billion, but
demanded surrender of some disputed territories, as well as oil-pumping
rights inside Kuwait (Freedman and Karsh, 1993, pp. 59–60).

On August 2, 1990, Iraq invaded and occupied Kuwait. The Iraqi military operation was a success: Kuwait was occupied in twelve hours. The
attack involved about 140,000 men and 1,800 tanks. The 16,000-strong
Kuwaiti army was not fully mobilized in order not to provoke Iraq, and
was subsequently not able to resist the Iraqi attack. The emir, however,
managed to escape to Saudi Arabia with most of the royal family. The
Kuwaiti air force had made some attacks on the advancing Iraqi divisions,
and some sporadic fighting occurred, particularly around the royal palace.

Contrary to the Iran–Iraq War, the first phase of this conflict was
less characterized by changes on the battlefield and more by those in the

political and diplomatic arenas. Two developments made the invasion look less like a success for Saddam. The first was that the international response, condemning the Iraqi action, included most Arab countries. At the meeting of the Arab League on August 10, Egypt proposed a resolution condemning the invasion, imposing economic sanctions on Iraq, and offering military support to Saudi Arabia. Twelve of the twenty delegates supported the resolution, and only Libya, the Palestinian Liberation Organization (PLO), and Iraq voted against it. The other development was the US deployment of military forces in Saudi Arabia. There had never been foreign forces in Saudi Arabia, and the thought that the Custodian of the Two Mosques should be defended by large US forces seemed odd. The United States, the world's largest oil consumer, felt indirectly threatened by the prospect of Iraq, having taken the Kuwaiti oil reserves, might be able to put political or military pressure on Saudi Arabia. "President Bush became convinced that the kingdom was vulnerable and that the United States could not afford to see an Iraqi takeover" (Freedman and Karsh, 1993, p. 86). When King Fahd agreed to the establishment of US forces on Saudi soil, the Operation Desert Shield started.

Already on the night of August 2, the UN Security Council had passed a unanimous resolution (660) condemning the invasion. On August 6, it decided to introduce economic sanctions against Iraq (Resolution 661),[7] and on August 18, it sanctioned an embargo of Iraq (Resolution 665). By mid-September, the US forces in Saudi Arabia had reached 150,000. The Iraqis were disturbed, and started building up forces in Kuwait and southern Iraq. In early October it seemed President George H.W. Bush was becoming impatient and in doubt about the effectiveness of the economic sanctions, as he stated: "Sanctions will take time to have their full intended effect. We shall continue to review all options with our allies, but let it be clear, we will not let this aggression stand. Iraq will not be permitted to annex Kuwait. And that's not a threat, it's not a boast, it's just the way it's going to be."[8] On October 30, a proposal for the additional forces needed to turn the operation into an offensive one was presented to the president by Colin Powell, chairman of the Joint Chiefs of Staff. "Bush reportedly concurred: 'If that's what you need, we'll do it'" (Freedman and Karsh, 1993, p. 208). On November 29, the UN Security Council passed a resolution sanctioning the use of all necessary means unless Iraq did not withdraw from Kuwait by January 15, 1991 (Resolution 678). Hectic international diplomatic activity followed until the last minutes before this deadline. No solution was reached, and on January 17, the air strikes commenced. Operation Desert Storm had begun. On February 24, a ground attack was launched; it lasted for 100 hours.

The UN Security Council boycott resolution of Iraq and the new regime in Kuwait in August 1990 immediately brought to a halt all oil flows from the two countries. The oil price skyrocketed from $18 per barrel to almost $30 per barrel in a couple of weeks. Other producers, particularly Saudi Arabia, quickly filled the gap. "On 19 August the Saudi Oil Minister, Hisham Nazer, announced that his country would increase production by 2 mbd with or without the blessing of OPEC" (Freedman and Karsh, 1993, p. 182). There was no shortage of oil. After a few weeks, the OPEC production was almost back at prewar level. Some additional barrels from non-OPEC producers balanced the market, although there were some elements of panic buying.

After conducting informal consultations among OPEC oil ministers from August 26 to 28, 1990, and convening a meeting of the OPEC Ministerial Monitoring Committee on August 29, OPEC issued the following press release:

> To clearly restate to the world that OPEC stands for market stability and regular supply of oil to consumers . . . That OPEC shall consequently increase production, in accordance with need, in order to maintain the above-stated objectives . . . This is a temporary arrangement, applicable only until such time as the present crisis is deemed to be over, and this arrangement shall not in any way compromise the provisions of the 1990 resolution, which is still valid. Once the present crisis is considered to be over, the Organization shall return to the July 1990 Resolution. (OPEC, 1990, pp. 310–311)

What were the oil-related reasons behind the outbreak and outcome of the Iraq–Kuwait conflict? Two questions arise regarding the relationship between the oil interests and the Gulf War. First, to what extent was the Kuwaiti overproduction (measured against its allocated OPEC quota) an important reason for Saddam Hussein to invade Kuwait? Second, to what extent was the fact that the annexation of Kuwait gave Saddam control over about 20 percent of world oil reserves an important reason for the United States and Saudi Arabia to try to evict Saddam from Kuwait?

As described above, Saddam, in his political attacks on the Gulf states during spring of 1990, focused on both the repayment of war loans from the Gulf states in connection with the Iran–Iraq War, and the low oil price caused by the overproduction by particularly Kuwait and the United Arab Emirates. The Kuwaiti drilling activity in the Rumaila oil field, which crosses the border between Kuwait and Iraq, was also a cause for Iraqi concern. However, the question is not whether these factors were a part of the Iraqi argument in the build-up toward the invasion, but whether Iraq would have abstained from attacking Kuwait had these factors not been present. In other words, were these factors necessary conditions for the outbreak of war? Freedman and Karsh (1993, p. 429) conclude that the "mistake in the Arab world as well as in the West was not to recognize the desperation of Saddam's situation." Meierding (2016, p. 281) points to Saddam Hussein's lack of alternatives. "Saddam was increasingly convinced that American opposition was implacable; if oil price manipulation failed to unseat his regime, the United States would eventually turn to assassination attempts, airstrikes, or an invasion in order to overthrow him. By the summer of 1990, attacking Kuwait appeared to offer the only possible means of escaping Iraq's economic crisis and resisting American pressure."

The previous support of Iraq in the war against Iran, and the importance of Arab unity, suggested that the other Arab countries would be reluctant to interfere once the Iraqi invasion was completed. Given Iraq's expansionist and imperial ambitions, the attack on Kuwait cannot be ascribed solely to the lack of some billions of dollars in loan remittance. Regarding Kuwait's and the United Arab Emirates' overproduction against their OPEC quotas, one should note that Iraq itself produced substantially above its allocated quota, and in fact did not accept its quotas for most of the 1980s. This argument was part of the rhetorical game connected with the invasion. The economic issues were used to legitimize the invasion rather than the fundamental reason for it. Saddam regarded the international and regional political situation as one in which he could get away with the invasion of Kuwait, and he took advantage of this perceived opportunity. It turned out that either he misread the situation or his opponents changed their minds as they saw the implications of his policy.

This leads to the question about the motives of the United States and the Gulf countries in opposing the invasion. Again, the problem of distinguishing different motives of individual actors appears. For the United States the normative argument of punishing the obvious breach of fundamental international norms of nonaggression, the political argument of securing the sovereignty of an important ally like Saudi Arabia, and the undesired situation of having Saddam in control of one-fifth of world oil reserves all pulled in the same direction. The answer was to eject Saddam from Kuwait. For the other OPEC countries, this was not so. The OPEC advocates of pressing the oil price higher got unexpected help from Saddam, while the low-price advocates (the Gulf countries) focused on the negative effects of another period of oil-market turmoil. This division of the OPEC members' interests was exposed at the OPEC meeting in Vienna in late August 1990, where several non-Gulf countries advocated not increasing production and thus fuel the price rise that followed the invasion. For the Gulf countries, the security interests were of utmost importance. Although it seemed unlikely that Saddam would push farther into Saudi Arabia, gambling the nations' sovereignty on the rationality of Saddam seemed foolish. Furthermore, with an acceptance of the annexation of Kuwait, Saddam would be in a position to increase the political and economic pressure on the Gulf countries, even without military threats toward them. In the longer run this could politically undermine the regimes in the Gulf countries and possibly pressed them to change their oil policy according to the interests of Saddam. As for Saudi Arabia, security has in several instances been important in explaining the kingdom's oil policy. The Saudi Arabian regime found itself in an unacceptable position with Saddam's army on its northern border, imposing potential threats in order to change Saudi Arabian oil policy, if not less likely threats of direct military attacks.

8.5   PERSIAN GULF AS A REGIONAL SECURITY COMPLEX

So far, we have discussed direct military conflicts between oil-producing states around the Persian Gulf. Interstate conflicts are, of course, more than just direct military warfare. The Cold War should serve as the most prominent example of non-militarized, but severe, interstate conflict. Also, on the regional level, such antagonistic relations between states can occur, without direct military confrontation. This brings us back to the starting point of this chapter. "Security is a relational phenomenon. Because security is relational, one cannot understand the national security of any given state without understanding the international pattern of security interdependence in which it is embedded" (Buzan, 1991, p. 187).

8.5.1   Defining the Persian Gulf Security Complex

Buzan finds that study of international conflicts often neglects the regional level. The fundamental theories in the field of international relations have thoroughly developed models of the formation of foreign policy of the individual states, and the defining characteristics of the international system of states, he says. "But there is also an important set of security dynamics at the regional level, and this often tends to get lost or discounted" (Buzan, 1991, p. 187). Regionalism in the study of international relations is primarily concerned with regional cooperation, inspired by the process of European integration which led to the present state of the European Union. One obvious reason for the lack of attention paid to the regional level was the global supremacy of the Cold War, which almost everywhere suppressed regional security conflicts. After the end of the Cold War, latent conflicts came to the surface in many regions. This triggered the development of a more comprehensive theory of the so-called regional security complex (Buzan and Wæver, 2003). With the exception of today's Great Powers, like the US, Russia and China, most countries primarily interact with their neighbors. Buzan and Wæver (2003, p.47) thus point to the regional level as *better* suited to grasp the dynamics of security among nations than the global level. "The pattern of amity and enmity is normally best understood by starting the analysis from the regional level, and extending it towards inclusion of the global actors on the one side and domestic factors on the other ... For most of the states in the international system, the regional level is the crucial one for security analysis." A *regional security complex* is constituted by states within a defined geographical area being more worried about each other than about any other states. They are in conflict with each other rather than with others. It is also likely that, if defensive alliances are formed, their perceived enemy is within the region, rather than outside of it.

Buzan and Wæver (2003, p.187), suggest that the "Middle East is a place where an autonomous regional level of security has operated strongly for several decades, despite continuous and heavy impositions from the global level." The dimensions of the security complex of the Middle East are numerous and intertwined. Buzan and Weaver identify at least three sub-complexes – the Maghreb, the Levant and the Persian Gulf. Gregory Gause III (2010, p.5) develops this division further. "There are important analytical questions about the international politics of the Middle East that can be answered only by taking this larger regional perspective. However, simply folding the Gulf States into the larger Middle East security complex runs the analytical risk of having Arab–Israeli questions drive the analysis of regional international politics." He finds that interstate relations among the countries in the Persian Gulf region have dynamics "quite separate" from the Arab–Israel conflict. Thus, he focuses on the Persian Gulf as a regional security complex in its own right, defined by a mutual sense of fear/threat felt by the Persian Gulf states toward each other.

Gause III (2010, p.4) classifies Iran, Iraq, Kuwait, Saudi Arabia, and the Gulf monarchies as the obvious members of the Persian Gulf security complex. These countries "focus intensely on each other and devote the bulk of their security resources to relations with each other, and have done so for decades." Turkey, Syria, Jordan, and Yemen all border the members of the complex, but are excluded as their security concerns and focus lie outside of the Gulf itself.

8.5.2 The Strategic Security Implications of the Two Wars

In February 1981, the Gulf monarchies – Saudi Arabia, Kuwait, Qatar, the United Arab Emirates, Bahrain, and Oman – formed the Gulf Cooperation

Council (GCC). Both the external (the outbreak of the Iran–Iraq in 1980) and internal threats (an uprising in Mecca in 1979) motivated the establishment of the GCC. The Iraqi attack on Kuwait in 1990 was also interpreted as a common security threat to the GCC states.

Economically, the Iran–Iraq War had a beneficial effect on all oil producers, as the oil price increased. The reduced production capacity of the belligerent states also gave room for increased production from other countries without putting pressure on the oil price. Politically, the benefits to the other Gulf countries were more dubious. The new regime in Iran represented Islamic fundamentalism, which was perceived as a threat to the royal family in Saudi Arabia and the emirs in the other Gulf countries. The Gulf countries provided Iraq with financial assistance (estimates vary between $25 and $65 billion) and sold so-called 'war-relief oil' on behalf of Iraq. The Gulf leaders viewed Iraq as the lesser of two evils, but were "no less concerned over potential Iraqi hegemony in the Gulf region" (Kechichian, 1990, p. 92). However, the Gulf countries were primarily concerned with preventing the war from spreading to their territories. In the first two years of the war, the GCC countries pursued a neutral strategy in their official statements. However, Saudi Arabia and Kuwait provided Iraq with financial support, while the United Arab Emirates (UAE) tried to preserve "an open and friendly line of communication with Tehran" (Kechichian, 1990, p. 95). This strategy was made somewhat difficult by the fact that Iran occupied parts of the UAE islands Abu Musa, Greater Tunb, and Lesser Tunb. The island conflict escalated in 1992 when the:

> Iranian authorities on Abu Musa suddenly demanded that the civilians entering the island to live on the Arab side have Iranian visa stamps in their passports . . . Although Iran backed down on the visa issue, the dispute continued in the years after 1992 through repeated exchanges of accusations between Tehran and Abu Dhabi . . . The Iranian statements were often very strong; for example, after the December 1992 GCC summit meeting, Tehran declared that if the UAE tried to take the islands, it would have to 'cross a sea of blood' to do so. (Rugh, 1996, p. 62)

The neutral strategy was abandoned during 1982: "By November 1982 . . . the council's attention was clearly focused on Iran's persistent intransigence in the war" (Kechichian, 1990, p. 97). Also, the rejection of mediation attempts by Iran led to the GCC countries' official support of Iraq. This also meant they kept a low profile when it was revealed that Iraq had used chemical weapons. At the beginning of the Iran–Iraq War, the GCC countries were militarily weak. This changed during the course of the war, as the US military guarantee to these countries was strengthened, and the GCC countries' own military power was enhanced. In addition, the GCC as a security organization had developed from nothing into a military alliance with a common defense strategy, weapons programs, and joint military exercises. "For the first time in this century, forces from all six states participated in cooperative military activities aimed at defending their territories . . . Whereas the Gulf War had initially posed a threat to the GCC states, the end result was a stronger, more unified military structure" (Kechichian, 1990, p. 108). The external threat posed by Iran strengthened the GCC's internal political cohesion.

The Iraqi attack on Kuwait in August 1990 demonstrated the inability of the smaller Gulf states to muster sufficient military resistance against the larger countries in the region. The then nine-year-old GCC cooperation had not altered this fact. The consequences of the Iraq–Kuwait War were that GCC cooperative efforts were intensified: "The second Gulf crisis opened a new era in GCC interstate relations. The small GCC countries, with the exception of Oman, became more inclined to follow Saudi foreign policy. The GCC states have accepted the Saudi perspective on Gulf security" (Al-Alkim, 1994, p. 89). There are, however, political differences between the Gulf countries. Some of these, as long as they remain unresolved, will represent a hindrance to the extension of cooperation between the Gulf states. "The border dispute that had the most damaging effect on the GCC was the Saudi–Qatari problem . . . the crisis culminated [in Abu al-Khufs] in an armed clash in August 1992, in which two Qataris and one Saudi were killed" (Al-Alkim, 1994, p. 81). The cooperation thus resembles one based on common fear rather than common interests: "The only bond holding the Sheikhs together was that their fears of Iran and Iraq were greater than their dislike of each other" (Heikal, 1993, p. 125).

8.5.3 Trans Border Threats

The perception of internal threats also contributed to the formation of the GCC. The members are all sheikhdoms, with a political front against countries with "revolutionary" leaderships, or socialist or Nasserite ideologies. The pan-Arabic idea was dead by this stage: "Divisions in the Arab world were nothing new, but signs of deeper fragmentation emerged in 1980, when the sheikdoms formed what amounted to a club for the rich. The Gulf Cooperation Council" (Heikal, 1993, p. 115). This interpretation implies that regional cooperation stands in conflict with broader cooperation. This is not necessarily true, but in this case the GCC underlines deeper societal differences between the Arab countries; between the oil-rich, and mostly small, scarcely populated countries, and the poorer and heavily populated countries.

The other aspect of the internal threats is the threat represented by Islamic fundamentalism, fostered by the regime in Tehran. The Islamic leaders do not need tanks and troops to constitute a threat to the Gulf regimes. The possibility of internal fundamentalist groups conducting sabotage or terrorist attacks, or challenging the secular regimes in other ways, is a more likely development. The bomb explosion in Riyadh on November 13, 1995, which killed five American citizens, underlined the seriousness of these threats. Although this was the first terrorist action of this kind in Saudi Arabia, it "suggested an ominous escalation of the conflict between the Saudi royal family and its Islamic opposition."[9] This underlines the complexity of interstate relations in the Middle East in general. According to Halliday (1991, p. 230):

> [I]nterstate competition is more complex than anywhere else in the world because it involves not just a bipolar conflict . . . but a set of interlocking conflicts – Arab–Israel, Iran–Iraq, Iraq–Syria, Iraq–Saudi Arabia, Saudi– Yemeni . . . The history of formal and informal treaty organizations in the region is one of weakness, incompleteness and failure: by the Arab League in the 1940s, by the Baghdad Pact – CENTO (Central Treaty Organization) in the 1950s and 1960s, by the 'Twin Pillar' approach in the Gulf in the 1970s, by the Gulf Cooperation Council and the Arab Cooperation Council.

8.5.4   The Role of the US

It is more controversial to include the United States as a member of the Middle East's security complex. External powers can obviously frame the regional security complex, but in line with Gause III (2010, p. 6), I find it reasonable to include the US. The US Fifth Fleet represents a tremendous military capacity devoted solely to the Middle East region, and particularly the oil flow from the Persian Gulf. US security involvement in the Persian Gulf region has been increasing since the 1970s. It became more militarized with the intervention in the Iraq–Kuwaiti war in 1990, and culminated in the invasion of Iraq in 2003. The latter also changed the structure of the security complex. Until 2003, the core of the security complex in the Persian Gulf was the struggle for dominance between Iran, Iraq and Saudi Arabia. The Iran–Iraq war from 1980 to 1988, and the Iraqi attack on Kuwait in 1990 fit into this frame. The US invasion of Iraq in 2003 effectively removed one of these three regional powers. What used to be a triangular power competition became a bilateral battle between Saudi Arabia and Iran, although constrained by the increased ambition of the US to control and dominate the region. The success of the US strategy is more questionable. "Even with its heavy military involvement, the United States has not been able to dictate completely the politics of the region, either before 2003 or after . . . The hegemon cannot always get its way" (Gause III, 2010, p. 8).

The general dilemma of US engagement in the security complex of the Persian Gulf was discussed at the end of the previous chapter. Inside the Persian Gulf security complex, US strategic options have been limited due to the erasure of Iraq as a great power. The US' room of maneuver by having two out of three allies among Iran, Iraq and Saudi Arabia, has been made impossible by the collapse of Iraq's economic and strategic strength. Today, the goal of keeping Saudi Arabia and Iran on friendly terms obviously depends on the relationship between those two countries (see next sub-section). The nuclear deal with Iran fits perfectly with this picture, as long as negative Saudi reactions are not too strong. The US balancing act would also be jeopardized by an overly expansive foreign policy strategy on behalf of Saudi Arabia. The Saudi engagement in the war in Yemen and Syria could easily jeopardize this two-horse US strategy. As both Iran and Saudi Arabia seem to have stable and consistent regimes,[10] an alternative US strategy of alienating one of them appears very risky. In May 2018, US President Donald Trump announced that the US was withdrawing from the Iran nuclear deal and set to reinstate the sanctions against Iran.

8.5.5 The Saudi – Iranian Rivalry

In his 2003 book on Saudi Arabia, Anthony H. Cordesman provides a detailed discussion of the Saudi Arabian strategic maneuvering of their two primary threats: Iran and Iraq (Cordesman, 2003, p. 44). Iraq is seen as the most serious potential threat. Saudi–Iranian relations are described as having steadily improved. However, Cordesman cautiously observes that there "are no certainties in the Gulf, however, and the continuing internal political turmoil forces Saudi Arabia to continue to perceive Iran as a potential threat." In religious terms, there have been tensions between Wahhabi and Shi'ite clerics for more than two centuries. Saudi-Iranian relations could hardly be described as friendly under the rule of the Shah in Iran, but with the Iranian revolution in 1979, Iran was perceived as actively hostile toward Saudi Arabia (Cordesman, 2003, p. 44). The Hajj incident in 1987 – where hundreds of Iranian pilgrims were killed at Mecca – froze diplomatic relations between the two countries for several years. Even though the US invasion in Iraq in 2003 removed Saddam Hussein as a threat to Saudi Arabia, the Shia government that was installed in the aftermath brought the Iraqi regime close to Iran. From a Saudi strategic perspective, this could be seen as going from bad to worse. Having two opponents made it possible to try to play them out against each other. With a weakened Iraq dominated by Iran, such a strategy was no longer possible. The Arab Spring really proved Cordesman's caution of 'no certainties' in the Gulf. The consequences of the Arab Spring are more relevant to the next chapter of this book, which is concerned with domestic conflicts. For the interstate strategic game discussed here, the Arab Spring added an important destabilizing dimension, as both Saudi Arabia and Iran have intervened in domestic conflicts in other countries in the region, Yemen and Syria being the most prominent examples. This is nothing new. "Revolutionary Iran has cultivated ties with Islamist groups across the Arab world . . . Saudi Arabia has encouraged the spread of its own brand of Wahhabi Sunni Islam across the Sunni Muslim world for decades" (Gause III, 2010, p. 10). But the almost failed states of Yemen and Syria made their interventions easier and more consequential, and brought the two countries in more direct confrontation with each other, although still by proxies. The rhetoric between the countries can be quite harsh, as was the case after the Saudi government executed a Shia cleric, Sheikh Nimr al-Nimr, in January 2016. The response of Iranian supreme leader, Ayatollah Ali Khamenei was: "The unjustly spilled blood of this oppressed martyr will no doubt soon show its effect and divine vengeance will befall Saudi politicians."[11]

8.6 OIL (CO-)OPERATION WITHIN REGIONAL CONFLICTS

During the period discussed in this chapter there has been a clear deterioration of the political coherence among the Arab oil producers. Oil wealth has not led to increased inter- or intrastate unity among this important sub-group of oil producers. Furthermore, the conflicts among the countries in the Persian Gulf region seems to be motived and driven by a very complicated set of factors. Oil as a single explanation of the conflicts described above, seems highly inadequate for several reasons. First, the security interests of the Gulf regimes have been given more weight than their economic interests. During intensified conflicts in the region, expenditure on arms, payments for foreign forces, and so on, has been carried out regardless of the costs. Oil has also been used to ensure alliances, such as when Saudi Arabia and Kuwait sold oil from their neutral sector in order to support the Iraqi war against Iran. Regarding the Saudi-Iranian rivalry, the proxy-wars and support of various terrorists and fighting groups can only have constituted an increasing economic burden for both countries over the last decade. Second, the warfare in the region has destroyed production capacity in the belligerent countries. The Iranian production in spring of 1978 of almost 6 mbd has never been replicated since, although the potential oil reserves are present. In spring of 1980, Iraq produced approximately 3.5 mbd; although production in the first half of 1990 approached this level, the subsequent attack on Kuwait reduced Iraqi production to about 0.5 mbd. The Kuwaiti loss of production has been more short-term. Contrary to what was predicted after the retreating Iraqi forces had set a substantial part of the Kuwaiti oil fields on fire, the country regained its production capacity during 1992, and by 1993 was back to the prewar level. Third, the wars have made internal OPEC negotiations over production quotas easier, as the belligerent producers have been unable to produce at full capacity and thus made room for increased production by other OPEC members. The political antagonism created between the OPEC members by the warfare seems to have had only short-term effects on the internal negotiations inside OPEC. Both Iran and Iraq, and later Iraq and Kuwait, have accepted the presence of each other's delegations at OPEC meetings. The rivalry between Saudi Arabia and Iran has been interpreted as influencing OPEC cooperation, but not drastically.[12] Apart from some incidents of political confrontation, 'business as usual' has been the norm at OPEC meetings conducted during military conflicts between members.

Conflicts in the Middle East and in the Persian Gulf in particular, affect the oil market, as soon as the news is carried through the Internet and into the screens on the New York Mercantile Exchange and the other oil exchanges. In the public, the presence of oil in the Middle East will always be confused with oil being the reason for conflicts. "Oil is a constant. It cannot explain why specific wars happen at specific times" (Gause III, 2010, p. 246). Oil has certainly been an important factor in several conflicts, but hardly as the cause itself (Meierding, 2016). More nuanced approaches are required, distinguishing between oil as a motive for conflict, a target or instrument in the conflict, or a consequence of the conflict. Instead of more refined statistical correlations, we need to ask the harder analytical question: *How* is oil related to war and conflict, globally, regionally and nationally. The latter is the topic of the following chapter.

NOTES

1. Militarized interstate disputes are historical cases of conflict in which the threat, display or use of military force short of war by one member state is explicitly directed toward the government, official representatives, official forces, property, or territory of another state. Disputes are composed of incidents that range in intensity from threats to use force to actual combat short of war (Jones, Bremer, and Singer, 1996, p. 163). See also: http://cow.dss.ucdavis.edu/data-sets/MIDs (accessed December 30, 2017).
2. Kamran Mofid in *The Independent*, 20 July 1988, cited in Hiro (1989, p. 251).

3. "Saudi Arabia's brilliant chief of operations was shunted aside for allowing the intercept and kill of the Iranian F-4" (Cordesman and Wagner, 1990, p.214, note 7).
4. *The Observer*, October 21, 1990, cited in Freedman and Karsh (1993, p.45).
5. Baghdad Radio, July 18, 1990, cited in Freedman and Karsh (1993, p.46).
6. Baghdad Radio, July 18, 1990, cited in Freedman and Karsh (1993, p.48).
7. Yemen and Cuba abstained.
8. BBC Radio 4, October 9, 1990, reprinted in Freedman and Karsh (1993, p.204).
9. *The Economist*, November 18, 1995.
10. It should be noted that Iran experienced large demonstrations and protest related to the presidential election in 2009. Inspired by the so-called Arab Spring there were new demonstrations in 2011. Also late in 2017 into 2018 there were protests against the regime in Iran. None of these amounted to serious reforms or changes in the political regime.
11. *The Guardian*, January 3, 2016 https://www.theguardian.com/world/2016/jan/03/irans-leader-vows-divine-vengeance-over-clerics-execution-in-saudi (accessed December 31, 2017).
12. In particular the Saudi refusal to sign a production agreement in Qatar in April 2016 was interpreted as part of the conflict with Iran, but it was also rejected by delegates. *Financial Times*, April 19, 2016, p.3.

9. Oil and domestic conflicts

9.1 OIL AND CIVIL WAR

The role of oil in political conflicts is of course not limited to the relationship between countries, but also has the potential to influence domestic political conflicts. Political conflicts on the domestic level can take many shapes and forms, and vary considerably as to their urgency and intensity. Oil can cause fierce parliamentary debates and be a regular topic of democratic decision-making processes in both oil-producing and oil-consuming states. It can also feature in internal discussions and conflicts over political strategies for the oil industry in the leadership of autocratic countries. In this chapter, we will limit the discussion to more ferocious political behavior either from the state or from domestic actors challenging the state.

The literature on natural resources and civil conflicts has focused on identifying general, causal mechanisms linking natural resources to the *outbreak, intensity* and *duration* of civil wars. The conceptual underpinning of these relationships builds upon the resource curse literature, as the curse is also assumed to trigger social conflicts. The political connection to resource curse literature is through the concept of rentier state discussed in Section 3.4. The fundamental political implication of oil richness is eloquently stated by Ross (2012, pp. 65–66) "the more petroleum that an authoritarian country produces, the less likely it will make the journey to democracy." With oil in the hands of autocratic rulers, and the welfare of the citizens dependent on oil revenues, the citizens will have an incentive for obedience and loyalty to the state. On the other hand, the prize of controlling the state, and thus the oil income, is greater. The general argument is that high value of oil as a commodity, implies that domestic actors may want to own and control it for their own enrichment, thus affecting the incentives and choices of individuals, societal groups and the state.

Oil revenues create a form of wealth worth fighting for, and those in control of political power are better able to gain access to this wealth, as pointed out by Collier and Hoeffler (1998, p. 563), "War occurs if the incentive for rebellion is sufficiently large relative to the costs." Their main conclusion was that resource wealth increased the risk of civil war, and prolonged the civil wars that broke out. Collier and Hoeffler's work triggered a vast number of other studies linking natural resources to civil war, in tandem with the resource course literature, and they remain two of the most influential authors in the field. They compiled a cross-national statistical analysis of the outbreak of civil wars in 161 countries dating back to 1960. They singled out primary commodity exports as the most important factors behind the risk for a country to experience civil war.

This literature falls broadly into two camps. The first emphasizes the incentives of the potential rebels. Low growth rates following the resource curse constitutes a low opportunity cost for rebellion and thus makes civil war more likely. The other initial strand of literature focuses on the effect of natural resources on the strength of the state. These studies suggest that systems of patronage and arrested democratic development following the formation of the rentier state weaken the state and encourage rebels to take up arms. Early examples were mostly large-N studies identifying a correlation between resource dependence and civil war (Collier and Hoeffler, 2002; Fearon and Laitin, 2003). The theoretical development of how the resource dependency and civil war were connected was somewhat less prominent.

9.1.1   Patterns of Correlation between Oil Revenues and Civil War

The overall correlation. The effect of resource wealth on civil war appears to be non-monotonic. Several studies identify an inverted U-relationship, meaning that the risk increases before decreasing after some point. The interpretation of this pattern varies, but most follow the argument of Collier and Hoeffler (1998) – that resource wealth yields a stabilizing force at some level, enabling the government to buy off or repress potential insurgents. At the same time, however, the prize of controlling the state should rise with the increase in oil income, and thus strengthen the incentive of potential rebels to pick up arms. Fearon (2005) uses non-parametric methods to examine what the data says about the functional form of the relationship (as non-parametric methods do not assume functional forms). Here he finds no evidence for the 'increasing-then-decreasing' pattern. Rather, the pattern seems to increase at a decreasing rate. He also notes that "few countries have more than 35 percent of GDP in primary commodity exports, so the relationship between civil war risk and commodity dependence is mainly positive" (Fearon, 2005, p. 486).

Variation in time. As discussed in Chapters 5 and 6, production of oil was dominated by international oil companies known as the Seven Sisters up until the 1970s The revenues collected by the host governments did not constitute an economic wealth of any magnitude. This changed dramatically when the producing countries gained market control, resulting in price increases and the nationalization of the oil industry in most of the large oil-producing countries during the first half of the 1970s. With the nationalization of the oil industry in several countries, the governments of these countries rapidly accumulated large oil revenues. It should be noted that the oil revenue of the oil states has varied considerably during the period from the 1970s until today. This fact does not seem to have been fully included in the statistical studies of the relationship between oil income and civil war. If oil revenues are the main cause of civil war, the incentives for rebels to take up arms would have increased dramatically with the oil price increase in the 1970s, fallen sharply with the oil price fall in the 1980s, and increased to unprecedented levels in the 2000s, when the oil price increased reaching over $140 per barrel in 2008.

Variation in space. When studies account for location, the results often change. When oil is found offshore, there don't seem to be any effects on the probability of conflict. As Ross (2012, p. 163) notes, these countries have less conflicts than countries without any oil at all. It is obviously harder for rebel groups to access offshore oil. The prevalence of conflict is higher with onshore oil discoveries or a combination of onshore and offshore discoveries (Ross, 2012, p. 163). Østby, Nordås, and Rød (2009) find that oil in poor regions (relative to national average) is more likely to spark conflict. Conflicts situated in regions with oil wealth also seem to last longer than conflicts in regions without oil wealth.

9.1.2 'An Embarrassment of Mechanisms'[1]

In this book, oil is our only focus. The literature on civil war also identifies a conflict-inducing effect from other kinds of natural resources apart from oil. Such resources include alluvial diamonds, other gemstones, other non-fuel minerals, as well as contraband. When it comes to oil, most studies identify a harmful – but conditional – effect of oil in the conflict equation. Oil helps trigger conflict in low- and middle-income countries, particularly when combined with the presence of marginalized ethnic groups. Compared to the discussion of resources and regime stability in Chapter 3, "Only petroleum is consistently correlated with less democracy and more corruption, but both petroleum and other mineral resources have been statistically associated with the onset or duration of civil war" (Ross, 2015, p. 250). While there is a consensus that oil and conflict are somehow related, the agreement seems to stop there.

Identifying statistical correlations between observed phenomena is only the first step in the analysis. The mechanisms creating the causal link between the phenomena also need to be identified, at least theoretically. But as Ross (2004, p. 36) observes "most scholars have little to say about causal mechanisms." He then goes on to suggest no less than seven possible mechanisms. Humphreys (2005) identifies six different mechanisms, partly overlapping with Ross' list. Other scholars also suggest various explanatory factors, but seldom with the aim of systematically proving or falsifying their empirical validity. The initial distinction by Collier and Hoeffler (2002) between rebel groups motivated by greed or grievance indicates two different mechanisms. The complete list of possible mechanisms proposed in the literature is far too long to be fairly accounted for here. However, a handful of suggested key mechanisms are worth identifying. First, three mechanisms relating natural resources to the *onset* of civil war:

- *Greedy rebels.* The natural resources encourage domestic groups to engage in quasi-criminal activity to benefit from the resource wealth independently from the state. To some extent, this contradicts the rentier state argument presented in Section 3.4. This should lead to local expulsion of the state. The natural resources also increase the 'prize' of capturing the state. This should lead to bids for state control. If the resources are concentrated in areas with a distinct ethnic population, they might encourage secessionist movements, as the resources provide the economic basis for an independent state.
- *Grievance.* Dependence on natural resources could also be associated with grievances rather than greed. This mechanism is the main opponent to the greed-based explanation in the literature. The development of natural resources can create inequalities among various domestic groups, especially if the resources are geographically concentrated. The production of oil might also cause grievance if it leads to environmental degradation or forced migration. The revenues from the resources might also be unjustly distributed among the citizens. As discussed in Chapter 3, countries dependent on a single commodity are vulnerable to terms of trade shocks or imbalances in commodity markets. Such effects can cause grievance in the whole population or among groups particularly hurt by the domestic effects of such volatilities.
- *Weak state.* Following the rentier state/resource curse theories, state capacity and structures may be weaker in resource dependent states. There are two main variants of this argument, both focusing on the state-society linkage: (i) Untaxed citizens have less control over their government. When the citizenry does not serve as a source of legitimate power, they do not hold the power to withdraw their support from unwanted leaders and governments. Resource dependent states thus have little need to respond to their demands, or create structures for engaging their citizens. (ii) The state-side variation of

this argument affirms that resource dependent states have weakened incentives to create strong bureaucratic institutions, and are more exposed to corruption.

The civil war literature also focuses on the role of natural resources in conflict *duration*. The main distinction here is between: (1) Natural resources as a reward in themselves, and (2) natural resources as 'conflict fuel' – either as start-up capital, or as a means of financing the rebels' need for guns and butter.

- *Feasibility*. Natural resources may provide financing for rebels in wars started for other reasons, enabling rebels to keep on fighting. In particular, if both sides have access to natural resources, their conflict can continue for a long time; asymmetric conflicts last shorter. This mechanism relates to the relative balance between the conflicting parties. Access to resources keep combatants alive, but also helps to protect assets and inflict damage on the other side. These effects influence the chance of victory and may affect how easy it is to negotiate settlements.
- *Rebel organization*. This is a newer line of research arguing that the prospect of gaining access to natural resources can affect the organizational structure of rebel groups. Concentrated resources like oil require more organizational cohesion and hierarchical structures than diffuse resources like coffee or cattle (Le Billon, 2001). We should expect a positive relationship between the cohesiveness of a rebel organization or its degree of hierarchy in oil-rich areas, and the duration of conflict.
- *Pork-barrel politics*. Natural resources help governments finance pork-barrel politics. While this is a general mechanism, it also relates to domestic conflicts. Available resource rents grease negotiation processes between factions and increase the likelihood of the leaders' adherence to a potential deal. Thus, under certain conditions natural resources can shorten an ongoing conflict or civil war, regardless of the initial reasons for the onset of the conflict.

9.1.3 Key Findings in the Literature

Collier, Hoeffler, and Rohner (2009), repeat the initial studies of Collier and Hoeffler mentioned above. In the new study they expand the period of investigation, nearly doubling the observations (to over 1,000), and introduce some additional variables. Their core argument from previous publications stands: Economic characteristics are the most important explanatory variables – namely the level, growth and structure of income. The new variables found to be both significant and important are (i) whether the country was under the security umbrella of France, and (ii) the proportion of male youths (15–29). They also find some (weaker) evidence for mountainous terrain. The explanation is this – a country under the French security umbrella, with only half the average proportion of young males, and without mountainous terrain, presents potential rebels with more resistance from a strong, foreign power as well as difficulty in recruitment and hiding.

Fearon (2005) identifies weaknesses in Collier and Hoeffler's first study and proposes an alternative explanation for the identified relationship between natural resources and civil war. His critique relates to the definition of the opportunity for financing rebellion. Collier and Hoeffler (2004, p. 565) see extortion of natural resources as creating the opportunity for rebel groups to take up arms against the government, and regard the ratio of commodity exports to GDP as a suitable proxy for measuring the role of natural resources.

Fearon (2005) finds this measure quite fragile; his altering of the sample frame from five-year intervals to yearly intervals largely removes the statistical relationship. While Fearon agrees that opportunity structures matter, he argues that primary commodity exports are a surrogate measurement for what is really the underlying cause, namely *weak states*. Oil producers tend to have weak state institutions compared to non-oil producers at the same level of GDP. This stems from a lack of incentives to develop sound administrative competence and bureaucratic capacity. Showing that investors' perception of the probability of states withdrawing or altering contracts is high for oil-producing states, he argues that oil producers develop less reliable state institutions. Oil revenues help against insurgents through financial resources, but produce lower bureaucratic capacity. Fearon's main argument for the weak-state hypothesis is that profit from natural resources requires control of national distribution and/or production systems. Only one of Ross' 13 most likely cases includes what he calls 'booty futures' – that is, small-scale extortion including the sales of future exploitation rights (Ross, 2004). According to Fearon, this is the most available rebel financing opportunity, and it is not that common.

Le Billon (2001) focuses on the importance of geography when investigating natural resources and armed conflict. He asserts that the end of the Cold War induced a change in the political economy of war, mainly because the larger states no longer lent assistance to states fighting proxy-wars in different parts of the world. Natural resources were one of many ways to fill the financial gap. Le Billon also claims that natural resources increase not only the risk of armed conflict, but also exacerbate regime

Table 9.1 *Relation between the nature/geography of a resource and the type of conflict*

		Concentration	
		Point	Diffuse
Location	Proximate	State control/coup d'état	Rebellion/rioting
	Distant	Secession	Warlordism

Source: Le Billon (2001, p. 573).

vulnerability by weakening the ability of states to peacefully resolve conflicts. Natural resources might induce conflict by themselves, or work through the state by weakening institutions.

Le Billon claims that motivation and the way resources are used to finance wars are the two main ways resources and conflicts are related. While few of the direct causes of wars can be attributed to natural resources alone, many conflicts affects the natural resources, and the resources influence the strategies and agendas of belligerents. The significance of resources also influences the course of conflicts since the localization of authority and motives for violence can be swayed by economic considerations. An interesting contribution is Le Billon's typology of resources, where he classifies natural resources on two dimensions: *location* (near/far from central government) and *concentration* (point/diffuse), and then identifies four different types of conflict/violence usually found in each of these four cells (cf. Table 9.1).

In this context, oil is a point resource. The oil-related domestic conflicts categorized as point/proximate are Angola, Chad and Congo. The point/distant oil cases are Angola/Cabinda, Caucasus, Nigeria/Biafra and Sudan. Le Billon's article also represents an alternative with respect to the attention paid to categorization and conceptualization of the relevant phenomena. This is because he "analyses the role of natural resources in armed conflict, through their materiality, geography and related socio-economic processes . . . and extends this approach in building a political ecological framework for the analysis of resource-linked armed conflicts" (Le Billon, 2001, p. 563). While Fearon (2005) contributes to a more nuanced understanding of the independent variable, the value of the natural resources, Le Billon (2001) creates a more fine grained understanding of how different resources create different types of conflicts.

Ross (2004) provides a contribution to the literature on civil war and natural resources using a comparative method in a small-N study, as he finds most studies unable to provide carefully specified and testable causal

Table 9.2   The role of oil for civil war onset, duration and intensity

Conflict	Onset	Duration	Intensity
Angola	No	Longer	Mixed
Colombia	No	Longer	Mixed
Congo Republic	Yes	Shorter	None
Sudan	Yes	Longer	Mixed

Source: Ross (2004, p. 49).

mechanisms, and that the quality of the data used for large statistical cross country N-studies is rather poor. He tests seven causal mechanisms on a sample of 13 'most likely' cases of resource-related civil war, and finds that a majority were influenced by natural resources. However, they were influenced through several different mechanisms operating simultaneously. This possibly explains some of the difficulty in achieving consistent empirical results in previous studies. Among the 13 cases, only four relate to oil resources: Angola, Colombia, Congo-Brazzaville and Sudan. The other cases were related to other natural resources, like diamonds. Table 9.2 shows the role of natural resources in the four oil-related cases with regard to onset, duration and intensity of civil wars.

This analytical design gets closer to identifying the causal mechanisms of the relationship between oil and civil war. Ross finds support for the claim that oil resources have plausibly influenced the onset and duration of civil wars, but the number of conflicts where the relationship is clearly observable seems to be limited.

9.1.4   Weaknesses and Critique

In order to count as a civil war, a rate of 1,000 battle deaths per year is required. Hegre and Sambanis (2006) attempt to test the robustness of variables usually attributed to civil war onset in the empirical literature. They find support for some aspects of the economic theory of civil war. Oil export and primary commodity dependence are both robustly associated with lower-level armed conflict (25 battle deaths per year), but not with civil war (1,000 battle deaths per year). A similar conclusion is drawn by De Soysa and Neumayer (2005) who dismiss both major oil exports and resource rent as predictors for the onset of civil war for the same reason. Specifically, they find that energy wealth increases the risk of civil war onset, but only after 1970 and only with the lower threshold of 25 deaths per year. Upon retesting the claim of Collier and Hoeffler (2004), they do not find evidence of a non-linear relationship suggesting that highly petroleum rich/dependent countries are able to prohibit riots. Overall, they conclude that oil matters, even when using alternative measures of resource rents, but the results are dependent on the conceptualization of civil war and the time-period in question.

A more fundamental critique has been directed against the indicator for dependency on natural resource income. This is usually measured as the share of GDP occupied by commodity export revenues, which captures the relative dependency of the country on the resource sector. "Capturing the concept this way became the standard not just for civil war studies but also for work on the effect of oil on regime type and durability" (Smith, 2016, p. 221). The relative relationship between income from oil exports and GDP is susceptible to changes in GDP. The civil war itself will often have a negative effect on GDP. This could be because of a reduction in oil exports, but it could also be caused by reduced activity in other sectors of the economy. If so, the importance of oil exports would increase their relative share of GDP due to the conflict itself. Shifting the indicator from resource dependency to resource abundancy does not solve this problem, as any measure of the relative value of the oil resources will be influenced by the same changes in relative value compared to other sectors. Brunnschweiler and Bulte (2009) take this argument one step further. Observing that the conventional measurement of resource dependence is endogenous to conflict, they use an instrumental variable approach and show that resource dependence is no longer associated with conflict. Rather, conflict increases dependence on resource extraction. Economic growth and peace result in diversification and low dependence on natural resources, even when countries are highly rich in natural resources. It is thus resource scarcity, rather than resource abundance, that drives the probability of conflict.

9.2   OIL AND TERRORISM

The previous section can give the impression that the study of the relationship between natural resources and civil war is somewhat overloaded with statistical analyses, which don't necessarily improve our understanding of the relationship or help us identify the true causal mechanisms producing the statistically identified correlations. In the case of the relationship between natural resources and terrorism, the field seems rather underdeveloped as it is barely empirically tested, and offers very little scholarly discussion of the role of oil in explaining the various aspects of terrorism (Lee, 2016, p. 2). One reason is that a clear definition of terrorism is harder to achieve than for civil war. Here, we will define terrorism in line with the definition used for the construction of the Global Terrorism Database. The database defines terrorism as "the threatened or actual use of illegal force and violence by a non-state actor to attain a political, economic, religious, or social goal through fear, coercion or intimidation" (IEP, 2016, p. 6).

As mentioned in the introduction to this chapter, the large literature on the relationship between natural resources and civil war is relevant and to some extent directly addresses the relationship between natural resources and other violent domestic conflicts. However, there are differences. The primary aim of rebels in a civil war is usually to overthrow the existing regime by some kind of warfare. The immediate aim of terrorists is usually to enhance support for their own political, ideological or religious cause, by using indiscriminate violence. Their ultimate aims can be similar to the aims of rebels, such as regime change, separation or independence. In civil wars, the belligerent parties are usually identifiable, while terrorists can seek to remain unidentified. The fine grained differences are not crucial for understanding the role of oil in this chapter, as the purpose here is to discuss the role of oil in domestic conflicts. Furthermore, violent domestic conflicts will often consist of both warring rebels and terrorist attacks. The recent history of the wars in Iraq, Afghanistan and Syria clearly demonstrate this.

9.2.1   Recent Trends in Terrorism

Over the last 50 years, there have been distinct changes in terrorism trends. In the 1970s, the annual average deaths from terrorist attacks were about 700 people. In the period between 1980 and 2011, terrorism caused an average of 7,000 deaths per year. Since 2011, the number of deaths has averaged over 27,000 people each year. Today, terrorism is a widespread phenomenon. In 2015, 92 countries experienced a terrorist attack, not necessarily with fatal victims (IEP, 2016, p. 15). Nevertheless, 95 percent of deaths from terrorist attacks were concentrated in Middle East, Africa, and South Asia.

Figure 9.1 shows a dramatic increase in the number of terrorist deaths since 2011. This increase is almost entirely concentrated in five countries: Iraq, Afghanistan, Niger, Pakistan and Syria. In the rest of the world, the increase in deaths due to terrorist incidents is modest. The five countries mentioned accounted for 72 percent of all deaths from terrorism in 2015 (IEP, 2016, p. 9).[2] The 10 percent reduction in terror victims from 2014 to 2015 is due to decreased activity by Boko Haram in Nigeria and ISIL in Iraq. Both terrorist groups have increased their activities elsewhere – ISIL to other parts of the Middle East and Europe, and Boko Haram, to Western Africa, in Niger, Cameroon and Chad (IEP. 2016, p. 9). The attacks by ISIL in Paris, Brussels and Ankara drove the deaths in OECD

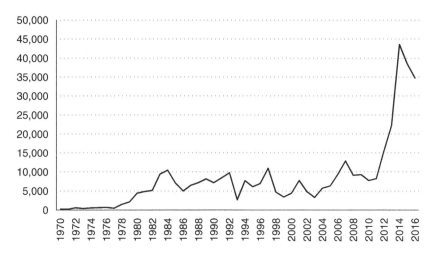

Source: Wikipedia – National Consortium for the Study of Terrorism and Responses to Terrorism (2017). Global Terrorism Database (globalterrorismdb_0617dist.xlsx). https:// www.start.umd.edu/gtd University of Maryland (accessed June 21, 2018).

Figure 9.1 Deaths following terrorist incidents 1970–2015

countries up to 577 from 77 in 2014. The activity of Taliban in Afghanistan increased in 2015, regarding both terrorist attacks and civil war activity. In 2015, four groups were responsible for 74 percent of all deaths from terrorism: ISIL (6,141 deaths), Boko Haram (5,478 deaths), the Taliban (4,502 deaths) and Al-Qaeda (1,620 deaths) (IEP, 2016, p. 49). In particular, ISIL and the Taliban are also engaged in civil war activities, with governments and/or other non-state groups. The total number of deaths involving these groups is much higher than those caused by terrorism. The number of battle deaths in conflicts involving ISIL and the Taliban has resulted in more than 40,000 deaths.

Although the empirical study of terrorism is less developed than studies of civil war, some general correlations emerge from the data. Two characteristics of a state seem to be associated with terrorist activity – "93 percent of all terrorist attacks between 1993 and 2014 occurred in countries with high level of state sponsored terror, involving extrajudicial killing, torture, and imprisonment without trial . . . over 90 percent of all terrorist deaths occurred in countries already engaged in some form of conflict whether internal or international" (IEP, 2016, p. 3). These observations suggest that terror is not an isolated phenomenon, but rather a part of wider political issues such as repressive political regimes and civil and international wars and violent conflicts. The direction of the causal mechanism can thus be hard to determine. For instance, does terrorism create or enhance the repressiveness of the regime, is it the other way around, or is it both? Furthermore, even though terrorism caused almost 30,000 deaths in 2015, its economic impact is limited. Terrorism is calculated to have cost the global economy about $90 billion in 2015, which is less than 1 percent of the total global economic impact of violence (IEP, 2016, p. 3).

9.2.2 The Role of Oil

Oil can relate to terrorism in various ways. Lee (2016) has suggested three categories of the relationship between oil and terrorism.

Motivation. Oil can motivate potential terrorists by the same mechanisms as suggested in the case of civil war. Oil income makes the state richer, thus triggering the greed of non-state actors who want to gain control or access to the state's wealth through terrorism. It also creates dissatisfaction and grievance among groups who lack access to the oil wealth of the state. The close concurrence between terrorism and other forms of political violence, as mentioned above, suggests that these motivating mechanisms present in the case of terrorism can be similar to the motivation of rebels taking up arms against the state (Collier and Hoeffler, 2004). In the case of separatist movements, oil can provide extra motivation for separation, as the presence of oil fields in regions with separatist inclinations creates a prize that justifies the fighting. If oil weakens state institutions, as suggested by Fearon (2005), the ability to fight terrorism is reduced, and thus potential terrorists are motivated.

Funding. Most terrorist attacks are rather cheap, although some are expensive, like the 9/11 attacks ($500,000) and the Bali bombing in 2002 ($50,000) (Kaplan, 2006). However, terrorist groups also need to support themselves. Terrorism conducted by 'lone wolves' are, of course, not burdened with high costs, but the large and dominant terrorist groups mentioned above (ISIL, Al-Qaeda, Boko Haram and the Taliban) are in fact large organizations. Such organizations need to spend money to recruit new members, build and maintain training camps, including provision of food and housing for members. Furthermore, elaborate terrorist attacks require equipment like guns, explosives, fake passports and communication devices (Freeman, 2011, p. 462). The Taliban and ISIL also have defined territorial ambitions, and thus have the need for regular battlefield weapons. In these cases, the necessity of financial assets increases dramatically. The potential control of an oil field is an obvious candidate in this respect. Freeman (2011, p. 465) divides terrorist funding into four general categories: State sponsorship, illegal activities, legal activities and popular support. The latter consist of various kinds of donations. For Islamic groups, charitable donations make up a large part of their revenues. State sponsorship was more common during the Cold War, when both of the superpowers supported rebel groups that today would be deemed terrorist organizations. According to Freeman, "state sponsorship has decreased significantly in recent years" (Freeman, 2011, p. 465). Oil enters this discussion as illegal or semi-legal funding. Kidnapping foreigners working in oil companies in the Middle East and demanding ransoms, threatening to attack oil facilities in exchange for money or simply confiscating oil trucks are some possible oil-related funding opportunities for terrorist groups. In the case of ISIL, its territorial control facilitates the possibility of running oil fields and selling crude oil, or even refined products. By the end of 2017, ISIL lost control over the territories it controlled in Iraq and Syria. The terrorist activity is likely to continue, but the ability to use control over oil production facilities to finance the activity is diminished.

Target. Natural resources can also be linked to terrorism to the extent that terror groups choose to target oil installations. There are many reasons for attacking oil installations. Oil is the most important traded commodity. Disrupting the flow of oil from the main oil fields, pipelines, tankers or other essential infrastructure, could rapidly influence the global oil price. Terrorist attacks on Saudi Arabian oil facilities or the shipment of oil through the Strait of Hormuz would immediately increase the oil price. The economic effect would be substantial, but the fear-inducing effect on the public would be modest. Compared to other potential targets, oil facilities are often in remote areas. Some of the oil platforms in the North Sea are several hundred kilometers offshore. In the Middle East and North Africa, some oil fields are located in the desert. Thus, these installations are hard to defend in the event of a terrorist attack. However, their very remoteness also tends to ruin the spectacular effect that could trigger widespread fear. As the aim of terrorist attacks is usually to create fear among ordinary citizens, attacking populous places in big cities serves the purpose far better. A number of attacks have been directed toward places like New York, Madrid, London, Paris and Bali. In these cases, the causal connection to oil is harder to identify and explain.

Lee (2016) has conducted both a large-N study of the relationship between oil and terrorism, concluding that oil income has a positive effect on terrorism.[3] He identifies 26 terrorist groups directly related to oil out of the 856 terrorist groups included in the Global Terrorism Database (GTD) (see IEP, 2016). This represents about three percent. Lee concludes that "most of these groups are linked to oil because they mainly target or have a record of attacking oil facilities . . . Moreover, many of these terrorist groups are located in oil rich regions. They emerge primarily because the oil wealth is not distributed equally" (Lee, 2016, p. 18).

The main link between oil and terrorism thus seems to be that oil is occasionally a target for terrorist attacks. Toft, Duero, and Bieliauskas (2010) present a study particularly focused on the energy related targets for terrorist attacks. They identify a class of terrorist targets which they call 'Energy Transmission Infrastructures' (ETI). This category of targets consists of oil and gas pipelines, tankers at sea, electricity pylons and substations. Thus, their focus is on the transmission part of the energy system. They used the same database as described above – the GTD – and found that of 15,254 terrorist incidents worldwide, 232 attacks were directed towards ETIs, or about 1.5 percent of global terrorism. Regarding geographical distribution, 71.2 percent were concentrated in four out of the 29 countries experiencing terrorist attacks related to ETI. The largest oil producers and key transit countries suffered 14 out of the 232 ETI related attacks. Their conclusion is that there is "no significant correlation between energy rich countries and numbers of ETI attacks" (Toft et al., 2010, p. 4,413). They then go on to ask why we have not seen more terrorist targeting against ETIs when these targets have apparent strategic value. They discuss four incentives to strike energy infrastructures:

Intimidation effect. Attacks on energy infrastructure can have dramatic and very costly effects for energy companies, states and the public: "In November 2007, the Managing Director of Shell Nigeria reported that MEND's [Movement for the Emancipation of the Niger Delta] attacks on the oil industry had amounted to losses of $61 million per day; a staggering amount that aggregates into billions lost annually" (Giroux, 2008, p. 17). A series of terrorist attacks in Saudi Arabia in May 2004 contributed to the rise in the global oil price, although the independent effect of these attacks on the price is hard to isolate and measure. When it comes to causalities, the picture is different. ETI related terrorist attacks have killed an average of 2.4 people per incident. By contrast, the New York World Trade Center attacks on September 11, 2001 killed 2,603 people, the 2015 Paris attacks killed 130 people, the Bali bombings in 2002 killed 202 people and the 2004 Madrid train bombings killed 192 people. Compared to these attacks, the ETI attacks are not that dangerous for humans. If one of the purposes of terrorism is to make people afraid of being killed, targeting ETIs is not an effective strategy.

Symbolism. Here, the point is the symbolic attachment between the target and the cause of the terrorist group. Toft et al. (2010, p. 4416) argue that nationalist-separatists are likely to attack physical targets linked to the state. They question whether ETIs have such a symbolic value for these groups. Left-wing terrorists are more likely to attach symbolic value to

ETIs as they could arguably represent the capitalist system. In the case of right-wing or racist groups the symbolic value of ETIs is less obvious and for political-religious groups the symbolic value seems limited (Toft et al., 2010, p. 4416).

Attack feasibility. This was also discussed above regarding targeting in general. Some part of the energy infrastructure is easily accessible, particularly over-ground pipelines and high voltage electricity power lines. However, to achieve more permanent damage, knowledge of the energy supply system in question seems necessary. The complexity of energy networks might be an obstacle to attacks.

Outside stakeholders. The final incentive discussed by Toft et al. (2010) is the relationship to outside stakeholders. Terrorist attacks on ETIs would not discriminate between supporters of the terrorist group and the primary target audiences. Thus, damaging the energy infrastructure could cause supporters to turn their backs on the terrorist group.

So far, we have described the general trends in terrorism and some general academic conceptualization and statistical analysis of the relationship between oil and terrorism. On this level, there is no strong argument for making oil a prominent cause of international or domestic terrorism. Oil mainly serves the role as a target, but even here the role is limited compared to other more intimidating targets. The studies referred to are mainly based on data before the post-2011 surge in terrorism. We thus need to look a bit closer at particular terrorist groups and their attitude toward oil resources.

9.2.3 Terrorist Groups and Oil

Al-Qaeda
Al-Qaeda was established in 1988 by Usama bin Laden (killed in 2011) and Abdullah Azzam (killed in 1989). The goal of Al-Qaeda is international Jihad and it was built up during the Soviet war in Afghanistan. The group has been responsible for attacks in London, Madrid, and most prominently, the 9/11 attack on the World Trade Center in New York in 2001. Following this attack, Al-Qaeda became the prime target of the NATO-organized 'War on Terror'. Many of the leaders of Al-Qaeda have been killed and the organizational structure has become more decentralized, sprouting local or regional terrorist cells and affiliated terrorist groups, such as Al-Shabaab (based in Somalia), Al-Nusrah Front (operating in Syria), the Abdullah Azzam Brigades (based in Lebanon) and Al-Qaeda in the Arabian Peninsula, in the Islamic Maghreb, and on the Indian sub-continent. "Al-Qa'ida and its affiliates undertook attacks in 12 countries in 2015, down from 14 the previous year and the peak of 16 countries in 2011.

In total, there were 1,620 deaths from the six most prominent al-Qa'ida affiliates in 2015" (IEP, 2016, p. 56).

Toft et al. (2010, pp. 4,416–4,418) have conducted a case study of Al-Qaeda's energy related terrorist attacks. They find with reasonable certainty that Al-Qaeda and its affiliates were behind eight terror attacks against ETIs between 1998 and 2008.[4] The attitude of the leadership of Al-Qaeda towards conducting terrorist attacks against oil installations has changed over the years. In a CNN interview in March 1997, Bin Laden provided a brief analysis of the oil market and the price mechanism. He was asked about the consequences for the oil price from a take-over of Saudi Arabia. He stated that oil:

[I]s a commodity that will be subject to the price of the market according to supply and demand. We believe that the current prices are not realistic due to the Saudi regime playing the role of a US agent and the pressures exercised by the US on the Saudi regime to increase production and flood the market that caused a sharp decrease in oil prices. (Hegghammer, 2002, p. 31).

Al-Qaeda's "Declaration of War against the Americans Occupying the Land of the Two Holy Places," published in August 1996, contains a separate section on the destruction of the oil industries. In this publication, Bin Laden cautions mujahedin soldiers not to attack the oil wealth, due to the need to preserve the oil resources for the forthcoming Islamic state. "I would like here to alert my brothers, the mujahidin, the sons of the nation, to protect this (oil) wealth and *not to include it in the battle* as it is a great Islamic wealth and a large economic power essential for the soon-to-be-established Islamic state, by Allah's permission and grace" (Hegghammer, 2002, p. 130, my italics).

After the US invasions of Afghanistan and Iraq in the early 2000s, the then-leading figure in Al-Qaeda in Saudi Arabia, Abdul Aiz al-Moqrin, permitted attacking oil-related targets on a case by case basis, since they were not under the control of the Muslim public (Toft et al., 2010, p. 4415). The issue was further elaborated in a document dated June 15, 2004, called "The Laws of Targeting Petroleum-Related Interests and a Review of the Laws Pertaining to Economic Jihad," authored by the cleric, Abd-al-Aziz bin Rashid al-Anzi. In this document, the argument is that, as long as Muslims do not control the oil, attacks are justified. They should, however, be based on a cost-benefit analysis. In such an analysis, attacking oil wells is too costly, since it risks "irreparable environmental damage, unrecoverable wealth loss, and potential bad coverage in Arab media." However, attacking oil export pipelines, oil tankers and refineries constitute a net benefit (Toft et al., 2010, p. 4,418).

These concrete observations lead to the conclusion that the Al-Qaeda leadership recognizes the dilemma of targeting their own key source of wealth, should their ambition of creating an Islamic State be successful. Environmental concerns are also included in the equation. The benefits of gaining control over operative oil fields have been a vital consideration for the more successful land-grabbing terrorist organization – ISIL.

ISIL

The Islamic State of Iraq and the Levant (ISIL) is also known under the acronym ISIS, Islamic State or Daesh. It is based in Syria and Iraq under the leadership of Abu Bakr al-Baghdadi. It emerged from Al-Qaeda in Iraq, but in February 2014 Al-Qaeda and ISIL broke ties. The aim of ISIL has been to control and re-establish the caliphate in the Levant region, which includes Israel, Iraq, Jordan, Lebanon and Syria. The organization had a strong military presence in the region from 2013 until 2018. During 2013, ISIL achieved rapid territorial expansion in Syria and Iraq. By the end of 2014, ISIL controlled an area of more than 100,000 square kilometers, with approximately 6–8 million people. As of January 2018, ISIL holds about 2 percent of their previously held territory after suffering heavy losses in late 2017. ISIL is thus more than a regular terrorist organization, in that the typical terrorist group usually lacks control over large geographical areas. On the other hand, ISIL does carry out a large number of terror attacks besides their more regular civil war battlefield operations. For this discussion about the role of oil in the activities of ISIL, the differences between their civil war and terror operations are less important.

In 2015, terrorist attacks by ISIL killed 6,141 people. ISIL increased the number of countries targeted and conducted attacks on 252 different cities in 11 countries. However, most of the attacks were in Iraq (81 percent) and Syria (15 percent). The cities of Baghdad, Ramadi, Mosul and Baiji accounted for one fourth of all ISIL attacks (IEP, 2016, p. 52).

Wikipedia lists over 100 terrorist incidents linked to ISIL from 2003 to late 2017.[5] Although specific information regarding the individual incidents is limited, the impression is that none of these is directly related to oil installations or ETIs in general. The most prominent targets were public places, police and military stations or other governmental groups or facilities. The listing of recent terrorist events thus seems to confirm the finding of the older academic studies discussed above – oil, or energy installations, are not among the most popular *targets* for terrorist attacks.

On the other hand, oil has played an important role in *financing* the battlefield and terrorist operations of ISIL. A number of income generating activities, such as taxation, extortion, ransom, donations and the antiquities trade, help to fund ISIL. However, crude oil is the most important source of revenue.[6] The areas controlled by ISIL in the fall of 2014 included several operating oil fields in western Iraq and eastern Syria. "ISIL is no longer desperate for donors' funding to continue and expand their operations given they now possess a loosely integrated and thriving black economy consisting of approximately 60 percent of Syria's oil assets and seven oil-producing assets in Iraq" (Al-Khatteeb, 2014). Estimates of the total revenue generated from oil sales at their 2015 peak vary from between $1 and $3 million per day (Kiourktsoglou and Coutroubis, 2015, p. 3).

ISIL sold most of the oil to local traders, at a highly discounted price, of between $25 and $60. The profitability was affected by the fall in the market price of oil, which dropped from over $100 per barrel in the summer of 2014, to less than $50 per barrel in the summer of 2015. A more severe threat to ISIL's oil income was the US and Iranian air strikes that started in August 2014. In September 2015, Russia also began airstrikes against ISIL. These airstrikes were primarily in support of ground forces of the Iraqi army and the forces of the Assad regime, respectively. However, in October 2015, airstrikes targeting ISIL controlled oil infrastructure were launched. As indicated above, the territory controlled by ISIL has, by the fall of 2017, been severely diminished. In Iraq, all oil fields have been lost. Also, large oil fields in Syria were lost in the fall of 2017.

Despite this, oil still remains a vital source of revenue. Johnston (2017) refers the estimation made by a spokesman for the US-backed coalition forces that "ISIS's oil revenues declined to $4 million per month as of early October from a peak of $40 million per month in 2015." Though a continuous fall in ISIL oil revenues is likely, Johnston (2017) argues that it is still "likely benefiting from taxing fuel consumption locally and charging fees for tanker trucks transiting ISIS-controlled areas."

9.3   FIGHTING FOR OIL – HOW DO WE KNOW?

The academic literature discussed in this chapter is primarily based on quantitative large-N studies identifying statistically significant correlations between the presence of oil and violent conflicts. The large number of observations (large-N) is derived by panel data, creating an independent observation for each country every year. This is, by now, standard operating procedure in quantitative social science. Such methods are supposed to increase the scientific certainty of the inferences regarding the causal relationship between the explanatory factors and the dependent variable, in this case between oil resources and violent conflicts.

A challenge in this literature is that the definitions of the phenomena underlying both the dependent and the explanatory factors are not self-explanatory, but subject to interpretation. For instance, what is oil dependence and how should we measure it? How do we define a civil war? Many concepts in social sciences have this ambiguous character. The challenge is harder with statistical analysis than most other methods, since it demands precisely measured concepts and variables. A possible consequence is that as the accuracy of the causal proposition increases with precise measures, the validity and reliability of the inference decreases. In some cases, just minor adjustments in the definition of key concepts and variables, or their measurements, change fundamental conclusions. The solution is to supplement the statistical analysis with studies of the same phenomenon using other methods. After having fought a war of methods, political science seems to be moving in the direction of acknowledging the value of mixing methods. Ross provides an example for how this could be done: "When investigating causal mechanisms empirically, even the best statistical analysis can only take us so far . . . Hence, I also use brief case studies to show that the associations I report in the cross-national data can plausibly explain outcomes at the country level" (Ross, 2012, p. 24). Case studies are able to discuss the historic, cultural, societal and political context of the causal relationship between the social and political phenomena under investigation. Such methods permit a much richer understanding of the complexity of human interactions, including those related to oil and conflict.

In the Middle East region, various political, economic, social, cultural, ethnic, tribal and religious differences influence the instigation, duration, and outcome of conflicts. All based on and determined by centuries of historical context. In this perspective, the presence of oil is a rather new phenomenon. I am tempted to ask a rhetorical question – if oil is so important, how could there have been so much conflict in this region before oil was discovered?

To contextualize the role of oil in explaining conflicts among groups and countries, we need to distinguish between oil as a *cause* of conflict, as an *instrument* in a conflict or as an *outcome* of conflict. To some extent, this overlaps with some of the conceptual work discussed above. But here I am less interested in the operative categorization for the purpose of conducting statistical analysis, and more in identifying the underlying features of *how* oil and conflict are related. The most important way oil and conflict are connected is that oil is identified as the reason for the conflict – its cause. If this were the case, there would be no conflict without the oil. This suggests a counterfactual approach. The analytical question to ask would be the opposite of what characterizes many statistical studies, where the aim is to identify a simultaneous presence of oil and conflict. In a counterfactual analysis, we would ask, 'how likely is that this conflict would have occurred without the presence of oil?' Statistically, and to some extent in comparative studies, you would do this by refuting alternative explanations for the conflict, until you are left with oil as the only possible candidate, or at least the most likely one. The counterfactual argument would turn this around – even without the oil, are there reasons to expect this conflict to go on?

Let's move to the role of oil as an instrument in conflicts. Here the argument is that oil is not necessarily the cause of the conflict, but influences the conflict by prolonging it. It seems reasonable to argue that the fact that ISIL gained control over several oil fields in Iraq and Syria, enabled the proclaimed caliphate to hold on to the territory and thus prolonged the conflict beyond what would have been possible without the control of the oil fields. The possibility of targeting oil fields as part of terrorist attacks or the battlefield operations of civil wars, also gives oil a role in the enactment of the conflict. The role of oil as an outcome of conflict relates to how oil can be the prize of the conflict, and hints at the distributional role of the oil wealth among the warring parties.

This brief discussion has no intention of refuting all previous studies of the relationship between oil and violent political conflicts. Rather the aim is simply to encourage the reader to reflect more deeply on fundamental aspects of *how* oil and conflict are related. In other words, to pursue the mechanisms. As Ross (2015, p. 253) observes, "Many studies offer theories about the processes that link resources to different outcomes, or the conditions under which they are most likely to occur. Yet few have tried to distinguish among these mechanisms and conditions to see which is valid." The general statistical approach seems to be in need of more nuanced approaches – possibly able to identify *what* it is about oil that creates conflict, not only the simultaneous statistically observed presence of oil and conflict.

NOTES

1. The heading of this section is taken from Humphreys (2005, p. 510).
2. The IEP (2016) is an annual report based on data collected and collated by the National Consortium for the Study of Terrorism and Responses to Terrorism (START). The report includes an index – The Global Terrorism Index (GTI) – which provides a comprehensive summary of the key global trends and patterns in terrorism since 2000. It produces a composite score between 0 and 10, where 0 represents no impact from terror and 10 the maximum impact level. The GTI covers 163 countries, covering 99.7 percent of the world's population.
3. Lee's statistical testing of the mechanisms he proposes is rigorous and interesting. The only weakness is that he only covers the period until 2006. As shown above, there was a dramatic increase in the level of terrorism activity after 2011.
4. They exclude possible attacks in Iraq since the reliability of data on perpetrators and incidents after the invasion in 2003 is particularly problematic.

5. https://en.wikipedia.org/wiki/List_of_terrorist_incidents_linked_to_ISIL (accessed October 30, 2017).
6. *Financial Times*, February 29, 2016, http://ig.ft.com/sites/2015/isis-oil/ (accessed October 31, 2017).

10. Climate change and the future of oil

10.1 THE ROLE OF OIL IN THE ENERGY SYSTEM

This chapter begins with a historic view on the role of oil in the overall energy system, and tries to extract some general predictions about the role of oil in the future energy system. In the previous chapters of this book, I mostly discussed various aspects of oil politics, from the point when it became the dominant primary energy source 70 years ago. Natural science, studying the climate changes of the earth, has concluded that the consequences of having fossil fuels (coal, oil and gas) remain the dominant primary energy sources for another 70 years, will have calamitous effects on the conditions for all kinds of life on the planet. The catchphrase for the future is the need for an 'energy transition', reducing the consumption of fossil fuels, coal, gas and oil, to a minimum. The second part of the chapter discusses the possibilities and obstacles for such a transformation, emphasizing the consequences for the oil industry.

10.1.1 The Energy System

In physics, the definition of energy is 'the ability to do work'. There are various forms of energy like kinetic energy (matter in motion), thermal energy, electrical and electromagnetic energy, nuclear energy and more. Energy can be transformed from one form to another – a steam turbine, for example, transforms thermal energy into kinetic energy. The energy system consists of primary energy sources; various forms of production; refinement or generation which transform the primary energy sources into secondary energy sources (such as electricity or gasoline); different types of transmission or distribution which bring the energy to the end-users; and finally, the use by end-consumers of the energy products to perform various energy services, such as heating, cooking, light or mobility. Table 10.1 demonstrates the part played by the various primary sources in the assorted sectors of energy consumption in the United States in 2017.

As Table 10.1 shows, the three fossil fuels – coal, natural oil and gas – constituted about 80 percent of US energy consumption in 2017, while

Table 10.1   Distribution of sources and sectors in the US energy system, 2017

SOURCE	%	Distributed by sector	%		SECTOR	%	Distributed by source	%
Petroleum	37	Transportation	72		Transportation	29	Petroleum	92
		Industrial	23				Natural gas	3
		Resid.&Com.	5				Renewable	5
		Electric power	1		Industrial	22	Petroleum	38
Natural gas	28	Transportation	3				Natural gas	45
		Industrial	35				Coal	5
		Resid.&Com.	28				Renewable	12
		Electric power	34		Residental & Commercial	11	Petroleum	16
Coal	14	Industrial	9				Natural gas	76
		Resid.&Com.	< 1				Coal	< 1
		Electric power	91				Renewable	8
Renewable	11	Transportation	13		Electric power	38	Petroleum	1
		Industrial	23				Natural gas	26
		Resid.&Com.	7				Coal	34
		Electric power	57				Renewable	17
Nuclear	9	Electric power	100				Nuclear	23

Note: Percentages might not add up, due to rounding.

Source: U.S. Energy Information Administration, *Monthly Energy Review* (April 2018), Tables 1.3, 1.4a, 1.4b, and 2.1–2.6. https://www.eia.gov/totalenergy/data/monthly/pdf/flow/css_2017_energy.pdf (accessed July 4, 2018).

nuclear and renewables split the remaining 20 percent. The uses of the primary sources are very different. Nuclear power (100 percent) and coal (91 percent) are totally or primarily used for electricity generation, while renewables and natural gas are employed in several consumer sectors. The primary concern in this book is oil or as named here petroleum. Oil is mostly used in two sectors – industry and transportation. The share of oil in the total consumption in the industrial sector is almost 40 percent, while oil is the dominant primary energy for transportation with a share in this consumer sector of more than 90 percent.[1]

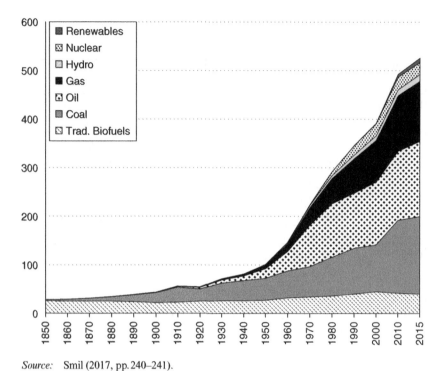

Source: Smil (2017, pp. 240–241).

Figure 10.1   Global primary energy consumption 1800–2015, values in EJ

10.1.2   Patterns of Consumption

Although the modern history of oil started in the late 1850s, it took almost a century before oil became the dominant energy source. Biofuels, such as wood, were the dominant form of energy until the middle of the 19th century, surpassed by coal around 1900. This was the first energy transition. The Industrial Revolution and the de-forestation of Europe reduced the role of biofuels and coal took over as the dominant energy source (see Figure 10.1). At the same time energy consumption started to increase more rapidly. After the Second World War, total consumption of coal was maintained, but the relative importance of coal declined, and oil became the dominant primary energy source.

The distribution of world consumption of primary energy in 2013 is shown in Table 10.2. The distribution of primary energy does not necessarily reflect, however, the importance of the various primary sources in the end use, or in energy service provision. This is because the energy

Table 10.2   World primary energy consumption in 2013 and IEA scenarios in million tons of oil equivalents (mtoe)

	Actual	Scenarios		
		Current Policies	New Policies	Sustainable Development
Year	2016	2040	2040	2040
Coal	3,755	5,045	3,929	1,777
Oil	4,388	5,477	4,830	3,306
Gas	3,007	4,682	4,356	3,458
Nuclear	681	997	1,002	1,393
Hydro	350	513	533	596
Bioenergy	1,354	1,728	1,801	1,558
Other Renewables	225	856	1,133	1,996
Total	13,760	19,298	17,584	14,084
Fossil-fuel share	81%	79%	75%	61%

Source: IEA (2017, p. 79).

efficiency and losses of the different primary sources vary according to the different technologies used for transferring them into the various energy services. Table 10.2 also includes the scenarios of the International Energy Agency (IEA). These are not to be taken as predictions, but rather as descriptions of possible future developments. In the *Current Policies* scenario, the effects of only policies for which implementing measures have been formally adopted are included. In the *New Policies* scenario, the likely effects of policies that have been announced are also included. This is the central scenario of the IEA. The *Sustainable Development* scenario attempts to capture the necessary measures required to limit the rise in global temperature to two degrees Celsius (IEA, 2017, pp. 37–39).

The importance of the different primary energy sources in the various consumption sectors differs from country to country. Table 10.3 illustrates the variation in primary energy consumption for the US, China, India and the EU. These four constitute 56 percent of total world energy consumption and are home to 48 percent of the world's population. The fossil fuel share is almost 90 percent in China, compared to 72 percent in the European Union. The fossil fuel mix also differs, with China having almost two-thirds of its energy consumption met by coal, while in the US and EU this share is about 15 percent.

Global oil consumption has become more and more concentrated in the transportation sector. Fifty years ago, oil was burned for heating

Table 10.3   Estimated primary energy consumption in 2016 (mtoe and percentage)

	US		EU		China		India	
	mtoe	%	mtoe	%	mtoe	%	mtoe	%
Coal	336	16	239	15	1957	65	402	45
Oil	796	37	524	33	552	18	222	25
Gas	643	30	381	24	172	6	47	5
Nuclear	219	10	218	14	56	2	10	1
Hydro	23	1	30	2	102	3	11	1
Bioenergy	101	5	154	10	112	4	200	22
Other Renewables	37	2	48	3	55	2	6	1
Total	2155	100	1594	100	3006	100	898	100
Fossil-fuel share	82		72		89		75	
Share of world consumption	16		12		22		7	
Share of world population	4		7		19		18	

Source: IEA (2017, annex).

and electricity generation. The latter use is almost nonexistent today, except in some oil-producing countries. Also the industrial use of oil as an input factor has been reduced, although almost a quarter of world oil consumption is still related to industrial production, primarily through processing in the petrochemical industry. Nearly all plastic products are made from petrochemicals. Oil is the basis for synthetic rubber and fabrics. Oil is estimated to be part of more than 6,000 miscellaneous consumer products. Oil is also part of the production of goods used in the industry sectors themselves, in building materials, for example, and in thousands of products used in various industries. These multiple products are made by the application of a number of different technologies and production processes. The dominant and growing consumer sector for oil products is transportation. Fifty-five percent of oil consumption is in transportation. About 14 percent of global greenhouse gas emissions comes from the transportation sector. Road transportation dominates the sector with 74 percent of oil consumption, aviation and marine transportation each cover about 11 percent of consumption and rail transport is responsible for the remaining 3 percent of oil consumption in the transportation sector (Summerton et al., 2016, p. 10).

10.1.3 Reducing Emission in the Industrial Sector

With more than 6,000 products containing oil, the diversity of production processes and the possibilities for non-emission substitutions are large, but highly varied. It follows that "a piecewise approach to reducing emissions is required, which is challenging to monitor, incentivize and control" (Brown et al., 2012, p. 1). Current industrial technological standards vary immensely across countries and regions. As a result, the transfer of technologies will both increase efficiency and reduce emissions. In some cases fuel switching is an option, in other cases product design and composition can be altered. This will be a matter of costs and profit margins. In most cases, changing fuel in existing industrial plants seems to be prohibitively costly, at least without government subsidies. Building new plants with non-fossil input will depend on investment in new technology. In the absence of subsidies, such investments will have to have a positive impact on companies' balance sheets within a reasonable period. Finally, the underlying trends in demand will also influence the possibility of reducing overall global oil consumption. For the industry sector, the IEA finds that: "Despite the growth in total demand, the oil intensity of GDP (i.e. the amount of oil used per unit of economic value) continues to decline . . . The industry sector, the second-largest contributor to global GDP and the second-largest oil consumer (when including petrochemical feed stocks), uses 30% less oil per unit of value added [than one and a half decades ago]." This effect is slower in the industry sector than in the service sector because "soaring demand for plastic products in developing economies more than offset further improvements and saturation effects in the industrialized countries" (IEA, 2015, p. 120). The industrial use of oil might increase further if "innovation in chemical products triggers further substitution away from other materials (metals, wood) or if a much higher number of EV [electric vehicles] are sold (electric vehicles tend to require more plastic than conventional cars)" (IEA, 2017, p. 168). IEA predicts an increase of 5 mbd from today until 2040, as they see "few substitution options away from oil available in the petrochemical industry, and with many of the easiest efficiency opportunities already captured" (IEA, 2015, p. 172).

10.1.4 Reducing Emissions in the Transportation Sector

In the transportation sector, a number of factors will influence the future demand for the various fuels. Continued technological improvement of the efficiency and emissions from all diesel and gasoline vehicles is possible, and thus emissions from new vehicles are likely to continue to fall.

However, the overall effect on emission can be offset as the number of cars increases. The number of new cars sold increased from 68.4 million in 2006 to 93.9 million in 2016. This represents an annual increase of 2.5 million cars or about 3.7 percent. Four-fifth of this increase was increase in sales of new cars in China. In 2005 the number of new cars sold in China was 33 percent of the number sold in the US, by 2016 this ratio was 156 percent. The number of vehicles in use in 2014 was 808 per 1,000 inhabitants in the US, 569 in the EU, 102 in China and only 22 per 1,000 inhabitants in India (OICA, 2017). If the trend of increased motorization continues in both China and India, the increase in the number of cars will offset improvement in efficiency and reduced emissions. Improved energy efficiency can have unintended consequences regarding consumption, as a more fuel-efficient car, and thus cheaper to use, can lead to increased driving, the so-called rebound effect. If so the positive effect on emissions is reduced or nullified (Sorell, 2007). This is further complicated in the transportation sector, since there is no linear relationship between high income and reduced emission. With a high income, two effects follow: a larger car, with a more gasoline consuming engine, and more cars in the same household. These effects can nullify the effect of technological improvements in the car engines themselves.

A more consequential technological change could be to abandon the internal combustion engine and switch to electric vehicles. So far the technology is ready for light vehicles, although with some limitations regarding battery technology putting limits on driving distance. The infrastructure is also lagging behind. More important is the lack of electric alternatives in heavy-duty road transportation and in aviation and maritime transportation. The technology will certainly develop further, and increase the reach of electric transportation. Still some caveats exists. The total sales of electric cars reached three million at the end of 2017. The annual growth rate of electric cars is likely to increase. The IEA (2017, pp. 164–165) made a strong upwards revision of the projection of electric cars and now projects 280 million electric cars in 2040, representing about 15 percent of the total car fleet. This would reduce oil demand by around 2.5 mbd. The effect on CO_2 emissions is more complicated. The US National Academy of Sciences discusses this issue in a large-scale report entitled, *Hidden Costs of Energy* (NAS, 2013). They balance the externalities of a reduction in urban emissions, safety issues and the environmental aspects related to battery recycling and disposal. They find that the positive impact of fuel switching in the consumption stage of the value chain depends on the type of primary energy fed into the electricity production. If coal is used to generate the electricity used in electric vehicles, the emission reduction from replacing the internal combustion engine with the electric engine is reduced and possibly lost. Even when considering the efficiency gains in the engine. "When the damages attributable to other parts of the life cycle were included, especially the emissions from the feedstock and the fuel (emissions from electricity production), the aggregate damages for the grid-dependent and all-electric vehicles became comparable to, or somewhat higher than, those from gasoline" (NAS, 2013, p. 202). A similar conclusion is reached by Holtsmark and Skonhoft (2014), comparing the direct emissions from driving gasoline cars with electric cars based on the present mix of input in electricity generation worldwide. In order to reduce emissions from the car fleet by introducing electric cars, the mix of energy sources in electricity generation will have to change reducing the share of fossil fuels. This is particularly important as the largest share of increase in new car sales is in China, with a share of coal in electricity generation of 82 percent, compared to the world average of 46 percent. The time horizon is also important. There is about one billion vehicles in the world. As indicated above this figure is increasing. One of the hardest obstacles to achieving a reduced global consumption of fossil fuels is the fact that for several decades many hundreds of millions of people will increase their energy consumption. This is a result of increased world population and the tendency to increased energy consumption as the level of economic welfare increases. IEAs most likely scenario is the so-called 'New Policies' scenario. In Table 10.2 this scenario suggests an increase in the use of all types of primary energy sources, although renewables represent the strongest growth. It implies a fossil fuel share of 75 percent in 2040. Even the sustainable development scenario ends up with a fossil fuel share in the global energy mix in 2040 of 61 percent. Within these global trends, there are important geographical differences that reflect variations in the level of industrialization and economic development. Countries and regions that are relatively industrialized and economically developed will reduce oil demand, whereas those that are still relatively less industrialized, and with populations aspiring to economic development, will likely increase their demand for oil (Figure 10.2).

10.2 THE ENERGY IMPLICATIONS OF CLIMATE POLICIES[2]

10.2.1 The United Nations Framework Convention on Climate Change

The United Nations Framework Convention on Climate Change, also known as the Paris Convention or just the Paris Agreement, was signed in December 2015, and as of January 2018, 172 of the 197 signatory

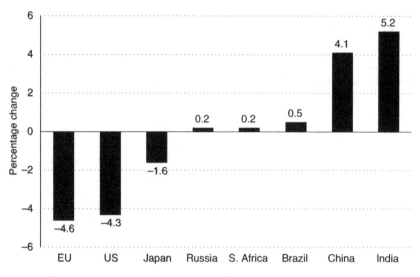

Source: IEA (2017, p. 163).

Figure 10.2   Change in oil demand in selected countries and regions in the New Policies scenario, 2016–2040

countries have ratified it. Although the ambition of the countries varies, the Convention will affect energy policy-making processes, both directly and indirectly in the future. Directly in terms of putting pressure on governments to honor promises of climate warming abatement action and indirectly in the sense that the general public will be more inclined to accept changes in energy usage, and energy producers will get incentives to 'decarbonize' their energy products. The aim of the Convention is to keep the global temperature rise this century well below 2 degrees Celsius above pre-industrial levels and to pursue efforts to limit the temperature increase even further to 1.5 degrees Celsius. The countries determine their own obligations by presenting so-called "nationally determined contributions" (NDCs). The countries will report on their fulfillment of the NDCs and are supposed to strengthen these efforts in assessments made every fifth year.

The structural conditions and economic consequences of changing national or regional energy systems vary dramatically. There are a large number of actors with strong interests and the capacity to exercise both economic and political power along the energy value chain. They may potentially halt, delay or alter the actual implementation of the Paris treaty. As indicated above, developments in consumption volumes and patterns will be most important. Market forces are vital, but they are influenced by power, politics and public policy outcomes. Transportation is the most important sector for oil consumption; changes in transport behavior, modes and technology will therefore be vital drivers. Both the behavior reactions from oil-producing countries and companies will influence the implementation of the Convention. Financial investors will be a decisive factor in shaping the production side of the oil system. If investments go down as a response to lasting low oil prices, and/or because investors decide to turn to green economy options, then the supply of oil will logically shrink. On the other hand, the growth and development aspirations of a rapidly growing population in developing countries are likely to stimulate demand, and thus increase exploration, production and subsequently the price. This will attract investors into further development of oil and the other fossil fuels.

In Table 10.3 I highlighted three countries, the United States, China and India, and the European Union. These four actors will be quite decisive if the Paris goal of 'well below 2°C' is to be achieved, as they represent half the population of the world and more than half the use of fossil fuels. Their indicated Nationally Determined Contributions (NDCs) vary considerably, with the EU's binding target of an at least 40 percent domestic reduction of greenhouse gas emissions by 2030 compared to 1990 being by far the most ambitious. China aims to achieve the peaking of carbon dioxide emissions by around 2030, and to increase the share of non-fossil fuels in primary energy consumption to approximately 20 percent (versus 12 percent in 2013). The US' commitment is a 17 percent reduction by 2020 (from the 2005 level of emissions) and to explore possible accelerated reductions further on, whereas India has committed itself to a 20–25 percent reduction over the same period. These policy positions combined are not going to result in implementing the 'well below 2°C' target. The procedure of setting more ambitious targets every five years, and developing a transparent and accountable system to follow up Paris and the five-year revisions, is therefore crucial for the implementation of the Paris Convention. In June 2017, the US President Donald Trump announced that the US would withdraw from the UN Framework Convention on Climate Change.

The Convention takes unequal levels of development into account by not committing developing, in particular the least developed, countries to combatting greenhouse gas emissions to the extent that developed countries are committed. Implementation of the agreement will "reflect equity and the principle of common but differentiated responsibilities and respective capabilities" (Agreement article 2). A major political issue in the years ahead will therefore be how to balance global goals for combatting GHG with national aspirations for economic development. China and India, with its combination of demographic growth and high economic growth potential, will be key actors. For both these countries, however, the vital factor in determining their follow-up of Paris is their consumption of coal (see Table 10.3). There is a considerable amount of potential for energy conservation in the carbon sector in China, but it is very much dependent on an increased investment in innovating and developing new technology (Boqiang and Xuan, 2015). In general, there are billions of oil consumers making individual decisions and calculations every day with implications for global oil consumption. The implementation of the Paris Convention will have to put in place various incentives, restrictions, regulations and legislation all over the world for these individuals to reduce their oil consumption. A large number of the oil-consuming individuals live in countries that provide them with a significant degree of freedom regarding their choices of energy consumption. In these cases, changes are best induced through mild incentives or changes in attitudes toward oil consumption at the societal, and not least the local level.

10.2.2 Producer Reactions

The structure on the producer side of the market is different from that on the consumer side. Compared to the billions of individual oil consumers, the top 10 producing countries cover two-thirds of the market, which obviously represents considerable power.

All of the top 10 producers, with the exception of the US, have a strong state involvement and control over their oil industry, and thus all decisions related to oil production, and subsequently the market-related reactions to the implementation of the Paris Agreement. Although there are important differences between Canada, Saudi Arabia and China regarding governmental control, one can argue that the economic aspects relevant for analyzing their reaction to Paris will be fairly similar. Most of the largest oil producers were against any type of international climate agreement, simply because it increases the likelihood of a reduced consumption of oil. Some producer countries were more active in their opposition to the Paris treaty than others. Here the focus is on the options available to oil-producing countries in the face of an increased potential for non-trivial negative effects on oil consumption following from implementation of the Paris Convention. The conclusion of the previous section was that such effects are hard to identify in the short run, but they might be more likely in the longer run. It should also be noted that the Paris Convention could create significant emission reductions without having a strong impact on the oil sector, for instance if the global coal consumption is reduced considerably.

Even so, it is fair to expect some kind of strategic reaction from oil producers, as the Paris Convention creates a new type of uncertainty for their long-term reliance on income from oil exports. Saudi Arabia's intention to diversify into financial operations is an illustration, though probably a non-typical one given the country's extraordinarily strong position as the world's largest oil exporter. When it comes to options related to the market and the oil industry of producing countries, Claes and Hveem (2016, pp. 202–203) outline three possible strategies to meet reduced demand induced by the Paris Agreement.

Competitive strategy: In this case, the oil producers meet the competition from other energy sources by reducing the price of oil. On average, the production costs in countries like Saudi Arabia and the other Gulf states are less than 10 US dollars per barrel. More important in the oil industry is the so-called replacement cost (the cost of replacing a consumed barrel with a new barrel), which represents the long-term costs of sustaining current production levels. The figure has been falling every year over the last three decades, with some exceptions. The technical and industrial potential for a long-term/low-price strategy is present. However, to what extent it is economically and politically viable is less obvious, but if the alternative is to be out of business, several key producers might find this strategy attractive. With moderate investments, several of the producers around the Persian Gulf can increase their production capacity.

Capitulation strategy: Models of resource economics suggest that oil-producing countries do not operate according to principles of market economics, but instead try to gain as much rent from their respective oil wealth as possible (cf. Section 2.1). If the expectation is that the consumers will turn away from oil in the long term, it could make sense to try to gain as much money as possible from the oil reserves, as soon as possible. This would imply immediately dumping as much oil as possible on the market. This would obviously bring the price down, so it is not entirely distinct from their competitive strategy, but it can be identified by the oil producers, thereby maximizing their production according to their installed production capacity and, if possible, to increase their production capacity even further.

Change-over strategy: This strategy moves us away from the pure market operations, and focuses on alternative courses of action in order to sustain current economic welfare levels. Several of the Middle East oil producers have pursued such a strategy for decades, though with little success. It is very difficult to turn resources and investments away from an extremely lucrative industry, such as oil production in the Middle East, into necessarily less lucrative sectors. A fall in oil prices might help such a strategy. Another aspect emerging is that some of these countries have natural conditions for alternative energy production, first and foremost solar power. It would obviously not be possible to replace the income from oil in the short run. But it is possible to imagine a breaking point, in which the long-term value of solar power, investment costs included, outweigh a losing battle to sustain world oil demand by cutting oil prices.

The three strategies are not that distinct from each other, but they can be empirically identified by investigating market behavior, production level and capacity change, as well as investments in alternative industries. Still, these factors can change even without any reference to the Paris treaty or climate change in general. Even so, the ambition for oil producers with large resource bases to prolong the horizon of the oil age can influence the likelihood and costs of replacing the consumption of fossil fuels with renewables. An oil price above $100 per barrel would make it much easier for renewables to compete than with an oil price below $50 per barrel. The available resources that can be produced profitably at $30 per barrel over the next decades are almost infinite. Aquilera and Radetzki (2016, p. 184) project an even greater "availability and lower long-term oil prices due to the shale and conventional oil [technological] revolutions . . . The price drop would give oil a major competitive advantage versus non-fossil alternatives, raising the costs of implementing policies to reduce carbon emissions."

For some of the key oil exporters, the income from oil exports is crucial for their economic activity in general, and thus for the welfare level of their societies. In addition, some of these countries are so-called rentier states (see Section 3.4), indicating that the state is economically independent of its inhabitants as it supports itself from oil income. In such cases, a reduction in oil income jeopardizes the political leadership. At the same time, some of these regimes have a huge potential for defending their positions, also against oil price drops. A recent illustration is the Saudi Arabian government's announcement to register Aramco, the state oil company, and by far the biggest producer in the world, at the Riyadh stock exchange. Selling a mere 5 percent of the company is assumed to raise $250 billion and support state finances currently running a budget deficit. In other words, the Kingdom disposes of a huge reserve of not only oil, but also financial resources. If it chooses, the Kingdom would be able to diversify its economy and make it less dependent on oil income in the future.

10.2.3   Investor Reactions

Investor decisions are a crucial factor in shaping the effects of the Paris Convention. Private investment decisions are also crucial to the prospect of sustained oil production in most producer countries, with the possible exception of several key producers in the Middle East. While the rig count of Saudi Arabia increased 15 percent from 2014 to 2015, it was almost cut in half in the US (OPEC, 2016, p. 91). If investments in the oil industry were to dry up, the industry would contract. The price of oil is an essential focal point for investors. With low prices, the time horizon will have to be extended in order to handle risk, and gain lifetime profits from the individual field investments. The price developments are not the only factor to consider in order to understand future behavior of investors and oil companies.

Contrary to the oil producers themselves, investors can rapidly change from oil to other assets. The role of investors, whether they sit inside the producing companies, provide capital to finance those companies or the oil services companies, or whether they consider investing in transportation modes, has an effect at all stages of the oil value chain. In many countries, oil production is a capital-intensive business. Therefore, a crucial variable in the premises forming investor decisions is what long-term strategies they adopt, among other things what time horizon they apply for their profit target and what risk they are prepared to take. The coal industry is already subject to substantial disinvestment. Moreover, several individual investors, as well as corporate managements, have signaled that they will invest in the transformation to a green economy. The standard assumption is that most investors still respond primarily to market forces, and their own profit aspirations and risk assessments rather than to political decisions like the Paris climate agreement. Can this change, and thus give the Paris Convention a significant impact on investors' behavior?

If we assume that investors are solely profit driven, the effect of a strict and global climate policy, could be compared to a rapid fall in the price of oil. Obviously, if oil consumption were to be severely restricted or made illegal, no one would pay for the oil. A more realistic scenario is that governments start to implement policies that make oil consumers switch to other fuels, in one way or another. In such a case, existing oil production would continue for some time, but investors would abandon prospects of investing in development of new commercial reserves, let alone the exploration for new resources. This would be an extreme parallel to the price drop in late 2014, which lasted until late 2016. Global investments in oil fell from $920 billion in 2014 to an estimated $620 billion in 2016. At the same time, investments in green energy increased in the entire carbon sector. Green investments increased six-fold from 2004 to 2015.[3] Given the political enforcement of policies aiming to reduce oil consumption, there is a possibility that investors will decide to move out of oil. A low oil price without such convincing political signals, would on the other hand, increase demand and bring back investments, and increase emission further down the road. The past is a story of very volatile oil prices; and some investors may bet on that pattern repeating itself. A good number of them are expecting price increases in the months or years to come; they may rely on the well-renowned consultancy firm Rystad Energy, which predicts a price rise to $95 per barrel by 2020.[4]

10.2.4   Achieving Emission Reductions

Summerton et al. (2016) make an elaborate attempt to estimate the effect on the oil market of governments' implementation of the Paris Convention. The study finds that implementation of vehicle efficiency standards in the period 2000 to 2015 has already reduced oil consumption by 5 billion barrels (Summerton et al., 2016, p. 6). Comparing two scenarios of oil demand in the transport sector to 2050 shows a stark difference. The 'business as usual' scenario assumes existing emission reduction policies, but adds no new initiatives. The 'technology potential' scenario includes the introduction of more emission-reducing technology-innovations for road transportation, passenger aviation and international shipping. "It assumes an extension of vehicle efficiency standards in markets with pre-existing policies, as well as an expansion of these policies to the rest of the world" (Summerton et al., 2016, p. 16). Table 10.4 summarizes these projections.

The Paris Convention was a major political and institutional achievement. However, its effect on the global oil system is uncertain and complex. The process leading from the Paris Convention to the end of oil is long and subject to a number of intervening factors. Even if consumers and investors also push for de-carbonization regarding oil, producer countries and the oil industry might contradict such efforts. How strong, and widespread the Paris effect will be on oil is therefore extremely difficult, if not impossible, to predict. The Summerton et al. (2016) study shows dramatic differences

Table 10.4   Global oil demand from transport, 2015 and two scenarios for 2050 (million barrels per day)

	2015	Business as usual	Technology potential
On-Road	38.2	67.1	30.6
Aviation	5.8	25.7	10.9
Marine	5.7	10.9	5.3
Rail	1.7	3.4	3.4
Total	51.4	107.1	50.2

Source: Summerton et al. (2016, p. 10).

between the two scenarios. The difference is the presence of strong emission reducing policies, not only in a few countries, but globally. And if strong emission-reducing policies are introduced, the use of oil or fossil fuels in general, will have to be replaced by different energy sources. "The choice then comes down to three sources of renewable energies: electricity generated by large wind turbines, by conversion of solar radiation . . . and biofuels" (Smil, 2017, p.153). Wind and solar power are primarily used for electricity generation. Oil is not. Thus, technological advances and the increase in use of these renewable energy sources will directly replace coal and gas, rather than oil. On the other hand, oil is dominant in the transportation sector. The technology of making modern cars that run on electricity has been improved, and sales of electric cars are increasing and will do so more rapidly in the future. The effect on emissions of this change is dependent on the source used for electricity generation. Today almost 40 percent of electricity generation is based on burning of coal, 22 percent comes from natural gas and 7 percent is down to oil. Electric cars based on the global energy mix of electricity generation are not thus emission-free. De-carbonizing oil consumption implies not only a switch of power source from oil to hydrogen or electricity, but also new motor vehicles, cars, ships, airplanes and new infrastructure in most parts of the transportation sector. Passenger cars are somewhat easier to run on electricity than trucks, ships and airplanes, but it is also possible to envision further technological advances for these methods of transportation as well. The Summerton et al. (2016) assumption of an expansion of emission reducing policies globally has not yet been manifested. In 2013, about two-thirds of all wind electricity originated in just four countries (United States, China, Germany and Spain), and two-thirds of solar electricity came from just five nations (Germany, Italy, China, Spain and Japan) (Smil, 2017, p.229).

Without a substantial impact on the global consumption of fossil fuels (oil, gas and coal), the Paris Convention will be a failure. The implementation of the agreement presupposes strong political measures in almost all developed countries. Clearly, this process may also be influenced by environmental activists and powerful commercial actors from both the fossil fuel industries and the emerging green industries. In democratic countries, the attitude of the electorate will influence the pattern and speed of change. On the international political scene, individual countries are reluctant to move ahead of other countries in introducing costly taxation or climate programs, for fear of losing competitiveness. In certain cases, domestic public opinion can override such fear. Rich countries are in a better position to take on risky climate policies than poor countries. Democratic consuming countries are more likely to experience such domestic pressure than autocratic regimes. This being said, the recent changes in Chinese energy policy are assumed to be the result of strong public opposition to local environmental degradation.

Three possible scenarios were elaborated above to capture likely responses to climate policies from oil producers. It can be assumed that producers with low costs of production will follow a competitive or capitulation strategy, while many of those producing at higher costs, and thus facing the prospect of continued prices below profitability, will pursue the change-over strategy. Politics is an intervening factor also among the producers.

The world is on the verge of another energy transition. But it is appropriate to end with some cautious remarks about what lies in store. "Energy transitions on the global scale – and that is the only scale that ultimately matters as far as decarbonization and prevention of an excessive temperature rise is concerned – remain inherently protracted affairs" (Smil, 2017, p. 175). "The process will be considerably more difficult than is commonly realized and that neither its pace nor its compositional and operational details are yet clear" (Smil, 2017, p. 233).

NOTES

1. Note that these figures covers the United States only. The various primary sources have different shares of the sectors of consumption in different countries.
2. This section is based on Claes and Hveem (2016).
3. *Aftenposten* (Norwegian), April 8, 2016.
4. 'The Global Oil & Gas Markets' Trends in a 1–5 Year Perspective – Opportunities and Challenges for Egypt.' Presentation by Henrik M. Poulsen, Rystad Energy, Cairo, February 13, 2017.

References

Abir, M. (1993). *Saudi Arabia: Government, Society and the Gulf Crisis.* London: Routledge.

Acemoglu, D., Johnson, S., and Robinson, J. (2001). The Colonial Origins of Comparative Development: An Empirical Investigation. *American Economic Review*, 91(5), 1369–1401.

Acemoglu, D., and Robinson, J. (2006). *Economic Origins of Dictatorship and Democracy.* Cambridge, UK: Cambridge University Press.

Adelman, M.A. (1972). *The World Petroleum Market.* Baltimore: Johns Hopkins University Press.

Adelman, M.A. (1977). Producers, Consumers, and Multinationals: Problems in Analyzing a Non-competitive Market. Working Paper MIT-EL77 038WP (World Oil Project). Cambridge, MA: MIT Energy Laboratory.

Adelman, M.A. (1982). OPEC as a Cartel. In D. Teece and J.M. Griffin (Eds), *OPEC Behavior and World Oil Prices.* London: George Allen & Unwin, pp. 37–63.

Adelman, M.A. (1986). The Competitive Floor to World Oil Prices. *The Energy Journal*, 7, 9–32.

Adelman, M.A. (1987). Economic Theory of Mineral Depletion with Special Reference to Oil and Gas. Paper presented at the IAEE Ninth International Conference, Calgary.

Adelman, M.A. (1993a). *The Economics of Petroleum Supply.* Cambridge, MA: MIT Press.

Adelman, M.A. (1993b). Modelling World Oil Supply. *Energy Journal*, 14(1), 1–23.

Adelman, M.A. (1995). *The Genie out of the Bottle – World Oil since 1970.* Cambridge, MA: MIT Press.

Adelman, M.A. (2004). The Real Oil Problem. *Regulation*, 27(1), 16–21.

Al-Alkim, H.H. (1994). *The GCC States in an Unstable World.* London: Saqi Books.

Al-Chalabi, F.J. (1989). *OPEC at the Crossroads.* Oxford: Pergamon Press.

Al-Khatteeb, L. (2014). The UN Strikes Back at ISIL's Black Economy. *The Huffington Post*, August 23, 2014. https://www.huffingtonpost.com/luay-al-khatteeb/the-un-strikes-back-at-isil_b_5702240.html?guccounter=1 (accessed July 1, 2018).

Alexeev, M., and Conrad, R. (2009). The Elusive Curse of Oil. *Review of Economics and Statistics*, 91, 586–598.

Alvik, I. (2015). Fundamental Principles of Petroleum Law. *Marius*, (456), 227–255.

Amen, T.G. (1996). The IPE of Energy and Oil. In D.N. Balaam and M. Veseth (Eds), *Introduction to International Political Economy*. New Jersey: Prentice Hall, page numbers unavailable.

Amuzegar, J. (1999). *Managing the Oil Wealth – OPEC's Windfalls and Pitfalls*. London: I.B. Tauris Publishers.

Andersen, J., and Ross, M. (2014). The Big Oil Change A Closer Look at the Haber–Menaldo Analysis. *Comparative Political Studies*, 47, 993–1021.

Andersen, S.S., and Austvik, O.G. (2000). Nasjonal handlefrihet – nye internasjonale rammebetingelser, Petroleum, makt og demokrati. *Report, from the Norwegian Power and Democracy Project*. http://www.sv.uio.no/mutr/publikasjoner/rapporter/rapp2000/Rapport21.html (accessed July 1, 2018).

Anderson, I.H. (1981). *Aramco: The United States and Saudi Arabia*. Princeton: Princeton University Press.

Aquilera, R.F., and Radetzki, M. (2016). *The Price of Oil*. Cambridge: Cambridge University Press.

Areklett, K. (2010). The Peak of the Oil Age – Analyzing the world oil production Reference Scenario in World Energy Outlook 2008. *Energy Policy*, 38(2010), 1398–1414.

Armstrong, C. (2017). *Justice and Natural Resources: An Egalitarian Theory*. Oxford: Oxford University Press.

Atkinson, G., and Hamilton, K. (2003). Savings, Growth and the Resource Curse Hypothesis. *World Development*, 31(11), 1793–1807.

Auty, R. (1993). *Sustaining Development in Resource Economies: The Resource Curse Thesis*. London and New York: Routledge.

Auty, R. (2001). The Political Economy of Resource-Driven Growth. *European Economic Review*, 45, 839–846.

Baland, J.M., and Francois, P. (2000). Rent-seeking and Resource Booms. *Journal of Development Economics*, 61, 527–542.

Baldwin, D.A. (1979). Power Analysis and World Power. *World Politics*, 31, 161–194.

Barnes, J., and Jaffe, A.M. (2006). The Persian Gulf and the Geopolitics of Oil. *Survival*, 48(1), 143–162.

Basosi, D., Garavini, G., and Trentin, M. (2018). *Oil Counter-shock: The Price Collapse of the 1980s*. London: I.B. Tauris.

Bates, R., and Lien, D.-H.D. (1985). A Note on Taxation, Development, and Representative Government. *Politics & Society*, 14, 53–70.

Benchekroun, H., and Withagen, C. (2011). The Optimal Depletion of Exhaustible Resources: A Complete Characterization. *Resource and Energy Economics*, 33, 612–636.

Bjorvatn, K., and Farzanegan, M. R. (2015). Resource Rents, Balance of Power, and Political Stability. *Journal of Peace Research*, 52, 758–773.

Black, J., and Nigar Hashimzade, G.M. (2017). *Oxford Dictionary of Economics* (5th edn). Oxford: Oxford University Press.

Blair, J.M. (1976). *The Control of Oil*. New York: Vintage Books.

Boqiang, L., and Xuan, X. (2015). Energy Conservation Potential in China's Petroleum Refining Industry: Evidence and Policy Implications. *Energy Conservation and Management*, 91, 377–386.

Boussena, S., and Locatelli, C. (2006). Le nouveau role de L'État dans l'industrie petrolière en Russie: le privé en tutelle? Retrieved from Laboratoire d'Economie de la Production et de l'Intégration Internationale Département Energie et Politiques de l'Environnement (EPE). https://halshs.archives-ouvertes.fr/halshs-00010435/document (accessed July 1, 2018).

Boyce, J.R. (2013). Externality Regulation in Oil and Gas. In J. Shogren (Ed.), *Encyclopedia of Energy, Natural Resources, and Environmental Economics*. London: Elsevier. https://www.sciencedirect.com/science/article/pii/B9780123750679000565 (accessed July 1, 2018).

BP (2017). BP Statistical Review of World Energy. https://www.bp.com/content/dam/bp/en/corporate/pdf/energy-economics/statistical-review-2017/bp-statistical-review-of-world-energy-2017-full-report.pdf (accessed July 1, 2018).

Brollo, F., Nannicini, T., Perotti, R., and Tabellini, G. (2013). The Political Resource Curse. *American Economic Review*, 103, 1759–1796.

Bromley, S. (1991). *American Hegemony and World Oil: The Industry, the State System and the World Economy*. Oxford: Polity Press.

Bronson, R. (2006). *Thicker than Oil: America's Uneasy Partnership with Saudi Arabia*. Oxford and New York: Oxford University Press.

Brown, T., Gambhir, A., Florin, N., and Fennell, P. (2012). Reducing CO_2 Emissions from Heavy Industry: A Review of Technologies and Considerations for Policy Makers. Briefing Paper, no. 7, February 2012 Imperial College London. https://www.imperial.ac.uk/media/imperial-college/grantham-institute/public/publications/briefing-papers/Reducing-CO2-emissions-from-heavy-industry---Grantham-BP-7.pdf (accessed July 11, 2018).

Brunnschweiler, C.N., and Bulte, E.H. (2008). The Resource Curse Revisited and Revised: A Tale of Paradoxes and Red Herrings. *Journal of Environmental Economics and Management*, 55, 248–264.

Brunnschweiler, C.N., and Bulte, E.H. (2009). Natural Resources and

Violent Conflict: Resource Abundance, Dependency and Onset of Civil Wars. *Oxford Economic Papers*, 61(4), 651–674.

Bull, H. (1977). *The Anarchical Society – A Study of Order in World Politics*. London: Macmillan.

Buzan, B. (1991). *People, States and Fear – An Agenda for International Security Studies in the Post–Cold War Era*. New York Harvester-Wheatsheaf.

Buzan, B., and Wæver, O. (2003). *Regions and Powers*. Cambridge: Cambridge University Press.

Bye, V. (1979). Nationalization of Oil in Venezuela – Re-defined Dependence and Legitimization of Imperialism. *Journal of Peace Research*, 16(1), 57–78.

Campell, C.J. (2005). *Oil Crisis*. Brentwood: Multi-Science Publishing.

Cappelen, Å., and Chaudhury, R. (2004). The Future of the Saudi Arabian Economy: Possible Effects on the World Oil Market. In D. Heradstveit and H. Hveem (Eds), *Oil in the Gulf*. London: Ashgate, pp. 41–62.

Cavalcanti, T.V. de V., Mohaddes, K., and Raissi, M. (2014). Commodity Price Volatility and the Sources of Growth. *Journal of Applied Econometrics*, 30(6), 857–873.

Caves, R. (1980). Industrial Organization, Corporate Strategy and Structure. *Journal of Economic Literature*, XVIII.

Chaudry, K.A. (1997). *The Price of Wealth: Economies and Institutions in the Middle East*. Ithaca: Cornell University Press.

Cherp, A., and Jewell, J. (2014). The Concept of Energy Security: Beyond the Four As. *Energy Policy*, 75, 415–421.

Church (1974). Church-commission hearings on *Multinational Corporations and the United States' Foreign Policy*. U.S. Senate 93. Congress 2nd session, 11 volumes. Washington, DC: U.S. Government Printing Office.

Claes, D.H. (2001). *The Politics of Oil-Producer Cooperation*. Boulder: Westview Press.

Claes, D.H. (2005). The United States and Iraq: Making Sense of the Oil Factor. *Middle East Policy*, 12(4), 9.

Claes, D.H. (2010). Global Energy Security: Resource Availability, Economic Conditions and Political Constraints. Paper presented at the SGIR 7th Pan-European International Relations Conference, Stockholm.

Claes, D.H. (2011). States and Firms in the International Oil Market. In D.H. Claes and C.H. Knutsen (Eds), *Governing the Global Economy – Politics, Institutions and Economic Development*. London: Routledge, pp. 292–311.

Claes, D.H. (2017). The Scramble for Arctic Oil and Natural Gas. In T.C.

Lehmann (Ed.), *The Geopolitics of Global Energy – The New Cost of Plenty*. Boulder: Lynne Rienner Publishers, pp. 85–104.

Claes, D.H., Goldthau, A., and Livingston, D. (2016). Saudi Arabia: Harnessing the Oil Market. In M. Leonard (Ed.), *Connectivity Wars – Why Migration, Finance and Trade are the Geo-Economic Battlegrounds of the Future*. London: European Council of Foreign Relations (ECFR), pp. 186–193.

Claes, D.H., and Hveem, H. (2009). Emerging National Oil Companies – Challengers or Partners? Paper presented at the 50th Annual Convention of the International Studies Association: Exploring the Past, Anticipating the Future, New York.

Claes, D.H., and Hveem, H. (2016). From Paris to the End of Oil. *Politics and Governance*, 4(3), 197–208.

Cleveland, C.J., and Morris, C. (2006). *Dictionary of Energy*. Oxford: Elsevier.

Colgan, J. (2013a). Fueling the Fire – Pathways from Oil to War. *International Security*, 38(2), 147–180.

Colgan, J. (2013b). *Petro-Aggression – When Oil Causes War*. Cambridge: Cambridge University Press.

Colgan, J. (2014). The Emperor Has No Clothes: The Limits of OPEC in the Global Oil Market. *International Organization*, 68(Summer), 599–632.

Colgan, J., Keohane, R.O., and van der Graaf, T. (2012). Punctuated Equilibrium in the Energy Regime Complex. *Review of International Organization*, 7(2), 117–143.

Collier, P., and Hoeffler, A. (1998). On Economic Causes of Civil War. *Oxford Economic Papers*, 50(4), 563–573.

Collier, P., and Hoeffler, A. (2002). Greed and Grievance in Civil War. CSAE Working Paper, WPS 2002–01, Oxford University. http://www.economics.ox.ac.uk/CSAEadmin/workingpapers/pdgs/2002-01text.pdf (accessed July 11, 2018).

Collier, P., and Hoeffler, A. (2004). Greed and Grievance in Civil War. *Oxford Economic Papers*, 56(4), 563–595.

Collier, P., Hoeffler, A., and Rohner, D. (2009). Beyond Greed and Grievance: Feasibility and Civil War. *Oxford Economic Papers*, 61(1), 1–27.

Cordesman, A.H. (2002). War with Iraq: A Cost–Benefit Analysis. *Middle East Policy*, 9(4), 23.

Cordesman, A.H. (2003). *Saudi Arabia Enters the Twenty-First Century – The Political, Foreign Policy, Economic, and Energy Dimensions*. Westport: Praeger.

Cordesman, A.H., and Wagner, A.R. (1990). *The Lessons of Modern War – Volume II: The Iran–Iraq War*. Boulder: Westview Press.

Corrales, J. (2013). The House that Chavez Built. *Foreign Policy* (March

7). https://foreignpolicy.com/2013/03/07/the-house-that-chavez-built/ (a ccessed July 1, 2018).

Corrales, J. (2015). Don't Blame It On the Oil. *Foreign Policy* (May 7). https://foreignpolicy.com/2015/05/07/dont-blame-it-on-the-oil-venezue la-caracas-maduro/ (accessed July 1, 2018).

Cramer, J.K., and Thrall, A.T. (2012). *Why Did the United States Invade Iraq?* London: Routledge.

Crawford, J. (2012). *Brownlie's Principles of Public International Law.* Oxford: Oxford University Press.

Crèmer, J., and Isfahani, D.S. (1991). *Models of the Oil Market.* Chur Switzerland: Harwood Academic Publishers.

Crystal, J. (1990). *Oil and Politics in the Gulf: Rulers and Merchants in Kuwait and Qatar.* Cambridge: Cambridge University Press.

Cuaresma, J.C., Oberhofer, H., and Raschky, P.A. (2011). Oil and the Duration of Dictatorship. *Public Choice*, 148, 505–530.

Dahl, C.A. (2004). *International Energy Markets – Understanding Pricing, Policies and Profits.* Tulsa: PennWell Corp.

De Soysa, I., and Neumayer, E. (2005). Resource Wealth and the Risk of Civil War Onset: Result from a New Dataset of Natural Resource Rents, 1970–1999. *Conflict Management and Peace Science*, 24(3), 201–218.

Deffeyes, K.S. (2005). *Beyond Oil: The View from Hubbert's Peak.* New York: Macmillan.

Derman, A.B., and Villarreal, D.J. (2013). United States. In E.G. Periera and K. Talus (Eds), *Upstream Law and Regulation – A Global Guide.* London: Globe Business Publishing, pp. 277–298.

Desta, M.G. (2003). The Organization of Petroleum Exporting Countries, the World Trade Organization, and Regional Trade Agreements. *Journal of World Trade*, 37(3), 523–551.

Desta, M.G. (2010). OPEC Production Management Practices under WTO Law and the Antirust Law of Non-OPEC Countries. *Journal of Energy Natural Resource Law*, 28(4), 439–463.

Doppelhofer, G., Miller, R.I., and Sala-i-Martin, X. (2000). Determinants of Long-Term Growth: A Bayesian Averaging of Classical Estimates (BACE) Approach. NBER Working Paper Series.

Dorraj, M., and English, J.D. (2012). China's Strategy for Energy Acquisition in the Middle East: Potential for Conflict and Cooperation with the United States. *Asian Politics and Policy*, 4(2), 173–191.

Downey, M. (2009). *Oil 101.* Echo Park: Wooden Table Press.

Downs, E.S. (2007). The Fact and Fiction of Sino–African Energy Relations. *China Security*, 3(3), 42–68.

Duffield, J.S. (2008). *Over a Barrel – The Costs of U.S. Foreign Oil Dependency.* Stanford: Stanford University Press.

Dunning, J.H. (1998). An Overview of Relations with National Governments. *New Political Economy,* 3(2), 280–284.

Dunning, T. (2008). *Crude Democracy.* Cambridge: Cambridge University Press.

Easterly, W., and Levine, R. (2003). Tropics, Germs, and Crops: How Endowments Influence Economic Development. *Journal of Monetary Economics,* 50, 3–39.

Eller, S.L., Hartley, P., and Medlock, K. B. (2007). *Empirical Evidence on the Operational Efficiency of National Oil Companies.* Houston: James A. Baker Institute for Public Policy, Rice University.

Engler, R. (1961). *The Politics of Oil – Private Power Democratic Directions.* Chicago: University of Chicago Press.

Esping-Andersen, G. (1990). *The Three Worlds of Welfare Capitalism.* Princeton: Princeton University Press.

Evans, J. (1990). *OPEC and the World Energy Market: A Comprehensive Reference Guide.* Essex: Longman.

Fattouh, B., and Sen, A. (2016). The Past, Present, and Future Role of OPEC. In T. van de Graaf, B.K. Sovacool, A. Ghosh, F. Kern, and M. Klare (Eds), *The Palgrave Handbook of the International Political Economy of Energy.* London: Palgrave Macmillan, pp. 73–94.

FEA (1975). *The Relationship of Oil Companies and Foreign Governments.* Federal Energy Administration. Washington: US Government Printing Office.

Fearon, J.D. (2005). Primary Commodity Exports and Civil War. *Journal of Conflict Resolution,* 49(4), 483–507.

Fearon, J.D., and Laitin, D.D. (2003). Ethnicity, Insurgency, and Civil War. *American Political Science Review,* 97(1), 75–90.

Finon, D. (1991). The Prospects for a New International Petroleum Order. *Energy Studies Review,* 3(3), 260–276.

Freedman, L., and Karsh, E. (1993). *The Gulf Conflict.* London: Faber & Faber.

Freeman, M. (2011). The Sources of Terrorist Financing: Theory and Typology. *Studies in Conflict & Terrorism,* 34(6), 461–475.

FTC (1952). *The International Petroleum Cartel.* Federal Trade Commission. Washington: US Senate.

Gause III, G. (2010). *The International Relations of the Persian Gulf.* Cambridge: Cambridge University Press.

Gautier, D.L., Bird, K.J., Charpentier, R.R., Grantz, A., Houseknecht, D.W., Klett, T.R., . . . Wandrey, C.J. (2009). Assessment of Undiscovered Oil and Gas in the Arctic. *Science,* 324(5931), 1175–1179.

Gelb, A. (1988). *Oil Windfalls: Blessing or Curse?* Oxford: Oxford University Press.

Gelb, A. (2011). Economic Diversification in Resource-Rich Countries. In R. Arezki, T. Gylfason, and A. Sy (Eds), *Beyond the Curse – Policies to Harness the Power of Natural Resources.* Washington: International Monetary Fund, pp. 55–80.

Giroux, J. (2008). Turmoil in the Delta: Trends and Implications. *Perspectives on Terrorism*, 2(8), 11–22.

Gleditsch, K.S., Salehyan, I., and Schultz, K. (2008). Fighting at Home, Fighting Abroad: How Civil Wars Lead to International Disputes. *Journal of Conflict Resolution*, 52(4), 479–506.

Goldthau, A., and Witte, J.M. (2009). Back to the Future or Forward to the Past? Strengthening Markets and Rules for Effective Global Energy Governance. *International Affairs*, 85(2), 373–390.

Golub, D.B. (1985). When Oil and Politics Mix – Saudi Oil Policy 1973–1985. *Harvard Middle East Papers*, 4.

Greer, D.F. (1984). *Industrial Organization and Public Policy.* New York: Macmillan Publishing Company.

Griffin, J.M.T., and David J. (1982). *OPEC Behavior and World Oil Prices.* London: George Allen & Unwin.

Gylfason, T. (2001). Natural Resources, Education, and Economic Development. *European Economic Review*, 45, 847–859.

Gylfason, T. (2011). Natural Resource Endowment: A Mixed Blessing? In R. Arezki, T. Gylfason, and A. Sy (Eds), *Beyond the Curse – Policies to Harness the Power of Natural Resource.* Washington: International Monetary Fund, pp. 7–34.

Gylfason, T., and Zoega, G. (2001). Natural Resources and Economic Growth: The Role of Investment. Discussion Paper Series – CEPR (Centre for Economic Policy Research) London.

Haber, S., and Menaldo, V. (2011). Do Natural Resources Fuel Authoritarianism? A Preappraisal of the Resource Curse. *American Political Science Review*, 105, 1–26.

Hall, R.E., and Jones, C.I. (1999). Why Do Some Countries Produce So Much More Per Worker Than Others? *Quarterly Journal of Economics*, 114, 83–116.

Halliday, F. (1991). The Gulf War and Its Aftermath: First Reflections. *International Affairs*, 67(2), 223–234.

Halvorsen, R., and Layton, D.F. (2015). *Handbook on the Economics of Natural Resources.* Cheltenham, UK and Northampton, MA, USA: Edward Elgar Publishing.

Hamilton, K., and Ley, E. (2011). Sustainable Fiscal Policy for Mineral-Based Economies. In R. Arezki, T. Gylfason, and A. Sy (Eds), *Beyond the Curse – Policies to Harness the Power of Natural Resources.* Washington: International Monetary Fund, pp. 131–148.

Hamm, K. (1994). The Refining Industry in the North Atlantic. *The Energy Journal*, 15, Special Issue, 179–193.

Hanisch, T.J., and G. Nerheim (1992). *Norsk Oljehistorie – fra vantro til overmot?* Oslo: Norsk Petroleumsforening / Leseselskapet.

Hardwicke, R.E. (1935). Rule of Capture and its Implications as Applied to Oil and Gas. *Texas Law Review*, 13(4), 391–422.

Hartwick, J.M. (1977). Intergenerational Equity and the Investing of Rents from Exhaustible Resources. *The American Economic Review*, 67(5), 972–974.

Hausmann, R., and Rigobon, R. (2003). An Alternative Interpretation of the 'Resource Curse': Theory and Policy Implications. Working Paper Series 129(9424): 2865. http://www.nber.org/papers/w9424 (accessed July 9, 2018).

Havranek, T., Horvath, R., and Zeynalov, A. (2016). Natural Resources and Economic Growth: A Meta-Analysis. *World Development*, 88, 134–151.

Hegghammer, T. (2002). Documentation on Al-Qa´ida – Interviews, Communications and Other Primary Sources 1990–2002. FFI-Report no. 2002/01393. Norwegian Defense Research Establishment. http://rapporter.ffi.no/rapporter/2002/01393.pdf (accessed July 2, 2018).

Hegre, H., and Sambanis, N. (2006). Sensitivity Analysis of Empirical Results on Civil War Onset. *Journal of Conflict Resolution*, 50(4), 58–33.

Heikal, M. (1993). *Illusions of Triumph – An Arab View of the Gulf War.* London: HarperCollins Publishers.

Helle, E. (1984). *Norges olje – de første 20 årene.* Oslo: Tiden Norsk Forlag.

Hellinger, D. (2006). Venezuelan Oil: Free Gift of Nature or Wealth of a Nation. *International Journal*, 55(68), 55–67.

Hendryx, F. (1959). A Sovereign Nation's Ability to Make and Abide by a Petroleum Concession Contract. *Platt's Oilgram News*, 28(April 28), 2–3.

Heubaum, H., and Biermann, F. (2015). Integrating Global Energy and Climate Governance: The Changing Role of the International Energy Agency. *Energy Policy*, 87, 229–239.

Hiro, D. (1989). *The Longest War – The Iran–Iraq Military Conflict.* London: Grafton Books.

Holtsmark, B., and Skonhoft, A. (2014). The Norwegian Support and Subsidy Policy of Electric Cars. Should it be Adopted by Other Countries? *Environmental Science and Policy*, 42(2014), 160–168.

Hotelling, H. (1931). The Economics of Exhaustible Resources. *The Journal of Political Economy*, 39(2), 137–175.

Howarth, S. (1997). *A Century in Oil – The "Shell" Transport and Trading Company 1897–1997*. London: Weidenfeld & Nicolson.

Hughes, L. (2014). *Globalizing Oil – Firms and Oil Market Governance in France, Japan, and the United States*. Cambridge: Cambridge University Press.

Humphreys, M. (2005). Natural Resources, Conflict, and Conflict Resolution – Uncovering the Mechanisms. *Journal of Conflict Resolution*, 49(4), 508–537.

Hveem, H. (1978). *The Political Economy of Third World Producer Associations*. Oslo: Universitetsforlaget.

IEA (2008). *World Energy Outlook 2008*. Paris: International Energy Agency (IEA).

IEA (2015). *World Energy Outlook, 2015*. Paris: International Energy Agency (IEA).

IEA (2017). *World Energy Outlook, 2017*. Paris: International Energy Agency (IEA).

IEP (2016). The Global Terrorism Index. Institute for Economics and Peace, University of Maryland. http://visionofhumanity.org/app/uplo ads/2017/11/Global-Terrorism-Index-2017.pdf (accessed July 9, 2018).

Inkpen, A., and Moffett, M.H. (2011). *The Global Oil & Gas Industry – Management, Strategy & Finance*. Tulsa: Penn Well Corporation.

Ishay, M. (2008). *The History of Human Rights: From Ancient Times to the Globalized Era*. Berkeley: University of California Press.

Jakab, É. (2015). Property Rights in Ancient Rome. In P. Erdkamp, K. Verboven, and A. Zuiderhoek (Eds), *Ownership and Exploitation of Land and Natural Resources in the Roman World*. Oxford: Oxford University Press, pp. 107–131.

James, A. (2015). The Resource Curse: A Statistical Mirage? *Journal of Development Economics*, 114, 55–63.

Jenkins, G. (1986). *Oil Economists' Handbook*. London: Elsevier Applied Science Publishing.

Jervis, R. (2012). Explaining the War in Iraq. In J.K. Cramer and A.T. Thrall (Eds), *Why Did the United States Invade Iraq?* London: Routledge, pp. 25–48.

Johnston, D., and Johnston, D. (2010). Petroleum Fiscal System Analysis – State of Play. *Oil, Gas & Energy Law Intelligence*, 8(4), 1–32.

Johnston, P.B. (2017). Oil, Extortion Still Paying Off for ISIS. https:// www.rand.org/blog/2017/10/oil-extortion-still-paying-off-for-isis.html (accessed July 2, 2018).

Jones, D.M., Bremer, S.A., and Singer, J.D. (1996). Militarized Interstate Disputes, 1816–1992: Rationale, Coding Rules, and Empirical Patterns. *Conflict Management and Peace Science*, 15, 163–213.

Kalicki, J.H., and Goldwyn, D.L. (2013). *Energy Security – Strategies for a World in Transition* (2nd edn). Baltimore: Johns Hopkins University Press.

Kaplan, E. (2006). Tracking Down Terrorist Financing. Council of Foreign Affairs. https://www.cfr.org/backgrounder/tracking-down-terro rist-financing (accessed October 28, 2017).

Karl, T.L. (1997). *The Paradox of Plenty – Oil Booms and Petro-States*. Berkeley: University of California Press.

Karl, T.L. (2004). Oil-Led Development: Social, Political, and Economic Consequences. *Encyclopedia of Energy*, 4, 661–672.

Kaufmann, D. (2017). Resource Governance Index. Natural Resource Governance Institute, New York. https://resourcegovernance.org/analy sis-tools/publications/2017-resource-governance-index (accessed July 10, 2018).

Kechichian, J.A. (1990). The Gulf Cooperation Council and the Gulf War'. In C.C. Joyner (Ed.), *The Persian Gulf War – Lessons for Strategy, Law, and Diplomacy*. New York: Greenwood Press, pp. 91–110.

Keohane, R.O. (1984). *After Hegemony – Cooperation and Discord in the World Political Economy*. Princeton: Princeton University Press.

Keohane, R.O. (1989). *International Institutions and State Power: Essays in International Relations Theory*. Boulder: Westview Press.

Keohane, R.O., and Nye, J.S. (1977). *Power and Interdependence – World Politics in Transition*. Boston: Little, Brown & Company.

Keohane, R.O., and Underdal, A. (2011). The West and the Rest in Global Economic Institutions. In D.H. Claes and C.H. Knutsen (Eds), *Governing the Global Economy – Politics, Institutions and Economic Development*. London: Routledge, pp. 51–69.

Kindleberger, C.P. (1973). *The World in Depression 1929–1939*. Berkeley: University of California Press.

Kiourktsoglou, G., and Coutroubis, A.D. (2015). ISIS Export Gateway to Global Crude Oil Markets. Maritime Business Forum, London Shipping Law Centre. http://www.marsecreview.com/wp-content/uploads/2015/03/ PAPER-on-CRUDE-OIL-and-ISIS.pdf (accessed July 10, 2018).

Kissam, L.T., and Leach, E.K. (1959). Sovereign Expropriation of Property and Abrogation of Concession Contracts. *Fordham Law Review*, 28(2), 177–214.

Kissinger, H. (1982). Foreword. In C.K. Ebinger (Ed.), *The Critical Link: Energy and National Security in the 1980s*. Cambridge: Ballinger Publishing Company, p. xx.

Kissinger, H. (1999). *Years of Renewal*. New York: Simon & Schuster.

Kisswani, K.M. (2016). Does OPEC Act as a Cartel? Empirical Investigation of Coordination Behavior. *Energy Policy*, 97(2016), 171–180.

Klare, M.T. (2004). *Blood and Oil: The Dangers and Consequences of America's Growing Dependency on Imported Petroleum*. New York: Metropolitan Books.

Klare, M.T. (2012a). Blood for Oil, in Iraq and Elsewhere. In J.K. Cramer and T. Thrall (Eds), *Why Did the United States Invade Iraq?* London: Routledge, pp. 129–144.

Klare, M.T. (2012b). The End of Easy Everything. *Current History*, 111(741), 24–28.

Klare, M.T. (2017). The Changing Geopolitics of Oil and Gas. In T.C. Lehmann (Ed.), *The Geopolitics of Global Energy – The New Cost of Plenty*. Boulder: Lynne Rienner Publishers, pp. 23–42.

Knutsen, C.H., Kotsadam, A., Olsen, E.H., and Wig, T. (2017). Mining and Local Corruption in Africa. *American Journal of Political Science*, 61(2), 320–334.

Kohl, W.L. (2010). Consumer Country Energy Cooperation: The International Energy Agency and the Global Energy Order. In A. Goldthau and J.M. Witte (Eds), *Global Energy Governance – The New Rules of the Game*. Berlin and Washington: Global Public Policy Institute/ Brookings Institution Press, pp. 195–220.

Kong, B. (2010). *China's International Petroleum Policy*. Santa Barbara: ABC-CLIO.

Kramer, B.M., and Anderson, O.L. (2005). The Rule of Capture – an Oil and Gas Perspective. *Environmental Law*, 35(4), 899–954.

Krasner, S.D. (1978). *Defending the National Interest – Raw Materials Investments and U.S. Foreign Policy*. Princeton: Princeton University Press.

Lahn, G., Marcel, V., Mitchell, J., Myers, K., and Stevens, P. (2007). Good Governance of the National Petroleum Sector. Royal Institute of International Affairs. https://www.chathamhouse.org/publications/ papers/view/108469 (accessed March 1, 2007).

Lallanilla, M. (2015). Peak Oil: Theory or Myth? Livescience. https://www. livescience.com/38869-peak-oil.html (accessed November 18, 2017).

Lambsdorff, J.G. (2002). Corruption and Rent-Seeking. *Public Choice*, 113, 97–125.

Le Billon, P. (2001). The Political Ecology of War: Natural Resources and Armed Conflicts. *Political Geography*, 20(5), 561–584.

Lee, C.-y. (2016). Oil and Terrorism: Uncovering the Mechanisms. *Journal of Conflict Resolution*, 62(5), 903–928.

Lee, L.-F. (2009). Sovereignty over, Ownership of, and Access to Natural Resources. In A.D. Tarlock and J. C. Dernbach (Eds), *Environmental Laws and their Enforcement* (Vol. Encyclopedia of Life Support Systems). Oxford: EOLSS Publishers/UNESCO, pp. 1–31.

Leite, C., and Weidmann, J. (1999). Does Mother Nature Corrupt? Natural

Resources, Corruption and Economic Growth. IMF Working Paper, no. 99/85.

Lenz, T.O., and Holman, M. (2013). *American Government*. Gainesville: University Press of Florida.

Lesage, D., van der Graaf, T., and Westphal, K. (2010). *Global Energy Governance in a Multipolar World*. Farnham: Ashgate Publishing.

Lewis, D. (1973). *Counterfactuals*. Oxford: Blackwell.

Lie, E., and Claes, D.H. (2018). The Counter-Shock in Norwegian Oil History. In D. Basosi, G. Garavini, and M. Trentin (Eds), *Counter-Shock: The Oil Counter-Revolution of the 1980s*. London: I.B. Tauris, pp. 199–217.

Lieber, R.J. (1992). Oil and Power After the Gulf War. *International Security*, 17(1), 155–176.

Likosky, M. (2009). Contracting and Regulatory Issues in the Oil and Gas and Metallic Minerals Industries. *Transnational Corporations*, 18(1), 1–40.

Livernois, J., and Thille, H. (2015). Empirical Evidence on the Theory of Nonrenewable Resource Economics. In R. Halvorsen and D.F. Layton (Eds), *Handbook on the Economics of Natural Resources*. Cheltenham, UK and Northampton, MA, USA: Edward Elgar Publishing, pp. 41–65.

Locke, J. (1689/1988). The Second Treatise of Government. In P. Laslett (Ed.), *Two Treatises of Government*. Cambridge: Cambridge University Press, pp. 265–429.

Luciani, G. (1990). *The Arab State*. London: Routledge.

Luciani, G. (2011). Price and Revenue Volatility: What Policy Options and Role for the State? *Global Governance*, 17(2), 213–228.

Lynch, M.C. (2002). Forecasting Oil Supply: Theory and Practice. *The Quarterly Review of Economics and Finance*, 42(2002), 373–389.

Mabro, R. (1992). OPEC and the Price of Oil. *The Energy Journal – IAEE*, 13(2), pp. 1–17.

Mabro, R. (1998). Rethinking OPEC. *Oxford Energy Forum*, 33. Oxford Institute of Energy Studies.

Mabro, R. (2005). The International Oil Price Regime: Origins, Rationale and Assessment. *The Journal of Energy Literature*, XI(1), 3–20.

Mahdavy, H. (1970). *Studies in Economic History of the Middle East*. London: Oxford University Press.

Malnes, R. (1983). OPEC and the Problem of Collective Action. *Journal of Peace Research*, 20(4), 343–355.

Marcel, V. (2006). *Oil Titans – National Oil Companies in the Middle East*. London: Royal Institute of International Affairs.

March, J.G., and Olsen, J.P. (1989). *Rediscovering Institutions: The Organizational Basis of Politics*. New York: The Free Press.

Maugeri, L. (2006). *The Age of Oil – The Mythology, History, and Future of the World's Most Controversial Resource*. Westport: Praeger.

McNally, R. (2017). *Crude Volatility – The History and the Future of Boom–Bust Oil Prices*. New York: Columbia University Press.

Mead, W.J. (1986). The OPEC Cartel Thesis Reexamined: Price Constraints from Oil Substitutes. *The Journal of Energy and Development*, 11(2), 213–239.

Mehlum, H., Moene, K., and Torvik, R. (2006). Institutions and the Resource Curse. *The Economic Journal*, 116, 1–20.

Meierding, E. (2016). Dismantling the Oil Wars Myth. *Security Studies*, 25(2), 258–288.

Mestad, O. (2015). Managing the Nation's Wealth – the Government Take and the Resource Curse. *Marius/Scandinavian Institute of Maritime Law Yearbook*, (456), 211–226.

Meyer, T. (2016). The World Trade Organization's Role in Global Energy Governance. In T. Van de Graf, B.K. Sovacool, A. Ghosh, F. Kern, and M.T. Klare (Eds), *The Palgrave Handbook of The International Economy of Energy*. London: Palgrave Macmillan, pp. 139–171.

Mills, R. (2008). *The Myth of the Oil Crisis – Overcoming the Challenges of Depletion, Geopolitics and Global Warming*. Westport: Praeger.

Mitchell, J.V. (2007). Energy and Norwegian Foreign Policy. In A. Holm and H. Thune (Eds), *Energipolitiske interesser og utfordringer*. Oslo: Norwegian Ministry of Foreign Affairs, page numbers unavailable.

Mitra, T., Asheim, G.B., Buchholz, W., and Withagen, C. (2013). Characterizing the Sustainability Problem in an Exhaustible Resource Model. *Journal of Economic Theory*, 148, 2164–2182.

Mommer, B. (2001). Venezuelan Oil Politics at the Crossroads. Monthly Commentary. Oxford Institute of Energy Studies. https://www.oxfordenergy.org/publications/venezuelan-oil-politics-at-the-crossroads/ (accessed July 2, 2018).

Mommer, B. (2002). *Global Oil and the Nation State*. Oxford: Oxford University Press.

Moore, M. (2015). *A Political Theory of Territory*. Oxford: Oxford University Press.

Moors, K. (2011). *The Vega Factor – Oil Volatility and the Next Global Crisis*. Hoboken: John Wiley & Sons, Inc.

Moran, T.H. (1981). Modelling OPEC Behavior: Economic and Political Alternatives. *International Organization*, 35(2), 241–272.

Morrison, K.M. (2015). *Nontaxation and Representation*. Cambridge: Cambridge University Press.

Morse, E.L. (2014). Welcome to the Revolution – Why Shale is the Next Shale. *Foreign Affairs*, 93(3), 3–9.

Morse, E.L., Lee, E.G., Dray, D.M., Bond, K., Fordham, T.M., and Fediuk, S. (2013). Energy 2020: Independence Day – Global Ripple Effects of the North American Energy Revolution. Citigroup. https://www.citivelocity.com/citigps/ReportSeries.action?recordId=16&src=Home&l=ri (accessed July 10, 2018).

Moses, J.W., and Letnes, B. (2017). *Managing Resource Abundance and Wealth – The Norwegian Experience*. Oxford: Oxford University Press.

NAS (2010). Hidden Costs of Energy: Unpriced Consequences of Energy Production and Use. National Academy of Science. http://www.ourenergypolicy.org/wp-content/uploads/2012/06/hidden.pdf (accessed July 10, 2018).

Naumov, A., and Toews, G. (2016). Revisiting the Relationship between Oil Prices and Costs in the Upstream Industry. VOX CEPR's Policy Portal. http://voxeu.org/article/oil-prices-and-costs-upstream-industry (accessed July 10, 2018).

Niblock, T. (2006). *Saudi Arabia: Power, Legitimacy and Survival*. London: Routledge.

Niblock, T. (Ed.) (1982). *State, Society and Economy in Saudi Arabia*. London: Croom Helm.

Nine, C. (2008). A Lockean Theory of Territory. *Political Studies*, 56(1), 148–165.

Nine, C. (2012). *Global Justice & Territory*. Oxford: Oxford University Press.

NOAA. (2017). What Lies Beneath: Mapping the Arctic Sea Floor. National Oceanic and Atmospheric Administration, US Department of Commerce. https://oceanservice.noaa.gov/news/weeklynews/aug09/arcticmap.html (accessed February 27, 2018).

Nolan, P.A., and Thurber, M.C. (2012). On the State's Choice of Oil Company: Risk Management and the Frontier of the Petroleum Industry. In D.G. Victor, D.R. Hults, and M. Thurber (Eds), *Oil and Governance – State-Owned Enterprises and the World Energy Supply*. Cambridge: Cambridge University Press, pp. 121–169.

Noreng, Ø. (1980). *The Oil Industry and Government Strategy in the North Sea*. London: Croom Helm.

Noreng, Ø. (2002). *Crude Power – Politics and the Oil Market*. London: I.B. Tauris.

Noreng, Ø. (2013). Global Resource Scramble and New Energy Frontiers. In A. Goldthau (Ed.), *The Handbook of Global Energy Policy*. Chichester: Wiley-Blackwell, pp. 159–175.

North, D.C. (1990). *Institutions, Institutional Change and Economic Performance*. Cambridge: Cambridge University Press.

Odell, P. (1986). *Oil and World Power*. Middlesex Penguin Books.

Odell, P. (1994). World Oil Resources, Reserves and Production. *Energy Journal*, 15 (Special Issue on The Changing World Petroleum Market), 89–114.

OICA. (2017). Sales of New Vehicles. http://www.oica.net/category/sales-statistics/ (accessed January 3, 2018).

Olson, M. (1965). *The Logic of Collective Action*. Cambridge: Harvard University Press.

OPEC (1990). *Official Resolutions and Press Releases – 1960–1990*. Vienna: OPEC.

OPEC (2003). OPEC production agreements: a detailed listing. *OPEC Review*, 27(1), 65–77.

OPEC (2016). Monthly Oil Market Report. April 2016. www.opec.org (accessed June 12, 2016).

OPEC (2017). Annual Statistical Bulletin. Vienna: OPEC. http://www.opec.org/opec_web/static_files_project/media/downloads/publications/ASB2017_13062017.pdf (accessed July 2, 2018).

Østby, G., Nordås, R., and Rød, J.K. (2009). Regional Inequalities and Civil Conflict in Sub-Saharan Africa. *International Studies Quarterly*, 53(2), 301–624.

Painter, D.S. (2012). Oil and American Century. *The Journal of American History*, 99(1), 24–39.

Palmer, M.A. (1992). *Guardians of the Gulf – A History of America's Expanding Role in the Persian Gulf, 1833–1992*. New York: The Free Press.

Papyrakis, E. (2016). The Resource Curse – What Have We Learned from Two Decades of Intensive Research: Introduction to the Special Issue. *Journal of Development Studies*, 53, 1–11.

Papyrakis, E., and Gerlagh, R. (2004). The Resource Curse Hypothesis and its Transmission Channels. *Journal of Comparative Economics*, 32, 181–193.

Parra, F. (2004). *Oil Politics – A Modern History of Petroleum*. New York: Palgrave Macmillan.

Pearce, D.W. (1983). *The Dictionary of Modern Economics*. London: Macmillan.

Pereira, E.G., and Talus, K. (2013). Upstream Regulation: An Introduction. In E.G. Periera and K. Talus (Eds), *Upstream Law and Regulation – A Global Guide*. London: Globe Business Publishing, pp. 7–13.

Pindyck, R. (1978). OPEC's threat to the West. *Foreign Policy*, 30, 36–52.

Pirog, R. (2007). *The Role of National Oil Companies in the International Oil Market*. Washington, DC: Congressional Research Service.

Pogge, T. (2002). *World Poverty and Human Rights*. Cambridge: Polity Press.

Quilès, P., and Gullet, J.-J. (2006). *Energie et Géopolitique*. Paris: Assemblée nationale.

Ramady, M., and Mahdi, W. (2015). *OPEC in a Shale Oil World*. Cham Heidelberg (Switzerland): Springer International Publishing.

Ramey, G., and Ramey, V.A. (1991). Technology Commitment and the Cost of Economic Fluctuations. NBER Working Papers no 3755, from National Bureau of Economic Research, Inc. https://econpapers.repec.org/paper/nbrnberwo/3755.htm (accessed July 2, 2018).

Ramey, G., and Ramey, V.A. (1995). Cross-Country Evidence on the Link Between Volatility and Growth. *The American Economic Review*, 85(5), 1138–1151.

Rawls, J. (1971). *A Theory of Justice*. Cambridge: Harvard University Press.

Ricardo, D. (1821/2001). *On the Principles of Political Economy and Taxation*. Kitchener: Batoche Books.

Richardson, J.J. (1981). Problems of Controlling Public Sector Agencies: The Case of Norwegian Oil Policy. *Political Studies*, 21(1), 35–50.

Robinson, D., and Qinhua, X. (2013). OIES-Renmin Roundtable Conference on Implications for China of North American Energy Independence. Oxford Institute of Energy Studies and Renmin University of China. https://www.oxfordenergy.org/wpcms/wp-content/uploads/2013/06/Summary-North-American-Energy-Independence-Beijing-March-2013.pdf (accessed July 2, 2018).

Robinson, J. (1988). *Yamani – The Inside Story*. London: Simon & Schuster.

Robinson, J.A., Torvik, R., and Verdier, T. (2006). Political Foundations of the Resource Curse. *Journal of Development Economics*, 106, 194–198.

Rodrik, D., Subramanian, A., and Trebbi, F. (2004). Institutions Rule: The Primacy of Institutions over Geography and Integration in Economic Development. *Journal of Economic Growth*, 9, 131–165.

Roncaglia, A. (1985). *The International Oil Market*. Basingstoke: Macmillan.

Ross, M.L. (1999). The Political Economy of the Resource Curse. *World Politics*, 51, 297.

Ross, M.L. (2001). Does Oil Hinder Democracy? *World Politics*, 53, 325–361.

Ross, M.L. (2004). How Do Natural Resources Influence Civil War? Evidence from Thirteen Cases. *International Organization*, 58(1), 35–67.

Ross, M.L. (2012). *The Oil Curse – How Petroleum Wealth Shapes the Development of Nations*. Princeton: Princeton University Press.

Ross, M.L. (2015). What Have We Learned about the Resource Curse? *Annual Review of Political Science*, 18(1), 239–259.

Ruggie, J.G. (1982). International Regimes, Transactions and Change:

Embedded Liberalism in Postwar Economic Order. *International Organization*, 36(2), 379–415.

Rugh, W.A. (1996). The Foreign Policy of the United Arab Emirates. *Middle East Journal*, 50(1), 57–70.

Rutledge, I. (2006). *Addicted to Oil – America's Relentless Drive for Energy Security*. London: I.B. Tauris.

Sachs, J.D. (2007). How to Handle the Macroeconomics of Oil Wealth. In M. Humphreys, J.D. Sachs, and J.E. Stiglitz (Eds), *Escaping the Resource Curse*. New York: Columbia University Press, pp. 173–193.

Sachs, J.D., and Warner, A. (1995). Natural Resource Abundance and Economic Growth. NBER Working Paper Series, 3, 54.

Sachs, J.D., and Warner, A. (2001). The Curse of Natural Resources. *European Economic Review*, 45, 827–838.

Sala-i-Martin, X. (1997). I Just Ran Two Million Regressions. *American Economic Review*, 87, 178–183.

Sampson, A. (1975). *The Seven Sisters: The Great Oil Companies and the World They Made*. London: Hodder and Stoughton.

Samuelson, P.A. (1954). The Pure Theory of Public Expenditure. *Review of Economics and Statistics*, 36, 387–389.

Samuelson, P.A. (1988). *Economics*. New York: McGraw Hill.

Sarbu, B. (2014). *Ownership and Control of Oil – Explaining Policy Choices across Producing Countries*. London: Routledge.

Schlager, E., and Ostrom, E. (1992). Property-Rights Regimes and Natural Resources: A Conceptual Analysis. *Land Economics*, 68(3), 249–262.

Schneider, S.A. (1983). *The Oil Price Revolution*. Baltimore: Johns Hopkins University Press.

Selvig, E. (1983). Statoil eller oljestat. *Marius*, no. 80. Oslo: Nordic Institute for Law of the Sea.

Selvik, K., and Stenslie, S. (2011). *Stability and Change in the Modern Middle East*. London: I.B. Tauris.

Selvik, K., and Utvik, B.O. (2016). *Oil States in the New Middle East*. New York: Routledge.

Sick, G. (1985). *All Fall Down – America's Tragic Encounter with Iran*. New York: Random House.

Simmons, M.R. (2005). *Twilight in the Desert – The Coming Saudi Oil Shock and the World Economy*. Hoboken: John Wiley and Sons.

Skeet, I. (1988). *OPEC: Twenty-five Years of Prices and Politics*. Cambridge: Cambridge University Press.

Skocpol, T. (1983). *Visions and Method in Historical Sociology*. Cambridge: Cambridge University Press.

Smil, V. (2017). *Energy Transition – Global and National Perspectives* (2nd edn). Santa Barbara: Praeger.

Smith, A. (1986). Re-shuffling the Decks of Domestic Reserves: Are Zealous Acquirers Picking Clean Bones? Paper presented at the Eighth Annual American IAEE Conference.

Smith, B. (2004). Oil Wealth and Regime Survival in the Developing World, 1960–1999. *American Journal of Political Science*, 48, 232–246.

Smith, B. (2015a). The Resource Curse Exorcised: Evidence from a Panel of Countries. *Journal of Development Economics*, 116, 57–73.

Smith, B. (2015b). Resource Wealth as Rent Leverage: Rethinking the Oil–Stability Nexus. *Conflict Management and Peace Science*, 34(6), 597–617.

Smith, B. (2016). Exploring the Resource–Civil War Nexus. In D.T. Mason and S.M. Mitchell (Eds), *What Do We Know About Civil Wars?* Lanham: Rowman & Littlefield Publishers, pp. 215–230.

Smoke, G. (1975). National Security Affairs. In F.I. Greenstein and N.W. Polsby (Eds), *International Politics, Handbook of Political Science* (Vol. 8). Reading, PA: Addison-Wesley, pp. 247–362.

Solow, R.M. (1974). Intergenerational Equity and Exhaustible Resources. *The Review of Economic Studies*, 41, 29–45.

Sorell, S. (2007). The Rebound Effect: An Assessment of the Evidence for Economy-Wide Energy Savings from Improved Energy Efficiency. London: UK Energy Research Centre. http://www.ukerc.ac.uk/publications/the-rebound-effect-an-assessment-of-the-evidence-for-economy-wde-energy-savings-from-improved-energy-efficiency.html (accessed July 2, 2018).

Stevens, P. (2012). Saudi Aramco: The Jewel in the Crown. In D.G. Victor, D.R. Hults, and M. Thurber (Eds), *Oil and Governance – State-owned Enterprises and the World Energy Supply*. Cambridge: Cambridge University Press, pp. 173–233.

Stevens, P., Lahn, G., and Koorshy, J. (2015). The Resource Curse Revisited. The Royal Institute of International Affairs. https://www.chathamhouse.org/publication/resource-curse-revisited (accessed July 2, 2018).

Stiglitz, J.E. (1976). Monopoly and the Rate of Extraction of Exhaustible Resources. *American Economic Review*, 66, 655–661.

Stiglitz, J.E., and Bilmes, L.J. (2008). *The Three Trillion Dollar War – The True Costs of the Iraq Conflict*. New York: W.W. Norton & Company.

Stijns, J.-P.C. (2005). Natural Resource Abundance and Economic Growth Revisited. *Resources Policy*, 30, 107–130.

Stocking, G.W., and Myron W. Watkins. (1948). *Cartels or Competition? The Economics of International Controls by Business and Government*. New York: Twentieth Century Fund.

Stokes, D., and Raphael, S. (2010). *Global Energy Security and American Hegemony*. Baltimore: Johns Hopkins University Press.

Stopford, J., and Strange, S. (1991). *Rival States, Rival Firms – Competition for World Market Shares*. Cambridge: Cambridge University Press.

Strange, S. (1988). *States and Markets*. London: Pinter Publishers.

Stritzel, H. (2007). Towards a Theory of Securitization: Copenhagen and Beyond. *European Journal of International Relations*, 13(3), 357–383.

Summerton, P., Pollitt, H., Billington, S., Facanha, C., Miller, J., Davies, G., . . . Unger, B. (2016). Oil Market Futures. April 2016. Cambridge: Cambridge Econometrics. https://www.camecon.com/how/our-work/oil-market-futures/ (accessed July 2, 2018).

Sydnes, A.K. (1985). Norges stillingtagende til nord-syd konflikten i oljemarkedet: Petroleumøkonomiske interesser og utenrikspolitiske orienteringer. The Fridtjof Nansen Institute Report 004–1985.

Szulecki, K. (2018). The Multiple Faces of Energy Security: An Introduction. In K. Szulecki (Ed.), *Energy Security in Europe – Divergent Perceptions and Policy Challenges*. London: Palgrave Macmillan, pp. 1–30.

Tamnes, R. (1997). *Oljealder. Bind 6 i Norsk utenrikspolitikks historie*. Oslo: Universitetsforlaget.

Terzian, P. (1985). *OPEC: The Inside Story*. London: Zed Books.

Thurber, M.C., Hults, D.R., and Heller, P.R.P. (2011). Exporting the "Norwegian Model": The Effect of Administrative Design on Oil Sector Performance. *Energy Policy*, 39(2011), 5366–5378.

Toft, P., Duero, A., and Bieliauskas, A. (2010). Terrorist Targeting and Energy Security. *Energy Policy*, 38(8), 4411–4421.

Tordo, S. (2011). National Oil Companies and Value Creation. Washington: The World Bank. https://siteresources.worldbank.org/INTOGMC/Resources/9780821388310.pdf (accessed July 2, 2018).

Torvik, R. (2002). Natural Resources, Rent Seeking and Welfare. *Journal of Development Economics*, 67, 455–470.

Tsui, K.K. (2011). More Oil, Less Democracy: Theory and Evidence from Crude Oil Discoveries. *The Economic Journal*, 121, 89–115.

Turner, L. (1983). *Oil Companies in the International System* (3rd edn). London: George Allen & Unwin.

Ulfelder, J. (2007). Natural-Resource Wealth and the Survival of Autocracy. *Comparative Political Studies*, 40, 995–1018.

UNCTAD. (2007). *World Investment Report. Transnational Corporations, Extractive Industries, and Development*. New York and Geneva: The United Nations.

US Department of State. (1993). *Foreign Relations of the United*

States – 1958–1960, Near East Region; Iraq, Iran; Arabian Peninsula. Washington: US Government Printing Office.

Useem, J. (2003). 'The Devil's Excrement'. *Fortune* (February 3).

USGS. (2008). *Circum-Arctic Resource Appraisal: Estimates of Undiscovered Oil and Gas North of the Arctic Circle.* Washington: United States Geological Survey (USGS).

van de Graaf, T., and Colgan, J. (2016). Global Energy Governance: A Review and Research Agenda. *Palgrave Communications*, 2, 15047.

van de Graaf, T., and Zelli, F. (2016). Actors, Institutions and Frames in Global Energy Politics. In T. van de Graaf, B.K. Sovacool, A. Ghosh, F. Kern, and M.T. Klare (Eds), *The Palgrave Handbook of the International Political Economy of Energy*. London: Palgrave Macmillan, pp. 47–72.

van der Ploeg, F., and Poelhekke, S. (2009). Volatility and the Natural Resource Curse. *Oxford Economic Papers*, 61(4), 727–760.

van der Ploeg, F., and Poelhekke, S. (2016). The Impact of Natural Resources: Survey of Recent Quantitative Evidence. *Journal of Development Studies*, 53, 1–12.

Vasiliou, M.S. (2009). *The A to Z of the Petroleum Industry*. Lanham: The Scarecrow Press.

Vernon, R. (1971). *Sovereignty at Bay – The Multinational Spread of U.S. Enterprises*. New York: Basic Books Inc.

Verrastro, F.A., Placke, J.A., and Hegburg, A.S. (2004). Securing U.S. Energy in a Changing World. *Middle East Policy*, XI(4), 1–25.

Victor, D.G. (2013). National Oil Companies and the Future of the Oil Industry. *Annual Review of Resource Economics*, 5, 445–462.

Victor, D.G., Hults, D.R., and Thurber, M. (2012). *Oil and Governance – State-Owned Enterprises and the World Energy Supply*. Cambridge: Cambridge University Press.

Victor, N.M. (2007). On Measuring the Performance of National Oil Companies (NOCs). Working Paper 64, Program on Energy and Sustainable Development. Stanford University.

Vivoda, V. (2008). *The Return of the Obsolescing Bargain and the Decline of Big Oil – A Study of Bargaining in the Contemporary Oil Industry*. Saatbrücken: VDM Verlag Dr. Müller Aktiengesellschaft & Co.

Waltz, K. (1979). *Theory of International Politics*. Reading: Addison-Wesley Publishing Company.

Weeks, J. (2012). Strongmen and Straw Men: Authoritarian Regimes, Domestic Politics, and International Conflict. *American Political Science Review*, 106(2), 326–347.

Wenger, A. (2009). Towards a More Sustainable Global Energy System: Integrating Demand-side and Supply-side Policies. In A. Wenger, R. Orttung, and J. Perovic (Eds), *Energy and the Transformation of*

International Relations – Toward a New Producer–Consumer Framework. Oxford: Oxford University Press / Oxford Institute for Energy Studies (OIES), pp. 331–363.

Willett, T.D. (1979). Conflict and Cooperation in OPEC: Some Additional Economic Considerations. *International Organization*, 33(4), 581–587.

Willoch, K. (1990). *Statsminister*. Oslo: Chr. Schibsted Forlag.

Wilson, P.W., and Graham, D.F. (1994). *Saudi Arabia – The Coming Storm*. New York: M.E. Sharpe.

Wolf, C. (2009). Does Ownership Matter? The Performance and Efficiency of State Oil vs. Private Oil (1987–2006). *Energy Policy*, 37, 2642–2652.

Wright, G. (2001). Resource-Based Growth Then and Now. Prepared for the World Bank Project "Patterns of Integration in the Global Economy".

Wright, G., and Czelusta, J. (2004). The Myth of the Resource Curse. *Challenge*, 47, 6–38.

Wright, J., Frantz, E., and Geddes, B. (2013). Oil and Autocratic Regime Survival. *British Journal of Political Science*, 45, 287–306.

Yergin, D. (1988). Energy Security in the 1990s. *Foreign Affairs*, 67(1), 110–132.

Yergin, D. (1991). *The Prize – The Epic Quest for Oil, Money and Power*. London: Simon & Schuster.

Index

Printed and bound by CPI Group (UK) Ltd, Croydon, CR0 4YY

23/04/2025

14660957-0005